Unbelievable Errors

In *Unbelievable Errors*, Bart Streumer defends an error theory about all normative judgements: not just moral judgements, but also judgements about reasons for action, judgements about reasons for belief, and instrumental normative judgements. This theory says that these judgements are beliefs that ascribe normative properties, but that these properties do not exist. It therefore entails that all normative judgements are false.

Streumer also argues, however, that we cannot believe this error theory. This may seem to be a problem for the theory, but he argues that it is not. Instead, he argues, our inability to believe this error theory makes the theory more likely to be true, since it undermines objections to the theory, it makes it harder to reject the arguments for the theory, and it undermines revisionary alternatives to the theory.

Streumer then sketches how certain other philosophical views can be defended in a similar way, and how philosophers should modify their method if there can be true theories that we cannot believe. He concludes that to make philosophical progress, we should sharply distinguish the truth of a theory from our ability to believe it.

Bart Streumer is Professor of Philosophy at the University of Groningen. He previously taught at the University of Reading. His work has appeared in journals such as the *Journal of Philosophy*, *Philosophy and Phenomenological Research*, *Philosophical Studies*, and the *Australasian Journal of Philosophy*.

T0346928

Unbelievable Errors

An Error Theory About All Normative Judgements

Bart Streumer

OXFORD
UNIVERSITY PRESS

OXFORD
UNIVERSITY PRESS

Great Clarendon Street, Oxford, OX2 6DP,
United Kingdom

Oxford University Press is a department of the University of Oxford.
It furthers the University's objective of excellence in research, scholarship,
and education by publishing worldwide. Oxford is a registered trade mark of
Oxford University Press in the UK and in certain other countries

First published 2017
First published in paperback 2023

Published in the United States of America by Oxford University Press
198 Madison Avenue, New York, NY 10016, United States of America

British Library Cataloguing in Publication Data
Data available

Library of Congress Cataloging in Publication Data
Data available

ISBN 978-0-19-878589-7 (Hbk.)
ISBN 978-0-19-889294-6 (Pbk.)

To Alma, Oscar, and Max

And if someone compelled him to look at the light itself, wouldn't his eyes hurt, and wouldn't he turn around and flee towards the things he's able to see, believing that they're really clearer than the ones he's being shown?

Plato, Republic, 515e

Preface

You cannot believe the view I will defend in this book. I therefore will not be able to convince you that this view is true.

We all make normative judgements: we all think from time to time that an action is right or wrong, that a state of affairs is good or bad, or that a consideration is a reason for or against a belief or an action. I will defend an error theory about such judgements. This theory says that normative judgements are beliefs that ascribe normative properties, but that normative properties do not exist. It therefore entails that all normative judgements are false. I will also argue, however, that we cannot believe the error theory. You may take that to be a problem for the theory, but I will argue that it is not. Instead, I will argue, it makes the theory more likely to be true.

This book is organized as follows. In chapter I, I will describe the four main views about normative judgements and properties: non-reductive realism, reductive realism, non-cognitivism, and the error theory. In chapters II to VII, I will give arguments against the first three views. These arguments together support the error theory. In chapter VIII, I will explain in more detail to which judgements the error theory applies. In chapters IX and X, I will argue that we cannot believe the error theory and that there is therefore no reason for us to believe this theory. In chapter XI, I will argue that this makes the error theory more likely to be true, since it undermines objections to the theory, it makes it harder to reject my arguments, and it undermines revisionary alternatives to the theory. In chapter XII, I will explain how my arguments can help us to make broader philosophical progress.

Plato made a sharp distinction between philosophy and rhetoric: whereas philosophy is the art of giving sound arguments for true conclusions, rhetoric is the art of convincing others with arguments, irrespective of whether these arguments are sound and of whether their conclusions are true. Philosophers rightly care most about whether an argument is sound, not about whether it convinces others. But they do tend to assume that a sound argument *can* convince others, at least if these others are sufficiently rational. I think we should give up this assumption. There may be sound arguments that cannot convince any-one, since we cannot believe their conclusions.

You may think that an error theory about all normative judgements is so obviously false that this book is not worth reading. But if I am right that you cannot believe this theory, you should think again. For in that case, the best explanation of your belief that the error theory is false may not be that the theory is actually false, but may instead be that you cannot believe the theory. If so, this book is worth reading. It cannot make you believe the truth about normative judgements and properties. But it may convince you that the truth about these judgements and properties is literally unbelievable.

Acknowledgements

Before I wrote this book, I tried out my arguments in a series of papers. For comments on these papers, I am grateful to Matt Bedke, Terence Cuneo, Jonathan Dancy, Max de Gaynesford, Jamie Dreier, David Enoch, Brian Feltham, Guy Fletcher, Philip Goff, Alex Gregory, Brad Hooker, David Hunter, Christopher Jay, James Lenman, Hallvard Lillehammer, Christian Nimtz, Jonas Olson, Derek Parfit, Michael Ridge, Debbie Roberts, Mark Schroeder, Nishi Shah, Michael Smith, Daniel Star, Philip Stratton-Lake, Jussi Suikkanen, Jonathan Way, Ralph Wedgwood, Daniel Whiting, many anonymous referees, and audiences at the University of Birmingham (twice), the British Society for Ethical Theory Conference (twice), the Dutch Practical Philosophy Conference (twice), Lund University, the Moral Philosophy Seminar at the University of Oxford, the Moral Sciences Club at the University of Cambridge, the Open University, the University of Reading (four times), the Reasons for Action Seminar at the University of London, the University of Sheffield, the University of Southampton (twice), the St. Louis Annual Conference on Reasons and Rationality, Stockholm University, Tilburg University, Uppsala University, and the Wisconsin Metaethics Workshop. I would also like to thank Marianna Bergamaschi Ganapini, Andrew Forcehimes and Robert Talisse, Alexander Hyun and Eric Sampson, and Hallvard Lillehammer and Niklas Möller for their helpful replies to my paper 'Can We Believe the Error Theory?'.

I wrote a first draft of this book at the University of Reading in 2012. I am grateful to the Arts and Humanities Research Council for a nine-month fellowship that enabled me to write this draft. For comments on this draft, I would like to thank the participants in a graduate class I gave about it in Reading in 2013, particularly Alex Gregory, Brad Hooker, and Philip Stratton-Lake. I wrote a second draft at the University of Groningen in 2014. For comments on this draft, I would like to thank Matti Eklund, Gunnar Björnsson, and audiences at the University of Bielefeld, Central European University, and Utrecht University. I am particularly grateful to the two referees for OUP, Tristram McPherson and

Graham Oddie, for their extremely helpful comments on this draft. And I would like to thank Peter Momtchiloff for his advice and encouragement.

When I was an undergraduate at the University of Groningen more than twenty years ago, I met my future wife Alma. If I had not met her when I did, I probably would not have written this book. I therefore dedicate it to her, and to our children Oscar and Max.

Bart Streumer
August 2016

Copyright Acknowledgements

Parts of this book are based on Streumer 2007 (© Springer Science + Business Media BV), Streumer 2008 (© Australasian Association of Philosophy, by permission of Taylor & Francis Ltd), Streumer 2010 (© Springer Science + Business Media BV), Streumer 2011 (© Springer Science + Business Media BV), Streumer 2013a (© The Journal of Philosophy Inc.), Streumer 2013b (© Oxford University Press), Streumer 2013c (© John Wiley & Sons Inc.), Streumer 2016a (© Koninklijke Brill NV), Streumer 2016b (© Taylor & Francis Ltd), and Streumer forthcoming (© Oxford University Press).

Book symposia

Further arguments, clarifications, and some changes of mind can be found in the symposia on this book that have appeared in the *International Journal for the Study of Skepticism* 8 (2018): 257–341, with contributions by Frank Jackson, Philip Stratton-Lake, and Mark Schroeder, and the *Journal of Moral Philosophy* 16 (2019): 687–754, with contributions by Anandi Hattiangadi, Daan Evers, and Christine Tiefensee.

Contents

I

Normative Judgements and Properties

Before I can defend the error theory, I first need to do some taxonomy.

1. Normative Judgements and Properties

Predicates are parts of sentences that say something about an object, often by ascribing a property to it. Consider the following sentence:

My desk is white.

The predicate in this sentence is the phrase 'is white', which ascribes the property of being white to the desk at which I wrote this book.[1] If this sentence is true, my desk satisfies the predicate 'is white'.

We can distinguish *normative* from *descriptive* predicates. Philosophers disagree about what makes a judgement or a property normative, but they usually agree about which predicates are normative and which are descriptive. Normative predicates include, for example, 'is right', 'is wrong', 'is good', 'is bad', and 'is a reason' (if this is equivalent to 'counts in favour'). Descriptive predicates include, for example, 'is a desk', 'is white', and 'is made of wood and steel'. Some predicates, such as 'is courageous' or 'is just', seem partly normative and partly descriptive. I will classify these predicates as normative. In other words, I will use the term 'descriptive' to mean *wholly* descriptive.

We can now say that

---

[1] The predicate can be taken to be either the term 'white', or the phrase 'is white', or the open sentence '___ is white'. This does not matter to my arguments.

A mental state is a *normative judgement* if and only if it can be expressed with a sentence that conceptually entails that something satisfies a normative predicate.[2]

This claim gives a necessary and sufficient condition for a mental state's being a normative judgement. As I will explain in §45, it is compatible with different views about what *makes* a mental state a normative judgement.

Which sentences express normative judgements if this claim is true? The clearest examples are sentences that apply a normative predicate to an object, such as:

Murder is wrong.

Euthanasia is permissible.

Keeping your promises is right.

But the following sentences also express normative judgements if this claim is true:

There is a reason for you to quit smoking.

You ought to keep your promises.

Some actions are wrong.

Either murder is wrong or euthanasia is permissible.

For these sentences also conceptually entail that something satisfies a normative predicate: the first entails that a consideration satisfies the predicate 'is a reason for you to quit smoking', the second entails that you satisfy the predicate 'is such that he or she ought to keep his or her promises', the third entails that an action satisfies the predicate 'is wrong', and the fourth entails that an action satisfies either the predicate 'is wrong' or the predicate 'is permissible'.[3]

Other examples are less clear-cut. Consider the following sentences:

If you want to be a doctor, you ought to study medicine.

Euthanasia is not wrong.

---

[2] I use 'express' to mean semantically express, not pragmatically convey (for example, via conversational implicature). Why I say 'conceptually entails' rather than 'entails' will become clear in §10. For related but slightly different suggestions about when a sentence is normative, see Maitzen 1998, pp. 361–2, and 2010, p. 295, and Brown 2014, p. 62.

[3] I here assume that in the first sentence the term 'reason' means a consideration that counts in favour.

If murder is wrong, so is euthanasia.

Either it is raining or murder is wrong.

Etiquette requires that male guests at formal dinners wear a tie.

This is a good knife.

There is a reason to believe that the Earth has existed for billions of years.

I will discuss these sentences in §§47–51.[4]
We can next say that

A property is *normative* if and only if it can be ascribed with a normative predicate,

and that

A property is *descriptive* if and only if it can be ascribed with a descriptive predicate.[5]

As before, these claims give a necessary and sufficient condition for a property's being normative or descriptive. As I will explain in §45, they are compatible with different views about what *makes* a property normative.

Some philosophers reject these claims because properties do not literally describe anything, or because they take normative predicates to describe the world just as much as other predicates do.[6] But the term 'descriptive' is merely a label. We could instead use the term 'non-normative', and say that

A property is *non-normative* if and only if it can be ascribed with a predicate that is not normative.

But if we said this, the claim that

---

[4] Parallel questions can be raised about certain complex predicates: for example, is the predicate 'is such that either it is raining or murder is wrong' normative? My answer is that a predicate is normative if and only if a sentence that applies this predicate to an object conceptually entails that this object satisfies a simple normative predicate (such as 'is wrong'). I will list the normative predicates that I take to be simple in §47.

[5] I here follow Jackson 1998, pp. 120–1. Just as I use 'express' to mean semantically express, I use 'ascribe' to mean semantically ascribe.

[6] For the first reason to reject these claims, see Suikkanen 2010, p. 88 n. 2. Jonathan Dancy gave the second reason in conversation. See also Dancy 2005, p. 142 n. 1.

Property P is *non*-normative

would not entail that

Property P is *not* normative.

For it may be possible to ascribe this property both with a normative predicate and with a predicate that is not normative. Since this would be confusing, I will continue to use the term 'descriptive'.

You may think that English and other natural languages do not contain enough predicates to ascribe all properties, in which case my claims imply that some properties are neither normative nor descriptive. I will discuss this in §9. You may also think that we should not distinguish normative from descriptive properties by appealing to predicates. Instead, you may think, we should appeal to what *makes* a property normative or descriptive. But as I have said, philosophers disagree about what makes a property normative. Since my claims are compatible with different views about this, they are a good starting point for a taxonomy. As Quine writes, we sometimes need to withdraw "to a semantical plane ... to find common ground on which to argue".[7]

2. Different Views

We can next distinguish different views about normative judgements and properties. According to *cognitivists*, normative judgements are beliefs that ascribe normative properties. Most cognitivists are *realists*, who think that normative properties exist. We can say that

A normative property is *irreducibly normative* if and only if it is not identical to a descriptive property.

Non-reductive realists take there to be irreducibly normative properties: they take there to be normative properties that are not identical to descriptive properties. By contrast, *reductive* realists agree that there are normative properties, but deny that these properties are irreducibly normative: they take them to be identical to descriptive properties. I will discuss these views in chapters II to V.

We can also say that

---

[7] Quine 1953, p. 16.

A property is *natural* if and only if we can discover empirically that an object has this property.

Naturalist realists think that normative properties are natural properties. But they may deny that normative properties are identical to descriptive properties.[8] By contrast, *non-naturalist* realists deny that normative properties are natural properties. But they can perhaps allow that normative properties are identical to descriptive properties.[9] I will explain in §30 why this does not matter to my arguments.

It may seem easy to show that there are no irreducibly normative properties. If I am currently thinking about the property of rightness, I can denote this property with the descriptive phrase 'the property that I am actually currently thinking about'.[10] I can then ascribe the property of rightness with the descriptive predicate 'has the property that I am actually currently thinking about'. By varying my thoughts, I can do the same for any other normative property. But that does not show that there are no irreducibly normative properties. Instead, it shows that we should say that

A property is *descriptive* if and only if it can *non-accidentally* be ascribed with a descriptive predicate,

where a predicate non-accidentally ascribes a property if and only if, holding fixed its meaning, it ascribes this property in every context of utterance.[11] My claim about normative properties should be revised in a similar way. Since these revisions do not affect my arguments, I will ignore them in what follows.

According to *non-cognitivists*, normative judgements are non-cognitive attitudes, such as attitudes of approval or disapproval. But as I will explain in §31, many non-cognitivists also take normative judgements to be beliefs that ascribe normative properties, since they accept minimalism about

---

[8] See, for example, Sturgeon 1985 and 2005. There are also realists, such as Brink 1989 and Shafer-Landau 2003, who think that normative properties are constituted by natural properties without being identical to them.

[9] See Dunaway 2015, who argues that the core commitment of non-naturalism is not that normative properties are not identical to descriptive properties, but that normative properties are metaphysically fundamental.

[10] See Jackson 1998, p. 119 n. 10. A similar example is given by Williamson 2001, p. 629. See also Sturgeon 2009, p. 77 n. 46.

[11] I here follow Dunaway 2015, p. 632.

beliefs and properties. And some philosophers defend hybrid views that combine elements of non-cognitivism with elements of cognitivism. I will discuss these views in chapter VI.

Some views do not fit neatly into this taxonomy. *Cognitivist expressivists* take normative judgements to be beliefs that do not represent the world. *Descriptive fictionalists* think that normative sentences ascribe normative properties but normative judgements do not. *Constructivists* think that what makes a normative judgement correct is that it would be the outcome of a certain construction procedure. *Constitutivists* think that what makes a normative judgement correct is that it is implied by a norm that is constitutive of being an agent. And *quietists* take there to be normative truths but reject certain realist claims about normative properties. I will discuss these views in chapter VII. There are also revisionary versions of reductive realism and non-cognitivism, which I will discuss in chapter XI.

As I have said, most cognitivists are realists. But there is also a version of cognitivism that is not realist: the error theory, according to which normative judgements are beliefs that ascribe normative properties, but normative properties do not exist.[12] That is the view I will defend in this book.

3. Who Are 'We'?

I take the following claims to be true:

(S)   For all possible worlds W and W*, if the instantiation of descriptive properties in W and W* is exactly the same, then the instantiation of normative properties in W and W* is also exactly the same.

(G)   There are no descriptively specified conditions in which people's normative judgements are guaranteed to be correct.

(A)   When two people make conflicting normative judgements, at most one of these judgements is correct.

I take these claims to be what we can call *central thoughts* about normative judgements and properties: I take (S), (G), and (A) to reflect the

---

[12] The name 'the error theory' is often used to refer to a view that is only about *moral* judgements and properties. I will discuss this view in §52. I reserve the name 'the error theory' for the error theory about all normative judgements that I defend in this book.

nature of these judgements and properties.[13] These claims will therefore play a central role in my arguments.

Since I am similar to others, I think that *we* take (S), (G), and (A) to be true, or would take these claims to be true if we understood them and considered them carefully, and I think that (S), (G), and (A) are central thoughts about *our* normative judgements and the properties they ascribe. Does 'we' include you? To find out, you will have to read this book. If while reading this book you agree that these claims are true, my arguments will have force for you. But if you do not, they will not. Any philosophical argument has to start from what we currently think. At this point a philosopher's 'we' means 'I and everyone who is like me'.[14] Though I doubt that you are sufficiently unlike me to reject (S), (G), or (A), I cannot be completely certain about this.

When I say that I take (S), (G), and (A) to be central thoughts about normative judgements and properties, I do not mean that a view about these judgements and properties must be compatible with these claims in order to be defensible. But I do mean that if a view is incompatible with one or more of these claims, it is revisionary: it is not a view about what normative judgements *currently* are and about the properties they *currently* ascribe, but a view about what normative judgements should *become* and about the properties they should *start* to ascribe. If there is no defensible view that is compatible with (S), (G), and (A), we should perhaps accept a revisionary view. But I will argue that there is a defensible view that is compatible with our central thoughts about normative judgements and properties: the error theory.

You may suspect that I take (S), (G), and (A) to be true partly because this enables me to defend the error theory. As Timothy Williamson writes, "philosophers have a powerful vested interest in persuading themselves and others that the intuitions which directly or indirectly favour their position are stronger than they really are".[15] But I do not think that this is why I take these claims to be true. Like everyone else, I cannot believe the error theory. When I started to see that that the error theory is the only defensible view that is compatible with (S), (G), and (A), I therefore became inclined to reject one of these claims. But I have

---

[13] When I say that these claims reflect the nature of normative properties, I mean that they reflect the nature that these properties *would need to have in order to exist*. I will leave this implicit in what follows.

[14] See Lewis 1989, pp. 82–5, and also 1983, p. x.   [15] Williamson 2007, p. 237.

resisted this inclination. For I think that we should not reject one of our central thoughts about a topic merely because we cannot believe the only defensible view that is compatible with these thoughts.

4. Reading This Book

This book presents a sustained argument for the error theory. If you have no firm ideas about the nature of normative judgements and properties, it is best to read it from beginning to end. But if you do have such ideas, you can also read this book in a different way. You can initially ignore the chapters in which I argue against a view you already reject: chapters II and III if you already reject non-reductive realism, chapters IV and V if you already reject reductive realism, chapter VI if you already reject non-cognitivism and hybrid views, and chapter VII if you already reject the other views I mentioned in §2. You can then continue reading from chapter VIII onwards. If you start to suspect that a different alternative to the error theory is true, you can turn to the chapter or chapters in which I argue against this alternative.

II

The Reduction Argument

Since the error theory is an unattractive view, I cannot defend it by describing its attractions. I will instead defend it by attacking its competitors. I will start with non-reductive realism.

5. The First Version of the Argument

I will give an argument against non-reductive realism that we can call the *reduction argument*. There are several versions of this argument. I will begin with a well-known version given by Frank Jackson, which is inspired by a more general argument given by Jaegwon Kim.[1]

Consider an action A_1 that has a certain normative property, such as the property of being right. Since anything that has normative properties also has descriptive properties, A_1 also has descriptive properties, which we can call $P_{A1-1}, P_{A1-2}, \ldots$. And the objects $O_1, O_2, \ldots$ that are part of the same possible world as action A_1 have descriptive properties as well, which for each object O_x we can call $P_{Ox-1}, P_{Ox-2}, \ldots$.[2] Action A_1 therefore satisfies the following predicate, which we can call predicate D_1:

'has descriptive properties $P_{A1-1}, P_{A1-2}, \ldots$, and is such that O_1 has descriptive properties $P_{O1-1}, P_{O1-2}, \ldots$, O_2 has descriptive properties $P_{O2-1}, P_{O2-2}, \ldots, \ldots$'.

---

[1] See Jackson 1998, pp. 122–3, and 2001, p. 655, and also Jackson and Pettit 1996, pp. 84–5. For Kim's more general argument, see Kim 1993, pp. 68–71, 149–55. For discussion, see van Roojen 1996, Williamson 2001, Shafer-Landau 2003, pp. 89–98, McNaughton and Rawling 2003, Dancy 2004a and 2005, Majors 2005, FitzPatrick 2008, pp. 198–201, Kramer 2009, pp. 207–12, Plantinga 2010, Suikkanen 2010, Brown 2011, Enoch 2011a, pp. 137–40, and Dunaway 2015. My presentation of the argument assumes that the number of objects and properties in all possible worlds is countably infinite. I take this to be merely a matter of presentation.

[2] I include descriptive relations among $P_{A1-1}, P_{A1-2}, \ldots$ and among $P_{Ox-1}, P_{Ox-2}, \ldots$.

Since a predicate that wholly consists of descriptive predicates is itself descriptive, predicate D_1 is a descriptive predicate.

Suppose next that actions A_1, A_2, ... are all the right actions there are in all possible worlds.[3] Just as action A_1 satisfies predicate D_1, actions A_2, A_3, ... satisfy similarly constructed predicates D_2, D_3, ... These actions therefore all satisfy the following predicate, which we can call predicate D^*:

'satisfies either predicate D_1, or predicate D_2, or ... '.

As before, since a predicate that wholly consists of descriptive predicates is itself descriptive, predicate D^* is a descriptive predicate.[4]

I said in §3 that we take the following claim to be true:

(S)   For all possible worlds W and W*, if the instantiation of descriptive properties in W and W* is exactly the same, then the instantiation of normative properties in W and W* is also exactly the same.[5]

If (S) is true, any action that satisfies predicate D^* also satisfies the predicate 'is right'. For otherwise there would be two possible worlds W and W* that have exactly the same instantiation of descriptive properties but that do not have the same instantiation of normative properties, which would contradict (S). And any action that satisfies the predicate 'is right' also satisfies predicate D^*. For actions A_1, A_2, ... are all the right actions there are in all possible worlds, and these actions satisfy predicates D_1, D_2, ..., which means that they satisfy predicate D^*.

This shows that the predicate 'is right' and predicate D^* are necessarily coextensive. Now consider the following criterion of property identity:

---

[3] I assume for simplicity that only actions can be right.

[4] Majors 2005, p. 483, objects that "this looks very much like the fallacy of composition". But since a phrase is descriptive if it contains only descriptive terms, I do not think it commits this fallacy.

[5] I take (S) to be a claim about strong global supervenience: in other words, I take (S) to say not only that if W and W* are descriptive duplicates they must have the same pattern of normative properties, but also that these normative properties must be paired up with descriptive properties in the same way. Strictly speaking, (S) should therefore be formulated as follows: for all possible worlds W and W*, every isomorphism between W and W* that preserves descriptive properties is an isomorphism that preserves normative properties (see Bennett and McLaughlin 2011, §4.3.2). I will leave this implicit in what follows.

(N)   Two predicates ascribe the same property if and only if they are necessarily coextensive.[6]

If this criterion is correct, the predicate 'is right' and predicate D* ascribe the same property. The normative property of being right is then identical to a descriptive property. And this argument can be repeated for any other normative predicate. It therefore shows that if (S) is true and (N) is correct, there are no irreducibly normative properties. In other words, it shows that if (S) is true and (N) is correct, non-reductive realism is false.

6. Is (N) the Correct Criterion of Property Identity?

Non-reductive realists often try to resist the reduction argument by rejecting (N). But this is harder to do than it may seem.

We can order criteria of property identity from *coarse-grained* to *fine-grained*. The most coarse-grained criterion says that

(1)   Two predicates ascribe the same property if and only if they are coextensive.

This criterion makes few distinctions between properties: for example, it entails that the predicates 'is an animal with a heart' and 'is an animal with kidneys' ascribe the same property.

By contrast, the most fine-grained criterion says that

(2)   Two predicates ascribe the same property if and only if they express the same concept.

This criterion makes many distinctions between properties: for example, it entails that the predicates 'is full of water' and 'is full of H_2O' ascribe different properties.

(N) is more fine-grained than (1), but more coarse-grained than (2). Unlike (1), (N) entails that the predicates 'is an animal with a heart' and 'is an animal with kidneys' ascribe different properties. For though these predicates are coextensive, they are not *necessarily* coextensive. And

---

[6] Strictly speaking, (N) should say that two predicates *that both ascribe a property* ascribe the same property if and only if they are necessarily coextensive. I will leave this implicit in what follows.

unlike (2), (N) entails that the predicates 'is full of water' and 'is full of H_2O' ascribe the same property. For though these predicates express different concepts, they are necessarily coextensive. We can therefore picture the relation between these criteria as follows:[7]

(1)	(N)	(2)
←		→
Most coarse-grained		Most fine-grained

Which criterion is correct depends on what we take properties to be. Some philosophers take properties to be what we can call *shadows of concepts*: they think that what it is for an object to have a certain property is that this object falls under a certain concept.[8] If so, (2) is the correct criterion of property identity. Other philosophers take properties to be what we can call *ways objects can be*: they think that what it is for an object to have a certain property is that this object itself is a certain way.[9] If so, predicates that express different concepts can ascribe the same property, which means that the correct criterion of property identity must be more coarse-grained than (2).

What should non-reductive realists take properties to be? Their disagreement with reductive realists is not about whether normative and descriptive predicates express different *concepts*. Both sides agree that they do. Instead, this disagreement is about whether sentences that contain normative predicates have the same *truthmakers* as certain sentences that contain only descriptive predicates. Reductive realists think they do, and

---

[7] I owe this picture to Ralf Bader.

[8] See, for example, Schiffer 2003, pp. 61–71. Some philosophers, such as Aune 2002, even take properties to *be* concepts. And there are also philosophers who deny that properties exist (see Quine 1953, and for discussion Armstrong 1980 and Devitt 1980) or who deny that objects and properties are different kinds of entity (see Ramsey 1925, and for discussion MacBride 2005 and Lowe 2006, pp. 101–18).

[9] There are three main versions of this view. According to the first, objects are non-repeatable entities, or *particulars*, and properties are repeatable entities, or *universals*, that are shared by the objects that have them (see, for example, Armstrong 1997; he reserves the phrase 'ways things are' for universals, but I use the phrase 'ways objects can be' more broadly). According to the second version, properties are sets of resembling particulars, or *tropes*, and objects are bundles of tropes (see, for example, Campbell 1990). And according to the third version, properties are sets of actual and possible objects (see, for example, Lewis 1986, pp. 50–69). Lowe 2006 defends a more complicated view, according to which objects instantiate kinds, with objects being particulars and kinds universals, and tropes (which Lowe calls 'modes') instantiate properties, with modes being particulars and properties universals.

non-reductive realists think they do not. Non-reductive realists therefore cannot take properties to be shadows of concepts. They must instead take them to be ways objects can be.[10]

I will argue that if properties are ways objects can be, (N) is the correct criterion of property identity. I will begin by discussing several purported counterexamples to (N).[11] Many non-reductive realists take these examples to show that the correct criterion is more coarse-grained than (2), but more fine-grained than (N). In other words, they take these examples to show that the correct criterion is where (C) is in this picture:

(1)   (N)   (C)   (2)

←——————————————————————————————————→

Most coarse-   *Most fine-*
grained   *grained*

But I will argue that if properties are ways objects can be, what (N) says about these examples is exactly right. I will also argue that the versions of (C) that non-reductive realists have put forward either do not contradict (N) or assume that properties are shadows of concepts. And I will argue that non-reductive realists cannot defensibly say that normative properties are an exception to (N).

Since triangles have both three sides and three angles, one purported counterexample to (N) that many non-reductive realists give is that

The predicates 'has three angles' and 'has three sides' are necessarily coextensive but ascribe different properties.

Since the predicates 'has three angles' and 'has three sides' clearly ascribe different properties, this example may seem to show that (N) is too coarse-grained. But consider the following figure:

[10] See Jackson 1998, p. 126, and Jackson 2003, p. 573.
[11] For Jackson's response to such examples, see Jackson 1998, pp. 15–17, 125–8, and 2003, p. 573. For general discussion of whether necessarily coextensive predicates ascribe the same property, see Sober 1982 and Lewis 1986, pp. 55–9.

This figure has three sides, but only two angles. That shows that the predicate 'has three sides' is not necessarily coextensive with the predicate 'has three angles'. The example should therefore be revised to:

> The predicates 'is a closed figure that has three sides' and 'is a closed figure that has three angles' are necessarily coextensive but ascribe different properties.[12]

Since the predicates 'is a closed figure that has three sides' and 'is a closed figure that has three angles' are necessarily coextensive, this revised example may also seem to show that (N) is too coarse-grained.[13] But consider figures with the following kind of shape:

Besides satisfying the predicates 'is a closed figure that has three sides' and 'is a closed figure that has three angles', these figures also satisfy the predicate 'is a triangle'. If the predicates 'is a closed figure that has three sides' and 'is a closed figure that has three angles' ascribed two different properties, why would the predicate 'is a triangle' not ascribe a third property? And suppose we defined a 'half-side' as half a side and a 'half-angle' as half an angle. If the predicates 'is a closed figure that has three sides', 'is a closed figure that has three angles', and 'is a triangle' ascribed three different properties, why would the predicate 'is a closed figure with six half-sides and six half-angles' not ascribe a fourth property? If properties are ways objects can be, this multiplication of properties has to stop somewhere. It seems most defensible to say that it stops at the

---

[12] Kramer 2009, pp. 210–11, claims that the predicates 'has three sides' and 'has three angles' are necessarily coextensive but ascribe different properties when the class of objects over which they range is implicitly narrowed to closed figures. But if this class is implicitly narrowed in this way, it must be possible to make this narrowing explicit by reformulating these predicates as 'is a closed figure that has three sides' and 'is a closed figure that has three angles', which Kramer agrees ascribe the same property. Of course, if this class is *not* implicitly narrowed in this way, the predicates 'has three sides' and 'has three angles' ascribe different properties. But in that case, as Kramer agrees, they are not necessarily coextensive.

[13] For simplicity, I ignore further phrases that we need to add to these predicates to make them necessarily coextensive, such as 'in two-dimensional space'.

start, and that the predicates 'is a closed figure that has three sides' and 'is a closed figure that has three angles' ascribe the same property. If so, what (N) says about this example is exactly right.[14]

In response, non-reductive realists sometimes put forward the following criterion of property identity:

(C1)   Two predicates ascribe different properties if and only if these properties consist of different parts.[15]

They then say that the predicates 'is a closed figure that has three sides' and 'is a closed figure that has three angles' ascribe properties that consist of different parts: they say that the first consists of being a closed figure and having three sides, and that the second consists of being a closed figure and having three angles. But they are then overlooking the fact that these predicates may instead ascribe a single property that consists of the same three parts: being a closed figure, having three sides, and having three angles. (C1) therefore does not contradict (N). If non-reductive realists do take (C1) to contradict (N), they seem to assume that we can read off the composition of a property from the composition of a predicate that ascribes it. That is something we can do only if properties are shadows of concepts.

A second purported counterexample to (N) that non-reductive realists sometimes give is that

The predicates 'has a shape' and 'has a size' are necessarily coextensive but ascribe different properties.

But if you learn that an object has a shape without learning which shape it has, all you have learned is that this object is extended in two- or three-dimensional space. And if you learn that an object has a size without learning which size it has, all you have learned is also that this object is

---

[14] See also Oddie 2005, pp. 148–51. According to Lowe 2006, predicates like 'is a triangle', 'is a closed figure that has three sides', and 'is a closed figure that has three angles' do not ascribe a property to an object, but instead say of an object that it instantiates a certain kind. This does not matter to my arguments, since I can reformulate these predicates as 'is triangular', 'is closed and has three sides', and 'is closed and has three angles'. Lowe agrees that these predicates ascribe properties, and that the predicates 'is triangular' and 'is trilateral' ascribe the same property (2006, p. 85).

[15] Alternatively, (C1) could say that two predicates ascribe different properties if and only if these properties have a different structure. What I say in what follows also applies to this version of (C1).

extended in two- or three-dimensional space. This suggests that if properties are ways objects can be, the predicates 'has a shape' and 'has a size' ascribe a single property: the property of being extended in two- or three-dimensional space. If so, what (N) says about this example is also exactly right.

In response, non-reductive realists sometimes put forward the following criterion of property identity:

(C2)   Two predicates ascribe different properties if and only if these properties have different determinates.

They then say that the predicates 'has a shape' and 'has a size' ascribe properties that have different determinates: they say that the determinates of the first are being square, or being circular, and so on, and that the determinates of the second are being one metre by one metre, or having a diameter of two inches, and so on. But they are then overlooking the fact that these determinates are also determinates of the property of being extended in two- or three-dimensional space. (C2) therefore does not contradict (N) either. If non-reductive realists do take (C2) to contradict (N), they seem to assume that we can read off the determinates of a property from the determinates of a predicate that ascribes it. As before, that is something we can do only if properties are shadows of concepts.

A third purported counterexample to (N), which has been given by Derek Parfit, is that

The predicates 'is the only even prime number' and 'is the positive square root of four' are necessarily coextensive but ascribe different properties.[16]

But consider the sentence

Two is the positive square root of four.

This sentence does not seem to ascribe a property to the number two. Instead, it seems to say that the number two is identical to the positive square root of four. For we can reformulate it as

The positive square root of four is two,

---

[16] Parfit 2011b, pp. 296–7; see also Olson 2014, pp. 93–4.

and we can formalize it as

$$2 = \sqrt{4}$$

Moreover, Parfit admits that the phrases 'the positive square root of four' and 'the only even prime number' both refer to the number two.[17] This makes it hard to see how he can deny that the predicates 'is the positive square root of four' and 'is the only even prime number' ascribe a single property: the property of being the number two.

Jonas Olson suggests that Parfit can deny this because whereas being the positive square root of four is "an interesting property" of the number two, the property of being the number two is not.[18] Of course, Olson is right that the sentence

Two is the positive square root of four

is more interesting than the sentence

Two is two.

But that is because the predicates 'is two' and 'is the positive square root of four' express different concepts. This only shows that these predicates ascribe different properties if we take properties to be shadows of concepts.[19]

A fourth purported counterexample to (N), which Olson himself has given, is that

Predicates that necessarily lack extension, such as 'is a round square' and 'is an even prime larger than two', are necessarily coextensive but ascribe different properties.[20]

But if properties are ways objects can be, the predicates 'is a round square' and 'is an even number larger than two' ascribe non-existent properties.[21] Do these predicates ascribe a single non-existent property or different non-existent properties? If properties are ways objects can

---

[17] Parfit 2011b, p. 297.   [18] Olson 2014, p. 94.

[19] As Oddie 2005, pp. 149–50, puts it: "What we have here, in addition to the number [two], are … two ways of *arriving* at the number [two], two different intellectual *procedures* which yield that number."

[20] Olson 2014, p. 93.

[21] If properties are ways objects can be, uninstantiated properties may exist, but *necessarily* uninstantiated properties do not, since they are not ways any object can be. Some philosophers who take properties to be ways objects can be also deny that uninstantiated properties exist: see, for example, Armstrong 1997, pp. 38–43.

be, this question does not make sense. It only makes sense if properties are shadows of concepts.

A final purported counterexample to (N), which has been given by Alvin Plantinga, is that if divine command theory is true,

> Predicate D* and the predicate 'is such that God commands everyone to perform it' are necessarily coextensive but ascribe different properties.[22]

But these predicates are necessarily coextensive only if God cannot fail to exist and cannot fail to command everyone to perform the actions that satisfy predicate D*. More fully stated, therefore, Plantinga's example is that

> Predicate D* and the predicate 'is such that a being who could not fail to exist and who could not fail to command everyone to perform the actions that satisfy predicate D* commands everyone to perform it' are necessarily coextensive but ascribe different properties.

Though I have great trouble imagining such a being, these predicates seem to me to ascribe the same property. Of course, Plantinga has no such trouble, and he disagrees. But that is because he accepts the following criterion of property identity:

> (C3)   The predicates 'is F' and 'is G' ascribe different properties if and only if we can believe that an object is F without believing that this object is G.[23]

This criterion clearly assumes that properties are shadows of concepts. If (C3) were correct, Moore's open question argument would be sound:

---

[22] Plantinga 2010, pp. 258–9, 262. Plantinga gives this example while arguing that the reduction argument leaves open the possibility that normative properties are supernatural properties, which he takes to be properties that involve God or Godlike beings. But the reduction argument aims to show only that if there are normative properties, these properties are identical to *descriptive* properties. And the property of being such that God commands everyone to perform it is a descriptive property. See also McNaughton and Rawling 2003, pp. 29–30.

[23] Plantinga 2010, pp. 260, 264. Plantinga endorses what he calls an 'abundant' view of properties. He initially says that those who hold this view often accept (C3), but he then goes on to treat (C3) as part of this view.

non-reductive realists could then defend their view simply by noting that, for any descriptive property, someone who thinks that an action is right can intelligibly ask whether this action has this descriptive property.[24] Everyone agrees that non-reductive realism cannot be defended in this way. I therefore conclude that, contrary to what many non-reductive realists think, what (N) says about these purported counterexamples is exactly right.[25]

7. Leibniz's Law

But non-reductive realists need not give up yet. They could also say that normative properties are an exception to (N): they could say that (N) is generally correct, except when a normative predicate is necessarily coextensive with a descriptive predicate. But they then need to explain why these properties are an exception to (N).

Jussi Suikkanen suggests that they can explain this by appealing to the following criterion of property identity, which is an application of Leibniz's law:

(C4) Two predicates ascribe different properties if and only if these properties have different higher-order properties.

---

[24] As Plantinga 2010, p. 265, recognizes.

[25] Three other purported counterexamples to (N) are worth mentioning. Russ Shafer-Landau says that if (N) were true, the two-place predicates 'is identical to' and 'is necessarily coextensive with' would ascribe the same relation (2003, p. 91). But these predicates are not necessarily coextensive, since 'is identical to' applies to properties and 'is necessarily coextensive with' applies to predicates. Shafer-Landau also says that "if being triangular and trilateral were identical properties, then presumably being biangular and bilateral would be identical, and so too would being angular and lateral" (2003, p. 91). But this is not true, since biangular figures have three sides, figures that have one angle have two sides, and figures that have one side have no angles. And Jonas Olson calls (N) 'Hume's dictum' and suggests that the predicates 'is Hume's dictum' and 'is the correct dictum about whether necessarily coextensive predicates ascribe the same property' are necessarily coextensive but ascribe different properties (2014, p. 94). But these predicates are not necessarily coextensive, since the claim Olson calls 'Hume's dictum' could have been someone else's dictum instead: in the (admittedly not very close) possible world in which Derrida rather than Hume made this claim, it is Derrida's dictum.

For as Suikkanen notes, many non-reductive realists endorse the following claims:

(1) We can know a priori that an action is right, but we cannot know a priori that an action has the property that is ascribed by predicate D*.

(2) The property of being right is *resultant*, in the sense that an action is made right by a subset of its descriptive properties, but the property that is ascribed by predicate D* is not resultant.

(3) The property of being right has intrinsic practical relevance, but the property that is ascribed by predicate D* does not have such relevance.[26]

If these claims are true, the property that is ascribed by the predicate 'is right' and the property that is ascribed by predicate D* have different higher-order properties, in which case (C4) entails that these predicates ascribe different properties.

But reductive realists reject (1), (2), and (3). They could endorse the following claims instead:

(1*) We can know a priori both that an action is right and that an action has the property that is ascribed by predicate D*.

(2*) The property of being right and the property that is ascribed by predicate D* are both resultant.

(3*) The property of being right and the property that is ascribed by predicate D* both have intrinsic practical relevance.

If these claims are true, the property that is ascribed by the predicate 'is right' and the property that is ascribed by predicate D* have the same higher-order properties, in which case (C4) entails that these predicates ascribe the same property. This shows that non-reductive realists cannot explain why normative properties are an exception to (N) *merely* by appealing to (C4). They also need to explain why (1), (2), and (3) are true and (1*), (2*), and (3*) are false.

They could say that (1) is true and (1*) is false because a single proposition cannot be knowable both a priori and a posteriori. But that is not true: for example, my knowledge that 7,895,679 + 6,941,356

[26] See Suikkanen 2010, pp. 101–3. For the notion of resultance, see Dancy 1993, pp. 73–7, 2004b, pp. 85–6, and 2005, p. 128.

= 14,837,035 is a priori if it is based on my own calculation, but a posteriori if it is based on your testimony. They could also say that (1) is true and (1*) is false because if we had complete a posteriori knowledge of the instantiation of all descriptive properties in all possible worlds, we could nevertheless fail to know which actions are right.[27] That is true, but it does not show that we cannot know a priori that an action has the property that is ascribed by predicate D*. For non-reductive realists should admit that we can know a priori both that an action is right and that the predicate 'is right' is necessarily coextensive with predicate D*, and that is enough to know that this action has the property that is ascribed by predicate D*.[28]

Non-reductive realists could say that (2) is true and (2*) is false because the relation of resultance between an action's rightness and this action's descriptive properties is what Suikkanen calls a "metaphysically robust, worldly making-relation", whereas the relation between the property that is ascribed by predicate D* and this action's descriptive properties is "a merely logical relation of entailment between the act having a set of [descriptive] properties and a disjunction being true of it because one of the disjuncts is a specification of those properties".[29] But the reduction argument does not identify the relation of resultance with the relation of entailment between predicate D* and its disjuncts. The argument is therefore compatible with the claim that resultance is a worldly making-relation. Of course, non-reductive realists may think that this relation is itself irreducibly normative. But I will argue in §13 that the reduction argument also applies to normative relations, including the relation of resultance.

Finally, non-reductive realists could say that (3) is true and (3*) is false because only normative properties can have intrinsic practical relevance. But reductive realists who endorse (3*) think that descriptive properties that are identical to normative properties also have intrinsic practical

---

[27] Suikkanen 2010, p. 101.

[28] Of course, in order to know which descriptive property predicate D* ascribes, we need to know which actions are right. You may think that this undermines the reduction argument. But as I will explain in §27, it does not: to refute non-reductive realism, the argument does not have to show which descriptive properties normative properties are identical to, but only that each normative property is identical to some descriptive property or other.

[29] Suikkanen 2010, p. 102 (I have replaced 'natural' with 'descriptive'). See also McNaughton and Rawling 2003, pp. 32–3.

relevance. If non-reductive realists deny this, they are saying that only *irreducibly* normative properties can have intrinsic practical relevance. They are then in effect merely asserting that (3) is true and (3*) is false. And they are then merely asserting that normative properties are an exception to (N) instead of explaining why these properties are an exception. I therefore conclude that non-reductive realists cannot explain why normative properties are an exception to (N) by appealing to (C4).

8. Indispensability to Deliberation

David Enoch suggests a different way in which non-reductive realists can try to explain why normative properties are an exception to (N). He thinks that philosophers who accept (N) do so because (N) follows from a general principle of parsimony, according to which

> (1)   We should posit the existence of an entity only if this entity is indispensable to our best explanations.[30]

Enoch argues that this principle should be expanded as follows:

> (2)   We should posit the existence of an entity only if either this entity is indispensible to our best explanations, or this entity is indispensible to deliberation, in the sense that its non-existence would undermine our reason to engage in deliberation.[31]

And he argues that irreducibly normative properties are indispensable to deliberation in this sense. If so, this may explain why normative properties are an exception to (N).[32]

Whether it does depends on whether we should accept (N) because it follows from (1). I did not defend (N) in this way: instead, I argued that what (N) says about several purported counterexamples is exactly right, and that the versions of (C) that non-reductive realists

---

[30] See Enoch 2011a, pp. 137–40. As Enoch notes, Brown 2011 seems to agree.
[31] This is what Enoch calls 'instrumental' indispensability (2011a, p. 69). He adds that deliberation is also 'intrinsically' indispensable, in the sense that opting out of deliberation altogether is "not a rationally acceptable option" (2011a, pp. 70–1).
[32] See Enoch 2011a, p. 140 n. 15.

have put forward either do not contradict (N) or assume that properties are shadows of concepts. It also depends on whether (1) should be expanded to (2). This can also be denied.[33] And it depends on whether irreducibly normative properties are indispensable to deliberation. That is what I will now deny.

Enoch argues that normative properties are indispensable to deliberation because deliberation is "an attempt to eliminate arbitrariness by discovering (normative) reasons" which "is impossible in a believed absence of such reasons to be discovered", because deliberation "feels like trying to make the *right* choice", and because the phenomenology of deliberation is similar "to that of trying to find an answer to a straightforwardly factual question".[34] This may show that normative properties are indispensable to deliberation. But it does not show that if normative properties were identical to descriptive properties, this would undermine our reason to engage in deliberation. It therefore does not show that *irreducibly* normative properties are indispensable to deliberation.

Enoch tries to show that they are by saying that normative properties seem very different from descriptive properties when they are considered "from the point of view of the deliberating agent". He writes:

When I ask myself what I should do, it seems that just answering 'Oh, pressing the blue button will maximize happiness' is a complete non-starter, it completely fails to address the question. Of course, given some background commitments it can be a better answer. If, for instance, I am already a convinced utilitarian, willing to commit myself to something like 'It always makes sense to perform the action that maximizes happiness', then 'Pressing the blue button will maximize happiness' seems like a reasonable answer to the question what I should do. But such background commitments are themselves paradigmatically normative.[35]

Reductive realists can agree, however, that when I ask myself what I should do, an answer that uses a descriptive predicate to ascribe a normative property fails to address my question if I do not believe that this predicate ascribes this property. For they can agree that normative and descriptive

---

[33] See Olson 2014, pp. 176–7, and McPherson and Plunkett 2015.

[34] Enoch 2011a, pp. 72–4.

[35] Enoch 2011a, pp. 107–8; see also p. 80, where Enoch similarly writes that "only normative truths can answer the normative questions I ask myself in deliberation".

predicates present properties in different ways. But they can say that if I *do* believe that this predicate ascribes this property, this answer *does* address my question. And they can make similar claims about my background normative commitments. This means that irreducibly normative properties are not indispensable to deliberation. I therefore conclude that non-reductive realists cannot explain why normative properties are an exception to (N) in this way either.[36]

We can now also draw a more general conclusion. I said in §6 that many non-reductive realists take the correct criterion of property identity to be where (C) is in this picture:

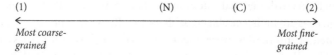

I have argued that what (N) says about several purported counterexamples is exactly right, and that the versions of (C) that non-reductive realists have put forward either do not contradict (N) or assume that properties are shadows of concepts. I have also argued that two possible explanations of why normative properties are an exception to (N) fail. I therefore conclude that if properties are ways objects can be, (N) is the correct criterion of property identity. Since non-reductive realists must take properties to be ways objects can be, this means that they cannot defensibly reject (N).

Why does not everyone agree with this conclusion? One reason for this may be the hold that a mistaken idea has on us: the idea that an object's name somehow reflects its essence. This idea is defended by Cratylus in Plato's eponymous dialogue. When it is made explicit, most of us will think that Socrates is right to mock it. But its hold on us may be hard to break completely.

9. Rejecting (S)

Non-reductive realists also try to resist the reduction argument in other ways. Some of them reject the claim that

---

[36] See also Lenman 2014, who argues in a different way that irreducibly normative properties are not indispensable to deliberation.

(S) For all possible worlds W and W*, if the instantiation of descriptive properties in W and W* is exactly the same, then the instantiation of normative properties in W and W* is also exactly the same.

One reason for rejecting (S) is that English and other natural languages may not contain enough predicates to ascribe all properties.[37] If so, my claims about normative and descriptive properties imply that some properties are neither normative nor descriptive. But we can get around this problem by saying that

A property is *descriptive* if and only if either it can be ascribed with a descriptive predicate or it cannot be ascribed with a normative predicate.[38]

If we say this, all properties are either normative or descriptive. That makes it very hard to reject (S). Could an object gain or lose a normative property without any descriptive change anywhere in its possible world? For example, could an action become right or cease to be right without any descriptive change anywhere in its possible world? It is hard to see how this could happen. And if you agree that this cannot happen, you are agreeing that (S) is true.

Non-reductive realists sometimes also reject the claim that

(S*) For all possible worlds W and W* and objects O and O*, if O in W and O* in W* have exactly the same descriptive properties, then O in W and O* in W* also have exactly the same normative properties.[39]

---

[37] As Sturgeon 2009, p. 75, writes, "as soon as we involve our representational powers in the formulation of a supervenience thesis in this way, the plausibility of the thesis is threatened if those powers are limited". Sturgeon also notes that it follows from some views about thick concepts that "there are natural (or supernatural) properties for which we lack descriptive terminology, and they seem to be properties that make an evaluative difference" (pp. 76–7).

[38] We could then call this property 'non-normative' rather than descriptive. But as I said in §1, this would be confusing, since the claim that property P is *non*-normative then would not entail that property P is *not* normative.

[39] Particularists such as Dancy 2004b reject (S*), at least if we do not include the instantiation of all descriptive properties in an object's possible world among this object's descriptive properties. Rosen unpublished also rejects (S*), and his reasons for rejecting (S*) commit him to rejecting (S) as well. For discussion, see Dreier unpublished and Väyrynen 2017.

But this does not matter to the reduction argument, since the argument appeals to (S) rather than to (S*). Moreover, in §12 I will give a version of the reduction argument that does not appeal to any claim about super-venience at all.[40]

10. Objections to Predicate D*

Some non-reductive realists try to resist the reduction argument by objecting to its use of predicate D*. They sometimes say that

(1)   Since predicate D* is infinitely disjunctive, it cannot be formu-
        lated in English or in another natural language.[41]

But the reduction argument requires only that there is a *possible* language in which predicate D* can be formulated, which may be a partly 'Lagadonian' language in which the objects or properties that are not named by any natural language are their own names instead.[42] You may object that if a property is its own name, this property is neither normative nor descriptive. But as before, we can get around this problem by saying that a property is descriptive if and only if either it can be ascribed with a descriptive predicate or it cannot be ascribed with a normative predicate.

Non-reductive realists also sometimes say that

(2)   Since there are no disjunctive properties, predicate D* does not
        ascribe a property.

But if properties are ways objects can be, properties are not themselves disjunctive or non-disjunctive. The only things that are disjunctive or

---

[40] Wedgwood 2007, pp. 212–20, rejects a version of (S) that replaces 'descriptive' with 'natural', and instead endorses what Schmitt and Schroeder 2011 call a 'world-relative' version of (S). To ensure that this world-relative version does not entail the version of (S) he rejects, Wedgwood rejects the S4 and S5 axioms of modal logic. But as Schmitt and Schroeder argue, the negation of the version of (S) that Wedgwood rejects is very implaus-ible. Moreover, the version of the reduction argument that I will give in §12 goes through even if we reject (S) and the S4 and S5 axioms of modal logic.

[41] See Brown 2011. Brown puts forward a version of the reduction argument that avoids what he calls a "needless detour" via language (p. 206) and that does not explicitly appeal to (N). But this version of the argument does appeal to the principle that we should "posit only so many properties as are required to distinguish possibilities" (p. 213). This principle entails (N), since necessarily coextensive predicates make the same distinction between possibilities.

[42] For the idea of a 'Lagadonian' language, see Lewis 1986, pp. 145–6.

non-disjunctive are the predicates with which they are ascribed.[43] More-over, if (N) is correct, many properties can be ascribed with either a non-disjunctive or a disjunctive predicate. For example, consider the non-disjunctive predicate

'is an additive primary colour'.

The property that this predicate ascribes can also be ascribed with the disjunctive predicate 'is green or red or blue'. Or consider the non-disjunctive predicate

'is a noble gas'.

The property that this predicate ascribes can also be ascribed with the disjunctive predicate 'is Helium or Neon or Argon or Krypton or Xenon or Radon'. Or consider the non-disjunctive German predicate

'ist ein Rind'.

Since the term 'Rind' applies to both cows and bulls, the property that this predicate ascribes can also be ascribed with the disjunctive English predicate 'is a cow or a bull'.[44] Similarly, if the non-disjunctive predicate 'is right' ascribes a property, this property can also be ascribed with predicate D*.

Graham Oddie makes a more specific version of this objection. Build-ing on work by Peter Gärdenfors, Oddie claims that a predicate ascribes a property only if this predicate carves out a convex region of what he calls a 'quality space', where a region R is convex if and only if any region between two subregions of R is itself also in R.[45] For example, suppose that we divide up a range of temperatures in the following way:

Cold	Warm	Hot

The predicates 'is cold', 'is warm', 'is hot', 'is cold or warm', and 'is warm or hot' then carve out convex regions of this quality space. Oddie

---

[43] Oddie 2005, p. 151, makes a similar point.
[44] A similar example is given by Antony 2003, pp. 9–10, though she uses the term 'Kuh'.
[45] See Oddie 2005, pp. 153–5, and Gärdenfors 2000 and 2014.

claims that these predicates therefore ascribe properties. But the predicate 'is cold or hot' does not carve out such a region, since the region carved out by 'is warm' is between two subregions of the region carved out by 'is cold or hot'. Oddie claims that this predicate therefore does not ascribe a property. And he thinks that non-reductive realists can similarly say that

(3)   Since predicate D* does not carve out a convex region of a quality space, it does not ascribe a property.

But whether a predicate carves out a convex region of a quality space may only tell us something about the concept it expresses. That is what Gärdenfors thinks: he takes properties to be "a special case of concepts" and calls what Oddie calls a quality space a "conceptual space".[46] Moreover, the predicate 'is right' *could* be necessarily coextensive with a predicate that carves out a convex region of a quality space: for example, if a simple version of utilitarianism is correct, the predicate 'is right' is necessarily coextensive with the predicate 'maximizes happiness'. Oddie's view therefore implies that whether there are irreducibly normative properties depends on which first-order normative view is correct. And that seems wrong: it seems that whether normative properties are identical to descriptive properties depends on the nature of these properties rather than on which first-order normative view is correct. I will return to this in §12.

Finally, non-reductive realists sometimes say that

(4)   Though predicate D* does ascribe a property, the property it ascribes is not descriptive.

They could try to defend (4) by saying that the specification of predicate D* depends on which actions have the normative property of being right.[47] But since predicate D* consists wholly of descriptive predicates, once it is specified this predicate ascribes a descriptive property. Of course, since this property can also be ascribed with the predicate 'is right', it is also normative. But that does not mean that it is not descriptive.

---

[46] Gärdenfors 2000, pp. 60, 101, and 2014, p. 25.
[47] See Majors 2005, p. 482.

Non-reductive realists could also try to defend (4) by saying that the sentence

(5)   Action A satisfies predicate D*

entails that action A satisfies the predicate 'is right'. They could say that if it is true that

A judgement is normative if and only if it can be expressed with a sentence that entails that something satisfies a normative predicate,

this means that (5) expresses a normative judgement. And they could say that if (5) expresses a normative judgement, predicate D* is a normative predicate. But they are then overlooking the fact that (5) does not *conceptually* entail that action A satisfies the predicate 'is right': it does not entail this in virtue of the concepts it expresses. I therefore think that (5) does not express a normative judgement.

When non-reductive realists object to the reduction argument's use of predicate D*, what they really have in mind may be that objects share a property only if there is a real resemblance between them, and that there is no real resemblance between the actions that satisfy predicate D*.[48] But since these actions all have the property of being right, non-reductive realists cannot defensibly say that there is no real resemblance between them. They may assume that a predicate ascribes a property only if this predicate somehow *reveals* the real resemblance between the objects that satisfy it. But I think we should reject this assumption. It is a remnant of Cratylus's idea that an object's name reflects its essence.

11. Preview

In the next chapter, I will give two further versions of the reduction argument. I will also defend the argument against several further objections.

---

[48] A claim along these lines is made by Majors 2005, p. 485, who writes that "if a property is of kind K, then the members of its extension must have something in common which is visible from level K".

III

Further Versions of the Reduction Argument

I will now continue my discussion of the reduction argument.

12. A Second and Third Version of the Argument

You may remain suspicious of predicate D*. I will therefore give two versions of the reduction argument that do not make use of this predicate. The first is as follows. Suppose that the correct first-order view about rightness is a simple version of utilitarianism, which says that

Necessarily, an action is right if and only if it maximizes happiness.

If this view is correct, the predicate 'is right' is necessarily coextensive with the descriptive predicate 'maximizes happiness'. If it is true that

(N)   Two predicates ascribe the same property if and only if they are necessarily coextensive,

this means that these predicates ascribe the same property. It therefore means that the property of being right is identical to a descriptive property.

Suppose next that equally simple first-order views are correct about all other normative properties. These views may say, for example, that

Necessarily, a consideration is a reason for a belief if and only if it increases the probability that this belief is true.

Necessarily, a state of affairs is intrinsically good to the extent that it contains happiness.

...and so on.

If such simple first-order views are correct, all other normative predicates are also necessarily coextensive with descriptive predicates. If (N) is correct, this means that all other normative properties are also identical to descriptive properties. This shows that

(1) If simple first-order normative views are correct, normative properties are identical to descriptive properties.

Now consider the following claim:

(W) Whether normative properties are identical to descriptive properties cannot depend on which first-order normative view is correct.

Of course, if normative properties are identical to descriptive properties, *which* descriptive properties they are identical to *does* depend on which first-order normative view is correct. For which descriptive properties they are identical to depends on

(2) which objects have which normative properties

and on

(3) which descriptive properties these objects have,

and a first-order normative view is, in part, a view about (2) and (3). But (W) does not deny this. (W) only says that *whether* normative properties are identical to descriptive properties cannot depend on which first-order normative view is correct. That seems true, since whether normative properties are identical to descriptive properties seems to depend on the nature of these properties rather than on (2) and (3). And since non-reductive realists think that the nature of normative properties prevents these properties from being identical to descriptive properties, they should agree that (W) is true.

Suppose that normative properties would be identical to descriptive properties if simple first-order normative views were correct, but not if more complicated first-order normative views were correct. In that case, whether normative properties are identical to descriptive properties would depend on which first-order normative view is correct, which would contradict (W). This means that if (W) is true and if it is true that

(1)   If simple first-order normative views are correct, normative
      properties are identical to descriptive properties,

it follows that normative properties are identical to descriptive properties
whether or not simple first-order normative views are correct. In other
words, if (W) and (1) are true, it follows that there are no irreducibly
normative properties.

Non-reductive realists could try to resist this version of the reduction
argument by rejecting (1). But they cannot reject (1) by objecting to the
argument's use of predicate D*, since this version of the argument does
not make use of predicate D* or any other infinitely disjunctive predicate.
And they also cannot reject (1) by rejecting the claim that

(S)   For all possible worlds W and W*, if the instantiation of descrip-
      tive properties in W and W* is exactly the same, then the
      instantiation of normative properties in W and W* is also exactly
      the same,

since this version of the argument does not appeal to (S) or to any other
claim about supervenience.[1]

---

[1] Dunaway 2015 also gives a version of the reduction argument that does not appeal to
(S). Suppose again that actions $A_1, A_2, \ldots$ are all the right actions there are in all possible
worlds, and suppose that we construct predicates $D_1, D_2, \ldots$ the way we did in §5. If (S) is
false, there are possible worlds that have the same instantiation of descriptive properties
but different instantiations of normative properties, which means that an action that
satisfies one of the predicates $D_1, D_2, \ldots$ may be right in one possible world but fail to be
right in a different possible world. But suppose that $W_1, W_2, \ldots$ are all the possible worlds
in which an action is right, with world W_1 being the world in which action A_1 is right,
and so on (and with possible worlds that contain more than one right action included
more than once in $W_1, W_2, \ldots$). We can then construct the following predicate, which we
can call predicate D**: 'either satisfies predicate D_1 *and is in* W_1, or satisfies predicate D_2
and is in W_2, or ...' Since W_1 is the possible world in which action A_1 is right, an action
cannot satisfy predicate D_1 *and be in* W_1 and fail to be right. Similar claims apply to
predicates $D_2, D_3, \ldots$ and possible worlds $W_2, W_3, \ldots$ It therefore follows that predicate
D** is necessarily coextensive with the predicate 'is right' whether or not (S) is true. And
if Dunaway is right that predicate D** is a descriptive predicate, it follows that normative
properties are identical to descriptive properties whether or not (S) is true. Dunaway
takes this to show that the core commitment of non-naturalism is not that normative
properties are not identical to descriptive properties, but is instead that normative
properties are metaphysically fundamental. But as I will explain in §30, what matters
to my arguments is only whether normative properties are identical to descriptive
properties.

Non-reductive realists could instead try to resist the argument by rejecting (W). They could say that (W) follows from a generalized version of the claim that

(W*)   Which metaethical theory is true cannot depend on which first-order moral view is correct,

and they could point out that some philosophers reject (W*). For example, Ronald Dworkin objects to irrealist metaethical views that these views contradict extremely plausible first-order moral claims, such as the claim that torturing children for fun is wrong.[2] Since this objection assumes that (W*) is false, it may also seem to assume that (W) is false.

But Dworkin's objection does not assume this. For instead of saying that *which metaethical theory is true* cannot depend on which first-order normative view is correct, (W) only makes the weaker claim that *whether normative properties are identical to descriptive properties* cannot depend on which first-order normative view is correct. And unlike irrealist metaethical views, neither the claim that

Normative properties are identical to descriptive properties

nor the claim that

Normative properties are not identical to descriptive properties

contradicts any first-order normative view at all.

Non-reductive realists may also say that though they themselves accept (W), their opponents do not accept (W) and therefore cannot appeal to this claim in order to reject non-reductive realism. But just as non-reductive realists accept (W) because they think that the nature of normative properties prevents these properties from being identical to descriptive properties, their opponents can accept (W) because they think that the nature of normative properties makes it the case that these properties *are* identical to descriptive properties. Moreover, we can put forward this version of the reduction argument even if we ourselves do not accept (W). Since the argument aims to show only

---

[2] See Dworkin 1996 and 2011. Similar views are defended by Nagel 1997 and Kramer 2009. I will return to this objection in §72.

that non-reductive realism is false, it requires only that non-reductive realists accept (W).

Non-reductive realists may still want to reject (W), perhaps as a defensive move in order to rescue their view.[3] If so, we can turn to another version of the reduction argument that does not make use of predicate D*. We can call normative truths that obtain independently of which objects have which descriptive properties *fundamental normative truths.*[4] These truths may have the following form:

> If certain objects have descriptive properties $P_1, \ldots, P_n$, then a certain object has normative property X.

Some examples may be:

> If an action maximizes happiness, then this action is right.

> If a consideration increases the probability that a belief is true, then this consideration is a reason for this belief.

> If a state of affairs contains happiness, then it is to this extent intrinsically good.

If the truth of such claims does not depend on which objects have which descriptive properties, these claims are fundamental normative truths.[5] By contrast, the truth of the claim that a particular action is right *does* depend on which objects have which descriptive properties, since it depends on this action's descriptive properties. Such a claim is therefore not a fundamental normative truth.

---

[3] Oddie 2005, pp. 141–80, gives an argument for the existence of irreducibly normative properties that entails that (W) is false. But Oddie does not give an independent argument against (W), and (W) seems to me more plausible than the premises of Oddie's argument (see §10).

[4] As Enoch 2011a, p. 146 n. 32, puts it: to reach these fundamental normative truths (or, as Enoch calls them, 'basic norms'), we "backtrack, so to speak, practical syllogisms to their major premises, until we reach such a major premise that is not itself the conclusion of a practical syllogism, or that is (roughly speaking) free of empirical content". See also Cohen 2008, pp. 229–73, who argues that there are "ultimate principles" that are "fact-insensitive" (by which he means that they are not made correct by descriptive facts), and Scanlon 2014, pp. 36–7, who thinks there are true "pure normative claims" according to which "whether *p* obtains or not, *should p* hold then it is a reason for someone in *c* to do *a*".

[5] You may object that these conditionals are not normative, since they do not ascribe normative properties. But my argument requires only that their consequents ascribe normative properties. I will discuss whether such conditionals are normative in §50.

Suppose that you are a non-reductive realist, and consider the complete list of what you take to be fundamental normative truths. Unless you are a particularist, this list will be finite.[6] And if this list is finite, it will be possible to construct, for each normative predicate, a finitely disjunctive descriptive predicate that is coextensive with this normative predicate if the fundamental normative truths are as you take them to be.

Now consider again the claim that

(S) For all possible worlds W and W*, if the instantiation of descriptive properties in W and W* is exactly the same, then the instantiation of normative properties in W and W* is also exactly the same.

If (S) is true, all fundamental normative truths are necessary truths. For suppose that some were not. In that case, there would be two possible worlds that have different fundamental normative truths. If these worlds had the same instantiation of descriptive properties, their different fundamental normative truths would make it the case that they had different instantiations of normative properties, which would contradict (S). Different possible worlds can therefore only have different fundamental normative truths if they have different instantiations of descriptive properties. But then these different normative truths do not obtain independently of which objects have which descriptive properties, and are therefore not fundamental.[7]

If all fundamental normative truths are necessary truths, and if the complete list of what you take to be fundamental normative truths is finite, it is possible to construct, for each normative predicate, a finitely disjunctive descriptive predicate that is *necessarily* coextensive with this normative predicate if the fundamental normative truths are as you take them to be. If (N) is correct, this commits you to the conclusion that there are no irreducibly normative properties. Particularists can perhaps avoid this conclusion by claiming that the complete list of fundamental normative truths is infinite. But other non-reductive realists cannot.

---

[6] For a defence of particularism, see Dancy 1993 and 2004b.

[7] Many non-reductive realists seem to agree that fundamental normative truths are necessary truths: see, for example, McNaughton and Rawling 2003, p. 33, Parfit 2011a, p. 129, and 2011b, pp. 307, 489–90, 747, and, more tentatively, Enoch 2011a, p. 146.

13. Does the Argument Apply to Normative Relations?

Some non-reductive realists try to resist the reduction argument by denying that it applies to normative relations, such as the relation of *being a reason for*, or the relation of resultance that I mentioned in §7.[8] To evaluate this denial, we can modify the first version of the argument.[9] We can say that

A relation is *descriptive* if and only if it can be ascribed with a descriptive two-place predicate,

that

A relation is *normative* if and only if it can be ascribed with a normative two-place predicate,

and that

A normative relation is *irreducibly normative* if and only if it is not identical to a descriptive relation.

Consider a fact F_1 that is a reason for an action A_1: in other words, a fact F_1 that stands in the relation of *being a reason for* to an action A_1.[10] Fact F_1 also has descriptive properties, which we can call $P_{F1-1}, P_{F1-2}, \ldots$, and action A_1 also has descriptive properties, which we can call $P_{A1-1}, P_{A1-2}, \ldots$. And the objects $O_1, O_2, \ldots$ that are part of the same possible world as fact F_1 and action A_1 have descriptive properties as well, which for each object O_x we can call $P_{Ox-1}, P_{Ox-2}, \ldots$.[11] Fact F_1 and action A_1

---

[8] See Dancy 2004a and FitzPatrick 2008, p. 201. Dancy actually says that "there is a worry that Jackson will be unable to capture the notion of a reason" (p. 233), and that "Jackson's descriptive metaphysics leaves him unable to capture the right-making relation" (p. 237). I take this to mean that he thinks that the argument does not show that the relation of *being a reason for* and the relation of right-making (which is a version of the relation of resultance) are identical to descriptive relations.

[9] As before, my presentation of the argument assumes that the number of objects and properties in all possible worlds is countably infinite. I take this to be merely a matter of presentation.

[10] I assume for simplicity that all reasons are facts and that these facts are reasons only for actions, not for attitudes.

[11] I include descriptive relations among $P_{F1-1}, P_{F1-2}, \ldots$, among $P_{A1-1}, P_{A1-2}, \ldots$ and among $P_{Ox-1}, P_{Ox-2}, \ldots$.

therefore satisfy the following two-place predicate, which we can call predicate R_1:

'___ has descriptive properties P_{F1-1}, P_{F1-2}, ..., and ___ has descriptive properties P_{A1-1}, P_{A1-2}, ..., and both are such that O_1 has descriptive properties P_{O1-1}, P_{O1-2}, ..., that O_2 has descriptive properties P_{O2-1}, P_{O2-2}, ..., ...'.

Suppose next that facts F_1, F_2, ... are all the facts that are reasons for action in all possible worlds, and that actions A_1, A_2, ... are all the actions that these facts are reasons for (with fact F_1 being a reason for action A_1, and so on).[12] Just as fact F_1 and action A_1 satisfy the two-place predicate R_1, facts F_2, F_3, ... and actions A_2, A_3, ... satisfy similarly constructed two-place predicates R_2, R_3, ... These facts and actions therefore all satisfy the following two-place predicate, which we can call predicate R^*:

'___ and ___ satisfy either the descriptive two-place predicate R_1, or the descriptive two-place predicate R_2, or ...'.

Just as we take (S) to be true, I think we also take the following claim to be true:

(S**)   For all possible worlds W and W*, if the instantiation of descriptive properties and relations in W and W* is exactly the same, then the instantiation of normative properties and relations in W and W* is also exactly the same.

If (S**) is true, any ordered pair of a fact and an action that satisfies predicate R^* also satisfies the predicate 'is a reason for'. For otherwise there would be two possible worlds W and W* that have exactly the same instantiation of descriptive properties and relations but that do not have the same instantiation of normative properties and relations, which would contradict (S**). And any ordered pair of a fact and an action that satisfies the predicate 'is a reason for' also satisfies predicate R^*. For facts F_1, F_2, ... are all the facts that are reasons for action in all possible worlds, and actions A_1, A_2, ... are all the actions that these facts are

---

[12] Of course, many facts stand in the relation of *being a reason for* to more than one action, and many actions are such that there is more than one fact that stands in the relation of *being a reason for* to them. These facts and these actions are included more than once in F_1, F_2, ... and in A_1, A_2, ...

reasons for. Since the ordered pairs of these facts and actions satisfy predicates $R_1, R_2, \ldots$, they also satisfy predicate R^*.

This shows that the predicate 'is a reason for' and predicate R^* are necessarily coextensive. Now consider the following criterion of relation identity:

> (N*) Two two-place predicates ascribe the same relation if and only if they are necessarily coextensive.

If this criterion is correct, the predicate 'is a reason for' and predicate R^* ascribe the same relation. The normative relation of *being a reason for* is then identical to a descriptive relation. And this argument can be repeated for any other normative two-place predicate. It therefore shows that if (S**) is true and (N*) is correct, there are no irreducibly normative relations.

Jonathan Dancy objects to this version of the argument that whereas the predicate 'is a reason for' ascribes an asymmetric relation, predicate R^* does not.[13] But a relation is asymmetric if and only if

> For all actual and possible objects X and Y, if X stands in this relation to Y, then Y does not stand in this relation to X.

In other words, a relation is asymmetric if and only if

> For all actual and possible objects X and Y, if the ordered pair (X, Y) satisfies a predicate that ascribes this relation, then the ordered pair (Y, X) does not satisfy this predicate.

Since predicate R^* is necessarily coextensive with the predicate 'is a reason for', these predicates are satisfied by exactly the same ordered pairs (F_x, A_x). This means that if the relation that the predicate 'is a reason for' ascribes is asymmetric, the relation that predicate R^* ascribes is asymmetric as well. I therefore conclude that the reduction argument does apply to normative relations.

14. Rampant Reductionism

Finally, non-reductive realists sometimes suggest that if the reduction argument is sound, it shows that *whenever* properties of kind X supervene

---

[13] See Dancy 2004b, p. 65.

on properties of kind Y, properties of kind X are identical to certain properties of kind Y.[14] Since they reject such rampant reductionism, they take this to show that there is something wrong with the argument.

But the reduction argument only shows that properties of kind X are identical to properties of kind Y if it is true that

(1) Necessarily, anything that has properties of kind X also has properties of kind Y,

and that

(2) For all possible worlds W and W*, if the instantiation of properties of kind Y in W and W* is exactly the same, then the instantiation of properties of kind X in W and W* is also exactly the same.

These claims are true of normative and descriptive properties, but they may not be true of other properties of kind X that supervene on properties of kind Y. For example, it may not be true that

Necessarily, anything that has mental properties also has physical properties,

and that

For all possible worlds W and W*, if the instantiation of physical properties in W and W* is exactly the same, then the instantiation of mental properties in W and W* is also exactly the same.

For there may be possible worlds that contain ghosts who have mental properties but no physical properties, or possible worlds in which certain objects have additional mental properties without any object having any additional physical property.[15]

Materialists therefore usually endorse a more restricted claim about supervenience, such as:

For all possible worlds W and W* that do not contain fundamental properties that are alien to the actual world, if the instantiation of

---

[14] A version of this objection is discussed by Majors 2005, p. 487.
[15] See Jackson 1998, pp. 11–12, 119, and Oddie 2005, p. 142.

physical properties in W and W* is exactly the same, then the instantiation of mental properties in W and W* is also exactly the same.[16]

If mental properties supervene on physical properties only in this more restricted sense, the reduction argument does not show that there are no irreducibly mental properties. The same applies to all other supervening properties of which (1) and (2) are not true. The reduction argument therefore does not support rampant reductionism.

15. Why Non-Reductive Realists May Remain Unmoved

In my experience, most non-reductive realists remain unmoved by the reduction argument. What explains this?

One explanation may be that they tacitly conflate properties with concepts. For example, Dancy writes that "the naturalist idea has to be that the subject matter of the fact that this action would maximize welfare could be the same as that of the fact that it would make the action right".[17] This claim about the 'subject matter' of facts seems to conflate facts with meanings of sentences, and thereby seems to conflate properties with concepts. And Parfit writes that if a normative and a non-normative claim "stated the same fact, they would give us the same information", in which case "this normative claim could not state a normative fact".[18] This slide from facts to information also seems to conflate properties with concepts.

A second explanation may be that many non-reductive realists take the reduction argument to support reductive realism, which is a view they reject for other reasons. I agree that there are good reasons to reject reductive realism. But the reduction argument only shows that

(1) If there are normative properties, these properties are identical to descriptive properties.

---

[16] See Lewis 1994, p. 293, and Jackson 1998, p. 14.

[17] Dancy 2005, p. 140. FitzPatrick 2008, pp. 180–1, also makes claims about the 'content' of moral and empirical facts.

[18] Parfit 2011b, p. 339. Parfit is perhaps better described as a quietist than as a non-reductive realist. I will return to this in §44.

This conclusion is compatible with the falsity of reductive realism, since it is compatible with the claim that

(2)   If there are normative properties, these properties are *not* identical to descriptive properties.

I will defend (2) in chapters IV and V. Even if there are good reasons to reject reductive realism, this therefore should not stop us from accepting the conclusion of the reduction argument.

A third and final explanation may be that non-reductive realists take the most defensible alternative to their view to be the error theory, which is a view they cannot bring themselves to believe.[19] I also cannot bring myself to believe this view. But I think that our inability to believe the error theory should not stop us from accepting the conclusion of the reduction argument either.

16. Conclusion

I conclude that non-reductive realism is false. This means that if there are normative properties, these properties are identical to descriptive properties.

---

[19] For the claim that the error theory is the most defensible alternative to non-reductive realism, see, for example, Enoch 2011a, p. 115.

IV

The False Guarantee
and Regress Objections

The reduction argument shows that if there are normative properties, these properties are identical to descriptive properties. But are they?

17. An Implication of Reductive Realism

According to reductive realists, they are. If so, an object's normative properties are not extra properties in addition to its descriptive properties. They are instead *among* its descriptive properties: they are those descriptive properties that can be ascribed with normative predicates. As Frank Jackson writes, if ethical properties are identical to descriptive properties, there is "no 'extra' feature that the ethical terms are fastening onto".[1]

Non-reductive realists disagree: they think that an object's normative properties *are* extra properties in addition to its descriptive properties. But that cannot be true if the reduction argument is sound. In the first version of the argument, the complicated formulation of predicate D* may have obscured this. But it is clear in the second version of the argument. If the predicate 'is right' is necessarily coextensive with the predicate 'maximizes happiness', and if

(N)   Two predicates ascribe the same property if and only if they are necessarily coextensive,

then the property of being right is not an extra property in addition to the property of maximizing happiness. Instead, the predicate 'is right' is another name for the property of maximizing happiness.

---

[1] Jackson 1998, pp. 124–5; see also Jackson 2005, p. 101.

Non-reductive realists may reply that the predicate 'maximizes happiness' is then *also* another name for the property of being right. That is true. But it does not show that the predicate 'is right' is *not* another name for the property of maximizing happiness. It therefore does not contradict my claim that if reductive realism is true, an object's normative properties are among its descriptive properties. If non-reductive realism is true, the difference between normative and descriptive properties is a difference in the nature of these properties. By contrast, if reductive realism is true, the difference between normative and descriptive properties is a difference in language, which is not matched by a difference in the nature of these properties.[2]

18. What Makes It the Case That a Certain Normative Predicate Ascribes a Certain Descriptive Property?

If a certain normative predicate ascribes a certain descriptive property, this cannot be a brute fact. There must be something that makes it the case that *this* normative predicate ascribes *this* descriptive property. What can make this the case?

Most reductive realists assume that

(P1)   What makes it the case that a certain normative predicate ascribes a certain descriptive property is that, in certain *descriptively* specified conditions, users of this predicate would apply it to objects that have this property.[3]

I will discuss this claim in §§19–21. You may instead think that

(P2)   What makes it the case that a certain normative predicate ascribes a certain descriptive property is that, in certain *normatively* specified conditions, users of this predicate would apply it to objects that have this property.

---

[2] Of course, it need not *only* be a difference in language: it may also be a difference, for example, in the way we experience these properties, or in the role these properties play in our deliberation. And this difference may explain the difference in language.

[3] Here and in what follows, I use 'apply' to mean sincerely apply.

I will ask in §22 whether reductive realists can endorse this claim. Finally, some reductive realists seem to assume that

(P3)   What makes it the case that a certain normative predicate ascribes a certain descriptive property is that the correct first-order normative view applies this predicate to objects that have this property.

I will discuss this claim in §23.

19. Descriptively Specified Conditions

There are two main versions of (P1). The first is outlined in most detail by Frank Jackson, making use of an idea by Frank Ramsey that was developed by Carnap and Lewis.[4] Consider the set of all moral judgements that people would make after maximum reflection.[5] If we write down these judgements as a long conjunction, this conjunction may, for example, say that

Happiness is good, and breaking one's promises is wrong, and virtuous people bring about good consequences without performing wrong actions, and...

We can then rewrite this conjunction as follows:

Happiness has the property of being good, and breaking one's promises has the property of being wrong, and people who have the property of being virtuous bring about consequences that have the property of being good without performing actions that have the property of being wrong, and...

[4] See Jackson 1998, pp. 129–62, and also Jackson 1992, pp. 485–6, 2000, 2005, pp. 102–4, 2009, pp. 442–9, and Jackson and Pettit 1995 and 1996. This version of (P1) fits with a descriptivist approach to reference determination, according to which a term's reference is determined primarily by implicit reference-fixing criteria that users of the term associate with it. For discussion of Jackson's view, see van Roojen 1996, Yablo 2000, pp. 16–19, Zangwill 2000, Schroeter and Schroeter 2009, and Horgan and Timmons 2009. For Lewis' development of Ramsey's idea, see Lewis 1970.

[5] Jackson 1998 calls this set 'mature folk morality'. As he puts it, mature folk morality is "what folk morality will (would) turn into in the limit under critical reflection" (p. 139; see also p. 133).

If we then replace all property names in this conjunction with variables $x_1, x_2, x_3, \ldots$, we get:

Happiness has x_1, and breaking one's promises has x_2, and people who have x_3 bring about consequences that have x_1 without performing actions that have x_2, and ...

Now suppose that there is exactly one set of descriptive properties that are related to each other the way $x_1, x_2, x_3, \ldots$ are related to each other. In that case, the following sentence is true:

$(\exists x_1) (\exists x_2) (\exists x_3) \ldots$ (Happiness has x_1, and breaking one's promises has x_2, and people who have x_3 bring about consequences that have x_1 without performing actions that have x_2, and ...) & $((\exists y_1) (\exists y_2) (\exists y_3) \ldots$ (Happiness has y_1, and breaking one's promises has y_2, and people who have y_3 bring about consequences that have y_1 without performing actions that have y_2, and ...) $\supset (x_1 = y_1$ & $x_2 = y_2$ & $x_3 = y_3$ & ...)).

This sentence's first conjunct is a so-called *Ramsey sentence*, which says that there is a set of properties that are related to each other the way $x_1, x_2, x_3, \ldots$ are related to each other. Its second conjunct adds that there is exactly one such set.[6]

According to Jackson, this modified Ramsey sentence tells us which descriptive properties moral predicates ascribe. For example, it tells us that the predicate 'is good' ascribes

The descriptive property x_1 such that $(\exists x_2) (\exists x_3) \ldots$ (Happiness has x_1, and breaking one's promises has x_2, and people who have x_3 bring about consequences that have x_1 without performing actions that have x_2, and ...) & $((\exists y_1) (\exists y_2) (\exists y_3) \ldots$ (Happiness has y_1, and breaking one's promises has y_2, and people who have y_3 bring about

---

[6] Since Jackson writes that folk morality is "the network of moral opinions, intuitions, principles and concepts whose mastery is part and parcel of having a sense of what is right and wrong" (1998, p. 130), you may think that this modified Ramsey sentence should contain only the normative judgements that we need to make in order to master a normative concept. But few normative judgements are such that we need to make them in order to master a normative concept. If the modified Ramsey sentence contained only these judgements, it would not have enough content to ensure that there is exactly one set of descriptive properties that are related to each other the way the variables $x_1, x_2, x_3, \ldots$ are related to each other. See also Smith 1994a, pp. 54–6, Schroeter and Schroeter 2009, pp. 8–9, and Horgan and Timmons 2009, pp. 229–31.

consequences that have y_1 without performing actions that have y_2, and ...) $\supset$ ($x_1 = y_1$ & $x_2 = y_2$ & $x_3 = y_3$ & ...)),

it tells us the predicate 'is wrong' ascribes

The descriptive property x_2 such that $(\exists x_1)$ $(\exists x_3)$ ... (Happiness has x_1, and breaking one's promises has x_2, and people who have x_3 bring about consequences that have x_1 without performing actions that have x_2, and ...) & $((\exists y_1)$ $(\exists y_2)$ $(\exists y_3)$ ... (Happiness has y_1, and breaking one's promises has y_2, and people who have y_3 bring about consequences that have y_1 without performing actions that have y_2, and ...) $\supset$ ($x_1 = y_1$ & $x_2 = y_2$ & $x_3 = y_3$ & ...)),

and so on.[7] If we extend this view to all normative properties, it assumes that what makes it the case that a certain normative predicate ascribes a certain descriptive property is that, after maximum reflection, users of this predicate would apply it to objects that have this property.[8]

The second main version of (P1) is outlined in most detail by Richard Boyd.[9] He writes:

Roughly, and for nondegenerate cases, a term t refers to a kind (property, relation, etc.) k just in case there exist causal mechanisms whose tendency is to bring it about, over time, that what is predicated of the term t will be approximately true

---

[7] These claims identify each normative property with its *realizer* property, which is the descriptive property that plays the role that the relevant x_i plays in the modified Ramsey sentence. Reductive realists can also identify each normative property with its *role* property, which is the descriptive property *of playing the role* that the relevant x_i plays in the modified Ramsey sentence. Jackson 1998, pp. 141–2, says that we should identify rightness with its realizer property. But Jackson 2000, p. 28, suggests that the predicate 'is right' ascribes the property *of having the realizer property*, which seems to be distinct from both the realizer property and the role property, and Jackson 2005, p. 104, suggests that it does not matter which of these properties the predicate 'is right' ascribes.

[8] Lewis 1989 defends a closely related view: he writes that something is a value if and only if "we are disposed, under conditions of the fullest possible imaginative acquaintance, to value it" (p. 77). If we apply this view to descriptive properties and extend it to all normative predicates, it assumes that what makes it the case that a certain normative predicate ascribes a certain descriptive property is that, in conditions of the fullest possible imaginative acquaintance, users of this predicate would be disposed to apply this predicate to objects that have this property.

[9] Boyd 1988 and 2003. This version of (P1) fits with an externalist approach to reference determination, according to which a term's reference is determined primarily by the environment that users of the term find themselves in. For discussion of Boyd's view, see, among others, Horgan and Timmons 1991 and 1992a, Merli 2002, van Roojen 2006, and Schroeter and Schroeter 2013.

of k. . . . When relations of this sort obtain, we may think of the properties of k as regulating the use of t (via such causal relations).[10]

Boyd then applies this general view about reference determination to moral predicates. If we extend this view to all normative predicates and take these predicates to ascribe descriptive properties, it assumes that what makes it the case that a certain normative predicate ascribes a certain descriptive property is that this property causally regulates the use of this predicate: in other words, that this property tends to cause users of this predicate to apply it to objects that have this property.[11]

Not all philosophers who endorse a version of (P1) are reductive realists: for example, Boyd is a naturalist realist who does not think that normative properties are identical to descriptive properties. But that does not matter here. What matters here is only whether reductive realists can endorse these versions of (P1).

20. The False Guarantee Objection

I will argue that if they do, they face what we can call the *false guarantee objection*. Consider first Jackson's view. As we have seen, if we extend this view to all normative properties, it assumes that

> What makes it the case that a certain normative predicate ascribes a certain descriptive property is that, after maximum reflection, users of this predicate would apply it to objects that have this property.

What is maximum reflection? It is tempting to give a normative answer to this question: it is tempting, for example, to equate reflection with *rational* reflection.[12] But then Jackson's view no longer assumes that a version of (P1) is true, and instead assumes that

> (P2)   What makes it the case that a certain normative predicate ascribes a certain descriptive property is that, in certain

---

[10] Boyd 1988, p. 195.

[11] Boyd's defence of this view assumes the correctness of a first-order normative view he calls "homeostatic consequentialism" (1988, pp. 203–6), though he adds that "the same sort of defense can be formulated on the basis of any of the other plausible competing moral theories" (1988, p. 222). He can therefore also be interpreted as assuming that (P3) is true. See also Boyd 2003.

[12] See Yablo 2000, p. 16.

> *normatively* specified conditions, users of this predicate would apply it to objects that have this property.[13]

Jackson's view only assumes that a version of (P1) is true if we give a descriptive answer to this question. We could say, for example, that people have reflected maximally if and only if they have considered all relevant descriptive information.[14] In that case, Jackson's view assumes that

> What makes it the case that a certain normative predicate ascribes a certain descriptive property is that, after considering all relevant descriptive information, users of this predicate would apply it to objects that have this property.

If this version of (P1) were true, the judgements about rightness that people would make after considering all relevant descriptive information would determine which descriptive property the predicate 'is right' ascribes. These judgements would then be guaranteed to be true.[15] More generally, this version of (P1) entails that

(1)   If people would make certain normative judgements after considering all relevant descriptive information, these judgements are guaranteed to be true.[16]

But suppose that Fred is a deeply depraved person, and suppose that, after considering all relevant descriptive information, he would apply the predicate 'is right' to actions that have the property of maximizing other people's suffering.[17] Is Fred's judgement that it is right to maximize other people's suffering then guaranteed to be true? Or suppose that it is impossible to maximize both equality and freedom, and suppose that, after considering all relevant descriptive information, liberals would apply the predicate 'is just' to institutions that have the property of

---

[13] At least, it assumes this if by 'rational' we mean more than just consistent and probabilistically coherent.

[14] Alternatively, we could say that they have reflected maximally if and only if they have considered all relevant descriptive information *and they have arrived at a consistent and coherent view.* This makes no difference to what follows.

[15] I assume here that these objects share exactly one descriptive property. If they do not, this is an additional problem for Jackson's view.

[16] As Schroeter and Schroeter 2013, p. 4, write, Jackson's approach to reference determination "seems to leave no room for error at the ideal limit".

[17] For simplicity, I assume that only actions can be right.

maximizing equality and conservatives would apply the predicate 'is just' to institutions that have the property of maximizing freedom.[18] Are liberals' and conservatives' conflicting judgements about justice then both guaranteed to be true?[19]

I think our answer to these questions is 'No'. This shows that instead of endorsing (1), we think that

(~1) If people would make certain normative judgements after considering all relevant descriptive information, these judgements are *not* guaranteed to be true.

Why may Jackson's view nevertheless seem attractive? First, because we may tacitly equate reflection with rational reflection. And second, because giving a person more descriptive information usually improves his or her normative judgements. But it need not always do so: for example, as Allan Gibbard notes, if a civil servant who refuses to accept bribes "dwelt vividly on all that he is forgoing", he would perhaps stop thinking that accepting bribes is wrong.[20]

Consider next Boyd's view. As we have seen, if we extend this view to all normative predicates and take these predicates to ascribe descriptive properties, it assumes that

What makes it the case that a certain normative predicate ascribes a certain descriptive property is that this property causally regulates the use of this predicate.

If this version of (P1) were true, the predicate 'is right' would ascribe whatever descriptive property causally regulates people's use of this predicate. If people applied this predicate to objects that have this property,

---

[18] For simplicity, I assume that only institutions can be just. I also assume that maximizing equality and maximizing freedom are descriptive properties.

[19] You may object that after considering all relevant descriptive information Fred would no longer think that it is right to maximize other people's suffering, and that after considering all relevant descriptive information, liberals and conservatives would no longer disagree about justice. But that does not matter: what matters is that Fred *could* continue to think this and that liberals and conservatives *could* continue to disagree. You may also object that if Jackson's view is true, a normative predicate ascribes a descriptive property only if *everyone* uses this predicate to ascribe this property. But then this view entails that the predicate 'is just', as liberals and conservatives use it, does not ascribe a descriptive property.

[20] Gibbard 1990, pp. 20–1.

their judgements about rightness would then be guaranteed to be true. More generally, this version of (P1) entails that

(2)   If people apply normative predicates to objects that have the descriptive properties that causally regulate their use of these predicates, their normative judgements are guaranteed to be true.

But suppose that Fred belongs to a deeply depraved community, and suppose that this community's use of the predicate 'is right' is causally regulated by the property of maximizing the suffering of people who do not belong to this community.[21] Is Fred's judgement that it is right to maximize these people's suffering then guaranteed to be true? Or suppose again that it is impossible to maximize both equality and freedom, and suppose that a liberal community's use of the predicate 'is just' is causally regulated by the property of maximizing equality, and that a conservative community's use of the predicate 'is just' is causally regulated by the property of maximizing freedom. Are these communities' conflicting judgements about justice then both guaranteed to be true?

As before, I think our answer to these questions is 'No'. This shows that instead of endorsing (2), we think that

(~2)   If people apply normative predicates to objects that have the descriptive properties that causally regulate their use of these predicates, their normative judgements are *not* guaranteed to be true.

Why may Boyd's view nevertheless seem attractive? I think there are two reasons for this. The first is Boyd's claim that

a term t refers to a kind (property, relation, etc.) k just in case there exist causal mechanisms whose tendency is *to bring it about, over time, that what is predicated of the term t will be approximately true of k.*[22]

---

[21] I here suppose that Fred's whole community is depraved because Boyd stresses that he takes reference determination to be a social phenomenon: what makes a predicate ascribe a certain property is that this property causally regulates a community's use of this predicate, not that it causally regulates a single person's use. You may object that the idea of such a community is far-fetched. But what matters here is only whether there *could be* such a community. And there have been actual communities with moral views that we consider depraved: for a brief survey, see Prinz 2007, pp. 187–95.

[22] Boyd 1988, p. 195 (italics added). Boyd also writes that "our moral judgements are, often enough, reflections of truths about the good" (1988, p. 205).

This prospect of approaching the truth may seem appealing. But we should not misunderstand the role it plays in this version of (P1). If this version of (P1) is true, it is not the case that

(3)   which normative judgements are true

determines

(4)   which descriptive properties causally regulate the use of norma-tive predicates.

It is the other way around: if this version of (P1) is true, (4) determines (3). More generally, if reductive realism is true, which normative judge-ments are true depends on which descriptive properties normative predicates ascribe. For if reductive realism is true, what makes it the case that an object has a normative property is that one of its descriptive properties can be ascribed with a normative predicate. Reductive realists therefore cannot appeal to the truth of certain normative judgements to explain what makes it the case that a certain normative predicate ascribes a certain descriptive property. If they did, their explanation would presuppose what it is meant to explain.

Mark van Roojen proposes a version of Boyd's view according to which a descriptive property's causal regulation of people's use of a normative predicate "is only relevant to the designation of that property when that regulation yields knowledge of the property", where knowledge "requires that our beliefs be non-accidentally true".[23] This prospect of approaching non-accidental truth may seem even more appealing. But as before, if reductive realism is true, which normative judgements are non-accidentally true depends on which descriptive properties normative predicates ascribe. Reductive realists therefore cannot appeal to the non-accidental truth of certain normative judgements to explain what makes it the case that a certain normative predicate ascribes a certain descriptive property.[24]

---

[23] van Roojen 2006, pp. 184, 176.

[24] van Roojen offers this proposal to defend Boyd's view against Horgan and Timmons' Moral Twin Earth argument (see Horgan and Timmons 1991, 1992a, 1992b, and Timmons 1999, pp. 32–70). He claims that since "the Twin Earth argument is a semantic objection to moral realism, we can make various realist metaphysical and epistemic assumptions without begging questions against it" (2006, p. 177; see also p. 171 n. 8). That may be true. My point here is only that if *reductive realists* assume that Boyd's version of (P1) is true in order to explain what makes it the case that a certain normative predicate ascribes a

A second reason why Boyd's view may seem attractive is that we may take it to be about the descriptive properties that *would* cause users of a normative predicate to apply it to certain objects *if* they held a certain first-order normative view. For example, David Merli suggests that Boyd's view assumes that

> What makes it the case that a certain normative predicate ascribes a certain descriptive property is that *if users of this predicate held the end-of-the-day normative view*, this property would causally regulate the use of this predicate.[25]

What is the end-of-the-day normative view? It is tempting to equate this with the *correct* normative view. But if we do this, Boyd's view no longer assumes that a version of (P1) is true, and instead assumes that

(P3)   What makes it the case that a certain normative predicate ascribes a certain descriptive property is that the correct first-order normative view applies this predicate to objects that have this property.

Boyd's view only assumes that a version of (P1) is true if we give a descriptive answer to the question of what the end-of-the-day normative view is. We could say, for example, that the end-of-the-day normative view is the view people would hold if they had considered all relevant descriptive information.[26] In that case, Boyd's view would assume that

> What makes it the case that a certain normative predicate ascribes a certain descriptive property is that, if users of this predicate had considered all relevant descriptive information, this property would causally regulate their use of this predicate.

But then it would face the same problem as Jackson's view.[27]

---

certain descriptive property, they cannot appeal to the non-accidental truth of certain normative judgements.

[25] Merli 2002, p. 222.

[26] As Brink 2001 writes, "causal regulation can and should be understood in *counterfactual* terms", which means that "a natural property N causally regulates a speaker's use of moral term 'M' just in case his use of 'M' would be dependent on his belief that something is N, were his beliefs in dialectical equilibrium" (pp. 168–9). By 'dialectical equilibrium' Brink means something similar to reflective equilibrium (see p. 169 n. 22), which requires not just consideration of all relevant descriptive information but also consistency and coherence.

[27] Similar claims apply to Boyd's restriction of his view to "nondegenerate cases". Which cases are nondegenerate? It is tempting to give a normative answer to this question: it is

21. What the False Guarantee Objection Shows

I said in §3 that we take the following claim to be true:

(G)   There are no descriptively specified conditions in which people's normative judgements are guaranteed to be correct.

Since (G) is a negative existential claim, it is hard to be completely certain that we take it to be true. The best we can do is consider the versions of (P1) that have actually been proposed. As we have seen, when we consider Jackson's version of (P1), we notice that we think that

(~1)   If people would make certain normative judgements after considering all relevant descriptive information, these judgements are not guaranteed to be true.

When we consider Boyd's version of (P1), we notice that we think that

(~2)   If people apply normative predicates to objects that have the descriptive properties that causally regulate their use of these predicates, their normative judgements are not guaranteed to be true.

And I think that we will have similar thoughts about all other versions of (P1). I therefore think that we do take (G) to be true.[28]

Versions of reductive realism that assume that (P1) is true are incompatible with (G). If I am right that (G) is a central thought about normative judgements, these versions of reductive realism are therefore revisionary: they are not views about what normative judgements *currently* are and about the properties they *currently* ascribe, but views about what normative judgements should *become* and about the properties they should *start* to ascribe. As I said in §3, if there is no defensible

tempting to say, for example, that a case is nondegenerate if and only if people in this case are sufficiently rational. But then Boyd's view would assume that a version of (P2) is true. His view only assumes that a version of (P1) is true if we give a descriptive answer to this question: if we say, for example, that a case is nondegenerate if and only if people in this case have considered all relevant descriptive information.

[28]   Whereas (G) is a claim about correctness, (~1) and (~2) are claims about truth. But this does not matter. Since reductive realists are cognitivists, they take normative judgements to be beliefs. A belief is correct if and only if it is true. If reductive realism is true, (G) therefore entails that there are no descriptively specified conditions in which people's normative judgements are guaranteed to be true.

view that is compatible with our central thoughts about normative judgements and properties, we should perhaps accept a revisionary view. But I
will argue later that there is a defensible view that is compatible with these
thoughts: the error theory. If so, the false guarantee objection refutes
versions of reductive realism that assume that (P1) is true.

Reductive realists could reply that we can use the predicate 'is water' to
ascribe the property of being H_2O without knowing that this predicate
ascribes this property, and without knowing that

(3)   What makes it the case that the predicate 'is water' ascribes the
property of being H_2O is that this property causally regulates our
use of this predicate.

They could say that we can therefore similarly use a normative predicate to
ascribe a certain descriptive property without knowing that this predicate
ascribes this property, and without knowing that a version of (P1) is true.[29]
But there is a crucial difference between (3) and (P1): unlike (P1), (3) is
compatible with our central thoughts about water. We do not think, for
example, that there are no descriptively specified conditions in which
people's beliefs about water are guaranteed to be true. By contrast, our
acceptance of (~1) and (~2) indicates that we *do* think that there are no
descriptively specified conditions in which people's normative judgements
are guaranteed to be correct. I therefore think that reductive realists cannot
avoid the false guarantee objection in this way.

Reductive realists could also reply that since the reduction argument
shows that normative properties are identical to descriptive properties,
there must be *something* that makes it the case that a certain normative
predicate ascribes a certain descriptive property, which means that *some*
version of (P1) must be true. But as I said in §15, the reduction argument
only shows that

If there are normative properties, these properties are identical to
descriptive properties.

It therefore only shows that

---

[29] See Sayre-McCord 1997, p. 280 n. 18 and p. 284 n. 21, Brink 2001, pp. 160–3, and van
Roojen 2004, pp. 175–6.

If there are normative properties, there is something that makes it the case that a certain normative predicate ascribes a certain descriptive property.

And this conclusion is compatible with the falsity of (P1). I therefore think that reductive realists cannot avoid the false guarantee objection in this way either.

The false guarantee objection resembles Terry Horgan and Mark Timmons's influential Moral Twin Earth argument against naturalist realism.[30] Suppose that there are two planets, Earth and Twin Earth. These planets are as much alike as possible, with one exception: whereas Earthlings' moral judgements are causally regulated by natural properties that make utilitarianism true, Twin Earthlings' moral judgements are causally regulated by natural properties that make a deontological moral view true. According to Horgan and Timmons, Boyd's view then entails that moral predicates on Earth and moral predicates on Twin Earth do not have the same meaning. But they think that when an Earthling says that maximizing happiness is always right and a Twin Earthling says that maximizing happiness is not always right, the Earthling and the Twin Earthling disagree. And they take this to require that these predicates *do* have the same meaning. Horgan and Timmons therefore conclude that Boyd's view is false. Unlike the Moral Twin Earth argument, however, the false guarantee objection does not derive a claim about meaning from a claim about disagreement. It therefore avoids certain replies to this argument.[31]

22. Normatively Specified Conditions and the Regress Objection

As we saw in §20, if we equate reflection with rational reflection, Jackson's view assumes that

(P2)   What makes it the case that a certain descriptive property can be ascribed with a certain normative predicate is that, in certain

---

[30] See Horgan and Timmons 1991, 1992a, 1992b, 2009, and Timmons 1999, pp. 32–70. For an earlier version of the argument, see Hare 1952, p. 148.

[31] For these replies, see Plunkett and Sundell 2013 and Dowell 2016.

normatively specified conditions, users of this predicate would apply it to objects that have this property.

This is not what Jackson actually thinks. But other realists do endorse versions of (P2). For example, David Brink writes that the reference of moral predicates

is fixed by an original intention to adopt the moral point of view – that is, to use moral language to pick out those properties, whatever they are, that make objects of assessment interpersonally justifiable.[32]

And he adds that

this account of moral semantics . . . is fiercely nonreductionist. To characterize the moral point of view in terms of interpersonal justification is to characterize it in ineliminably normative terms.[33]

In other words, Brink assumes that what makes it the case that a certain moral predicate ascribes a certain property is that, if users of this predicate made moral judgements that are interpersonally justifiable, they would apply these predicates to objects that have this property.

Since Brink is not a reductive realist, he can endorse this version of (P2).[34] But if reductive realists endorsed a version of (P2), they would face what we can call the *regress objection*. Suppose, for example, that Jackson equated reflection with rational reflection. In that case, his view would entail that whether

Action A is right

depends on whether

The judgement that action A is right is such that we would make it after maximum rational reflection.

Since 'is such that we would make it after maximum rational reflection' is a normative predicate, the property of being such that we would make it after maximum rational reflection is a normative property. If Jackson equated reflection with rational reflection, his view would therefore entail that whether

---

[32] Brink 2001, p. 175.   [33] Brink 2001, p. 176.

[34] Brink does not think that normative properties are identical to descriptive properties, but that moral properties are constituted by natural properties (1989, pp. 156–60, and 2001, p. 157).

The judgement that action A is right is such that we would make it after maximum rational reflection

depends on whether

The judgement *that the judgement that action A is right is such that we would make it after maximum rational reflection* is such that we would make it after maximum rational reflection,

which, in turn, depends on whether

The judgement *that the judgement* that the judgement that action A is right is such that we would make it after maximum rational reflection *is such that we would make it after maximum rational reflection* is such that we would make it after maximum reflection,

and so on. This is the start of an infinite regress.

Some infinite regresses are benign. Consider the truth regress: the regress from 'p is true' to 'it is true that p is true' to 'it is true that it is true that p is true', and so on. This regress is benign because the direction of determination is from the first claim to the last: the truth of the first claim makes the second claim true, the truth of the second claim makes the third claim true, and so on. But if Jackson equated reflection with rational reflection, the direction of determination would be the other way around: the truth of the last normative judgement would make the next-to-last normative judgement true, the truth of the next-to-last normative judgement would make the second-to-last normative judgement true, and so on. Since the infinity of the regress would ensure that there is no last normative judgement, this would make it indeterminate whether any of these judgements are true. Similar claims apply to other versions of (P2). I therefore conclude that reductive realists cannot endorse (P2).[35]

---

[35] You may think that Jackson could avoid the objection by including judgements about rationality in the modified Ramsey sentence. But this misses the point: the point of the objection is that if whether a normative judgement is included in the modified Ramsey sentence depends on whether people would make this judgement after maximum rational reflection, this leads to a regress that makes it indeterminate which judgements are included in the modified Ramsey sentence in the first place.

23. Can Reductive Realists Appeal to the Correct First-Order Normative View?

Some reductive realists seem to endorse neither (P1) nor (P2). For example, Peter Railton argues that if we imagine a version of you who has "unqualified cognitive and imaginative powers, and full factual and nomological information about [your] physical and psychological constitution, capacities, circumstances, history, and so on", your *interests* are what this version of you would want you to seek in your actual condition and circumstances.[36] He takes X to be *intrinsically non-morally good* for you if and only if X would satisfy one of your interests, without reference to any of your other interests.[37] And he argues that the property of being right is the property of maximizing people's intrinsic non-moral good, taking each person's intrinsic non-moral good into account equally.[38] This version of reductive realism assumes that a certain first-order normative view is correct: it assumes the correctness of a view that Railton describes as "consequentialist, aggregative, and maximizing".[39]

Another reductive realist who seems to endorse neither (P1) nor (P2) is Mark Schroeder, who argues that for any proposition R, person X, and action A,

> For R to be a reason for X to do A is for there to be some *p* such that X has a desire whose object is *p*, and the truth of R is part of what explains why X's doing A promotes *p*.[40]

---

[36] Railton 1986, p. 11.

[37] Railton 1986, pp. 11–13. These interests are what Railton calls your 'objectified subjective interests'. He distinguishes these interests from your 'objective interests', which are the "reduction basis for [your] objectified subjective interests, namely, those facts about [you] and [your] circumstances that [this version of you] would combine with his general knowledge in arriving at his view about what he would want to want were he to step into [your] shoes" (p. 11). Railton actually defines intrinsic non-moral goodness in terms of your objective interests.

[38] Railton 1986 first defines rationality from a social point of view as "what would be rationally approved of were the interests of all potentially affected individuals counted equally under circumstances of full and vivid information" (p. 22), and he then equates rightness with what is rational from a social point of view. He regards this as a 'reforming definition' of rightness, which may not fit with all our present beliefs about rightness (see Railton 1986, p. 32, and 1989, pp. 157–9).

[39] Railton 1986, p. 40 n. 31.

[40] Schroeder 2007, p. 59. This is meant to be a 'constitutive explanation' of what it is for R to be a reason for X to do A: an identity claim the right hand side of which elucidates the nature or structure of the left hand side (2007, pp. 64–5).

This version of reductive realism also assumes that a certain first-order normative view is correct: it assumes the correctness of the view that there is a reason for you to do A if and only if doing A helps to satisfy your desires.

Railton and Schroeder therefore both seem to assume that

(P3)   What makes it the case that a certain normative predicate ascribes a certain descriptive property is that the correct first-order normative view applies this predicate to objects that have this property.

Since they defend their versions of reductive realism partly by arguing that a certain first-order normative view is correct, they may seem to avoid the false guarantee and regress objections.[41]

But what makes a first-order normative view correct? Non-reductive realists would say that

(1)   What makes a first-order normative view correct is that the objects to which this view ascribes normative properties really have these properties.

But reductive realists cannot say this: if reductive realism is true, what makes it the case that an object really has a normative property is that one of its descriptive properties can be ascribed with a normative predicate. This means that if reductive realists endorsed (1), this would return them to the question we started with: what makes it the case that a certain normative predicate ascribes a certain descriptive property? It would therefore return them to the choice between (P1) and (P2).

Alternatively, reductive realists could say that

(2)   What makes a first-order normative view correct is that this view is supported by sound arguments.

---

[41] As we saw in §20, if Boyd's view appeals to our end-of-the-day normative view and if we equate this with the correct normative view, Boyd's view also assumes that a version of (P3) is true. Sayre-McCord 1997, p. 291, similarly writes that "what a moral term refers to, if anything, is determined by whether, in light of the best moral theory, the use of that term can be seen as appropriately regulated by instances of a normatively significant kind". And Brink 2001, p. 162, writes that which natural properties moral predicates refer to "is a matter of substantive moral theory that we articulate and defend by familiar dialectical methods" and that claims about the identity of moral properties to certain natural properties are "to be assessed on substantive moral grounds".

But an argument that supports a first-order normative view must either have premises that are together normative or rely on a suppressed normative bridge principle.[42] What makes these premises or this bridge principle correct? As before, non-reductive realists would say that what makes these premises or this bridge principle correct is that the objects to which they ascribe normative properties really have these properties.[43] But as before, if reductive realists said this, that would return them to the question we started with: what makes it the case that a certain normative predicate ascribes a certain descriptive property? It would therefore return them to the choice between (P1) and (P2).

Finally, some reductive realists may want to say that

(3)   What makes a first-order normative view correct is that it is the best first-order normative view.

But since 'is the best first-order normative view' is a normative predicate, they would then run into the regress objection again.

Reductive realists may think that this begs the question against their view: they may think that I am assuming that a first-order normative view cannot be correct, or that the arguments for a first-order normative view cannot be sound, or that there is no best first-order normative view. And they may think that I am therefore in effect assuming that realism is false. But I am not assuming this. I am merely pointing out that if reductive realists endorse (P3), this returns them to the choice between (P1) and (P2). Pointing this out does not beg the question against realism.

24. Why Reductive Realism Is False

Are there any real alternatives to (P1) and (P2)? I do not think there are. Any seemingly different assumption that reductive realists could make would, I think, return them to the choice between (P1) and (P2).

---

[42] Why I say that these premises are *together* normative will become clear when I discuss Hume's law in §48. By a 'normative bridge principle' I mean a claim that posits a necessary connection between certain descriptive properties and certain normative properties.

[43] You may doubt that a normative bridge principle ascribes a normative property. But such a principle entails that there is a possible world in which something has a normative property, which means that it can only be true if this property exists. I will discuss this in §50.

If reductive realists assume that a version of (P1) is true, their view runs into the false guarantee objection. And if they assume that a version of (P2) is true, their view runs into the regress objection. I therefore think that the false guarantee and regress objections together show that

> If reductive realism is true, there is nothing that makes it the case that a certain normative predicate ascribes a certain descriptive property.

But as I said in §18, if normative predicates ascribe descriptive properties, there must be something that makes it the case that a certain normative predicate ascribes a certain descriptive property. I therefore conclude that these objections together show that reductive realism is false: they show that if there are normative properties, these properties are not identical to descriptive properties.

25. Preview

But realists may not give up yet. In the next chapter, I will ask whether there is a way in which they could get around my arguments.

V

Further Defences of Realism

There are several ways in which realists could try to get around my arguments.

26. Underspecified Descriptive Predicates

The following possibility may occur to reductive realists: what if, for each normative predicate, there is a descriptive predicate that people with different first-order normative views *must* all agree is necessarily coextensive with this normative predicate? Would this avoid the false guarantee and regress objections?

Reductive realists could say, for example, that people with different first-order normative views must all agree that the predicate 'is right' is necessarily coextensive with the descriptive predicate 'has the descriptive property that rightness is necessarily coextensive with'. This means that if

(N)   Two predicates ascribe the same property if and only if they are necessarily coextensive,

these predicates ascribe the same property. And they could say that it is clear what makes it the case that these predicates ascribe the same property: what makes this the case is the truth of (N) together with the meaning of the predicate 'has the descriptive property that rightness is necessarily coextensive with'.

But this would be cheating. The predicate 'has the descriptive property that rightness is necessarily coextensive with' is *underspecified*, in the sense that which descriptive property it ascribes depends on which actions have the property of being right. Suppose that I think that an action is right if and only if it maximizes happiness, and that you think that an action is right if and only if it maximizes happiness without killing anyone. Which descriptive property the predicate 'has the descriptive property that rightness is necessarily coextensive with' ascribes will then depend on whose first-order normative view is correct. If my view is correct, this predicate ascribes the property of maximizing happiness. If your view is correct, it ascribes the property of maximizing happiness without killing anyone. And if yet another first-order normative view is correct, it ascribes yet another descriptive property.

If reductive realists appeal to an underspecified descriptive predicate like 'has the descriptive property that rightness is necessarily coextensive with', they will therefore need to say more about which descriptive property this predicate ascribes. And when they try to say more, they will run into the false guarantee objection or the regress objection.

27. Can Reductive Realists Appeal to the Reduction Argument?

Reductive realists could also try to avoid these objections by appealing to the reduction argument: they could say that this argument shows that normative properties are identical to descriptive properties.

But consider the first version of the reduction argument. If this version is sound, which descriptive property the predicate 'is right' ascribes depends on which descriptive property predicate D^* ascribes. And which property predicate D^* ascribes depends on which actions have the property of being right. Like the predicate 'has the descriptive property that rightness is necessarily coextensive with', predicate D^* is therefore underspecified. That does not undermine the reduction argument: to refute non-reductive realism, the argument does not have to show which descriptive properties normative properties are identical to, but only that every normative property is identical to some descriptive property or other. But it does mean that reductive realists cannot avoid the false guarantee and regress objections by appealing to this argument.

Non-reductive realists may now say that if the reduction argument fails to show that reductive realism is true, it also fails to show that there are no irreducibly normative properties. But that is not so. If the reduction argument is sound, it shows that

(1) If there are normative properties, these properties are identical to descriptive properties.

Since (1) is compatible with the claim that normative properties do not exist, (1) can be true even if reductive realism is false. And showing that (1) is true is enough to show that there are no irreducibly normative properties.

Non-reductive realists could reply that the claim that there are no irreducibly normative properties is equivalent to the claim that

(2) Normative properties are identical to descriptive properties,

and they could say that (2) can only be true if it is true that

(3) There is something that makes it the case that a certain normative predicate ascribes a certain descriptive property.

If the reduction argument fails to show that (3) is true, they could say, it therefore also fails to show that there are no irreducibly normative properties.

But (2) can be interpreted in two different ways. It can be interpreted as having existential import, in which case it is equivalent to the claim that

(4) There are normative properties that are identical to descriptive properties.

Reductive realists are committed to (4), and (4) can only be true if (3) is true. But the claim that there are no irreducibly normative properties does not entail (4), since it is compatible with the claim that normative properties do not exist.

Alternatively, (2) can be interpreted as lacking existential import, in which case it is equivalent to the claim that

(1) If there are normative properties, these properties are identical to descriptive properties.

(1) is equivalent to the claim that there are no irreducibly normative properties. But (1) does not entail (3). Instead, (1) only entails that

(5) *If there are normative properties*, there is something that makes it the case that a certain normative predicate ascribes a certain descriptive property.

And (5) is compatible with the negation of (3), since it is compatible with the claim that normative properties do not exist. The reduction argument therefore shows that non-reductive realism is false, but not that reductive realism is true.

28. Can Non-Reductive Realists Appeal to the False Guarantee and Regress Objections?

Non-reductive realists could also try to resist the reduction argument by saying that the false guarantee and regress objections explain why normative properties are an exception to (N). But I do not think that these objections explain this. To explain why normative properties are an exception to (N), the false guarantee and regress objections would have to show that

There are normative properties that are not identical to descriptive properties.

And as I have said, that is not what these objections show. Instead, they only show that

If there are normative properties, these properties are not identical to descriptive properties.

If non-reductive realists take these objections to explain why normative properties are an exception to (N), they are ignoring the possibility that normative properties do not exist. This makes them move too easily from objections to reductive realism to the conclusion that non-reductive realism is true.

29. Can Reductive Realists Say That the Difference Between Normative and Descriptive Properties is a Difference in the Nature of These Properties?

Reductive realists could also try to avoid the false guarantee and regress objections by denying that if their view is true, the difference between normative and descriptive properties is a difference in language that is not matched by a difference in the nature of these properties. They could defend this denial by rejecting my claims that

A property is *normative* if and only if it can be ascribed with a normative predicate

and that

A property is *descriptive* if and only if it can be ascribed with a descriptive predicate.

But these claims are hard to reject. If a property is descriptive, how could it fail to be possible to ascribe this property with a descriptive predicate? And if a property is normative, how could it fail to be possible to ascribe this property with a normative predicate? Of course, there are possible worlds in which people do not have a language that contains such predicates. But in any possible world there is a *possible* language that contains such predicates: namely, the language we have in the actual world. Similarly, if a predicate is descriptive and ascribes a property, how could this property fail to be descriptive? And if a predicate is normative and ascribes a property, how could this property fail to be normative? Of course, this property may be *both* descriptive *and* normative. But that does not mean that it is *not* descriptive or *not* normative.

Reductive realists could also try to defend this denial by endorsing what William FitzPatrick calls a 'dual aspect view' of normative properties. FitzPatrick, who is a non-naturalist realist, suggests that

the very properties and facts we typically refer to as natural are also inherently value laden ... [T]o reject naturalism ... is not, then, to deny that objective ethical standards are rooted in familiar facts and features of human life, but only to insist that they are rooted in the irreducibly evaluative dimension of these facts and features of human life.[1]

If reductive realists endorsed this view, they could say that

(1)   Descriptive properties that are identical to normative properties have a normative dimension that other descriptive properties lack.

But what does this mean? It may mean merely that

(2)   Descriptive properties that are identical to normative properties can be ascribed with normative predicates, but other descriptive properties cannot.

---

[1]   FitzPatrick 2008, p. 196 (italics removed).

But endorsing (2) would not enable reductive realists to say that the difference between normative and descriptive properties is a difference in the nature of these properties. Alternatively, (1) may mean that

(3)   Descriptive properties that are identical to normative properties have a certain second-order normative property that other descriptive properties lack.

But endorsing (3) would not help reductive realists either. For if their view is true, this second-order normative property must also be identical to a descriptive property. Finally, (1) may mean that

(4)   Descriptive properties that are identical to normative properties have a normative part that other descriptive properties lack.

But endorsing (4) also would not help reductive realists. For if properties have parts, these parts are themselves properties. The normative parts of these descriptive properties are therefore themselves normative properties. And as before, if reductive realism is true, these normative properties must also be identical to descriptive properties.

Finally, reductive realists could try to defend this denial by becoming naturalist realists: by saying that normative properties are identical to *natural* rather than to descriptive properties. Naturalist realism need not imply that the difference between normative and natural properties is a difference in language that is not matched by a difference in the nature of these properties. But it lacks this implication only if it takes a non-reductive form: if it says that an object's normative properties are extra properties in addition to its other natural properties.[2] Though such a view avoids the false guarantee and regress objections, it faces the reduction argument instead.

Reductive realism is an identity claim: it says that each normative property is identical to a certain descriptive property. Such claims clearly should not be interpreted as saying that different entities are a single entity, but as saying that different words or phrases pick out the same entity. That is why if reductive realism is true, the difference between normative and descriptive properties is a difference in language that is not matched by a difference in the nature of these properties.

---

[2]   A view of this kind is defended by Sturgeon 1985, pp. 58–61, and 2005, p. 98.

30. Conclusion

I conclude that these attempts to get around my arguments fail. The reduction argument shows that

(1)   If there are normative properties, these properties are identical to descriptive properties,

and the false guarantee and regress objections show that

(2)   If there are normative properties, these properties are not identical to descriptive properties.

These claims together entail that normative properties do not exist. In other words, they entail that realism is false.

I said in §2 that it does not matter to my arguments whether or not normative properties are natural properties. I can now explain why this does not matter: it does not matter because it does not affect the truth of (1) and (2).

VI

The Symmetry Objection

If the arguments I have given so far are sound, normative properties do not exist. But normative judgements may nevertheless be beliefs that ascribe such properties.

31. Cognitivism and Non-Cognitivism

Cognitivists think that they are. By contrast, non-cognitivists think that normative judgements are non-cognitive attitudes, such as attitudes of approval or disapproval. But many of them also take these judgements to be beliefs that ascribe normative properties. For they accept minimalism about truth, beliefs and properties: they think that the sentence '"p" is true' expresses the same attitude as the sentence 'p', that a sentence expresses a belief if and only if it can be true, and that an object has a property if and only if this property can be ascribed to it with a true sentence.[1]

Consider the judgement that euthanasia is wrong. If non-cognitivism is true, this judgement is a non-cognitive attitude, such as an attitude of disapproval of euthanasia. Non-cognitivists who accept minimalism think that this attitude can be expressed not only with the sentence

Euthanasia is wrong,

but also with the sentence

'Euthanasia is wrong' is true.

---

[1] Horwich 1993 proposes a minimalist account of the truth of normative judgements, and Blackburn 1998, pp. 77–83, and Gibbard 2003, p. 18, endorse such an account (though not in the way Horwich proposes). For discussion of the relation between non-cognitivism and minimalism, see Jackson, Oppy, and Smith 1994, Smith 1994b and 1994c, Divers and Miller 1994 and 1995, and Dreier 1996 and 2004.

They therefore take the judgement that euthanasia is wrong to be not only an attitude of disapproval, but also a belief. And if they disapprove of euthanasia themselves, they take euthanasia to have the property of being wrong. For this property can be ascribed to it with the sentence 'Euthanasia is wrong', which they take to be true.

Minimalism makes it hard to say what cognitivists and non-cognitivists disagree about. I will initially take cognitivism to be the following view:

> Normative judgements represent the world. Whether these judgements accurately represent the world wholly depends on what the world is like: it depends on whether objects in the world have the normative properties that these judgements ascribe to them.

And I will take non-cognitivism to be the following view:

> Normative judgements do not represent the world. These judgements ascribe normative properties to objects in the world, but whether these objects have these properties does not wholly depend on what the world is like.[2]

Everyone agrees that if a normative judgement ascribes a *descriptive* property, part of this judgement represents the world. For example, suppose that Susan thinks that Fred's dishonesty is wrong. Susan's normative judgement then ascribes the descriptive property of being dishonest to Fred.[3] This part of her judgement clearly represents the world. But Susan's judgement also ascribes the normative property of being wrong to Fred's dishonesty. I will take cognitivists and non-cognitivists to disagree about whether this *normative* part of Susan's judgement represents the world.

Is this an accurate description of the disagreement between cognitivists and non-cognitivists? Non-cognitivists may think it is not, since it ignores minimalism about representation.[4] They could also make other objections to my description of their view. I will return to this in §34.

---

[2] Ridge 2014, pp. 79–80, similarly takes cognitivism to be the view that normative judgements have "genuinely representational content", but he adds that this content must be identical to the content of the normative claim that would express the judgement.

[3] I here assume that being dishonest is a descriptive property.

[4] See Dreier 2004, p. 29.

32. Asymmetry

I said in §3 that we take the following claim to be true:

(A)   When two people make conflicting normative judgements, at most one of these judgements is correct.[5]

For example, suppose that Fred thinks euthanasia is permissible but Susan thinks it is impermissible.[6] We may then think that Fred's judgement is correct, or we may think that Susan's judgement is correct, or we may think that neither judgement is correct. But we will not think that *both* judgements are correct: we take conflicts between normative judgements to be what I will call *asymmetrical*.[7]

We do not take (A) to be true of judgements that differ in an imprecise way. If Susan thinks euthanasia is wrong but Bob thinks it is deeply wrong, we do not think that at most one of these judgements is correct. We also may not take (A) to be true of judgements about dilemmas. If Sophie cannot save both of her children, and if Fred thinks she ought to save her daughter but Susan thinks she ought to save her son, we may not think that at most one of these judgements is correct. But we *do* think that

When two people make conflicting normative judgements that do not differ in an imprecise way and that are not about a dilemma, at most one of these judgements is correct.

Since this complication does not matter to my arguments, I will ignore it in what follows.

As I said in §3, I take (A) to be a central thought about normative judgements: I take (A) to reflect the nature of these judgements. We can see this by comparing normative judgements to likes and dislikes.

---

[5] Claims along these lines are made, for example, by Brink 1989, pp. 29–30, Smith 1994a, p. 39, Parfit 2006, p. 328, and 2011b, p. 413, FitzPatrick 2008, pp. 169–70, and Schroeter and Schroeter 2013, pp. 7–8. You may think that 'is correct' is a normative predicate. If so, this does not matter to my arguments.

[6] Here and in what follows, I take Fred to think that euthanasia is *always* permissible and Susan to think that euthanasia is *always* impermissible.

[7] I assume that normative judgements conflict if one of these judgements entails the negation of the other judgement. For example, the judgement that euthanasia is impermissible entails that euthanasia is not permissible, which is the negation of the judgement that euthanasia is permissible. Why I distinguish euthanasia's being impermissible from its not being permissible will become clear in §54.

Suppose that Bob likes peanut butter but Kate dislikes it. We may then share Bob's like, or we may share Kate's dislike, or we may share neither like or dislike. But we do *not* take the following claim to be true:

(L)   When two people have conflicting likes or dislikes, at most one of these likes or dislikes is correct.

I think that this is part of what distinguishes normative judgements from likes and dislikes: just as (A) reflects the nature of normative judgements, the negation of (L) reflects the nature of likes and dislikes.

Cognitivism is clearly compatible with (A). For if cognitivism is true, Fred's and Susan's conflicting normative judgements represent the world in incompatible ways: Fred's judgement ascribes the property of being permissible to euthanasia and Susan's judgement ascribes the property of being impermissible to euthanasia. Since euthanasia cannot have both of these properties, their judgements then cannot both be correct.[8] More generally, if cognitivism is true, (A) follows from the claim that

(I)   When two people have mental states that represent the world in incompatible ways, at most one of these mental states is correct.

Is non-cognitivism also compatible with (A)? Most non-cognitivists will want to say that it is.[9] But since non-cognitivists think that normative judgements do not represent the world, they cannot explain how their view is compatible with (A) by appealing to (I).[10] They will instead have to explain this in a different way.

33. Quasi-Realist Explanations

They could try to explain how their view is compatible with (A) by making use of Simon Blackburn's work. Consider the following claim:

(M)   What makes an action right or wrong is not that we approve or disapprove of this action.

---

[8] I here assume that a belief is correct if and only if it is true.

[9] Some early non-cognitivists, such as Ayer 1946, may not have wanted to say this. If I am right that (A) is a central thought about normative judgements, this makes such views revisionary.

[10] I assume for now that non-cognitivists are not minimalists about representation. I will drop this assumption in §34.

You may think that non-cognitivism is incompatible with (M): you may think that if normative judgements are attitudes of approval or disapproval, what makes an action right or wrong is that we approve or disapprove of it. But Blackburn disagrees. He claims that (M) expresses the following attitude:

(M*) Disapproval of treating our own attitudes of approval or dis-
      approval as reasons to approve or disapprove of an action.[11]

If (M) expresses this attitude, non-cognitivism is clearly compatible with (M). Blackburn also argues that sentences that contain unasserted normative clauses express higher-order attitudes of approval or disapproval, that we can regard changes in our own attitudes of approval or disapproval as improvements, and that the truth of a normative judgement is its membership of a set of attitudes of approval or disapproval that cannot be further improved.[12] He thinks that non-cognitivists can thereby 'earn the right' to say that normative judgements are beliefs that ascribe normative properties, especially if they also accept minimalism.[13] They then become what Blackburn calls *quasi-realists*.[14]

Non-cognitivists could try to explain how their view is compatible with (A) in a similar way. They could say, for example, that (A) expresses the following attitude:

(A*) Disapproval of two people approving and disapproving of a
      single thing.

[11] Blackburn 1984, p. 218, 1993, pp. 153, 157, 172–3, and 1998, pp. 311–12. Blackburn occasionally says that moral judgements are attitudes of approval or disapproval (1984, p. 192), but he often simply calls them 'attitudes' (1984, pp. 167, 188) or 'conative' states or stances (1993, pp. 168, 178). He rightly says that "approval and attitude are natural terms to work with, but it would not matter if neither fitted exactly or if better terms for the state in question existed", as long as "the state is worth distinguishing from belief, or at least from belief with representational truth conditions thought of realistically" (1993, p. 184).

[12] For Blackburn's interpretations of sentences that contain unasserted normative clauses, see Blackburn 1984, pp. 189–96, 1993, pp. 125–7, 182–97, and 1998, pp. 70–7. For his account of the truth of normative judgements as membership of a set of attitudes of approval or disapproval that cannot be further improved, see Blackburn 1984, pp. 197–202. He does not wholeheartedly endorse this account, however, and Blackburn 1998 appeals more directly to minimalism about truth.

[13] Blackburn 1998, pp. 77–83, 294–8. He stresses, however, that before non-cognitivists can accept minimalism "the commitments must first be understood in other terms" (p. 80). See also Blackburn 1996, pp. 86, 92, and 1999, p. 217.

[14] See Blackburn 1984, 1993, and 1998. Blackburn takes his quasi-realism so far that he denies that his view is a version of non-cognitivism: see Blackburn 1996, pp. 82–3, and 1998, p. 85.

As before, if (A) expresses this attitude, non-cognitivism is clearly compatible with (A).[15]

But does (A) really express this attitude? Suppose again that Bob likes peanut butter but Kate dislikes it. Now suppose, however, that Bob and Kate belong to a community in which everyone has the following attitude:

(L*)   A dislike of two people liking and disliking a single thing.

And suppose that, in this community's language, the attitude described by (L*) can be expressed by saying that

(L)   When two people have conflicting likes or dislikes, at most one of these likes or dislikes is correct.

This imagined community then endorses (L) in exactly the same way in which, according to this explanation, we endorse (A). But it is hard not to feel that *something* about the way we endorse (A) is missing from the way this community endorses (L). This is evidence that the way we endorse (A) is different from the way this imagined community endorses (L). In other words, it is evidence that (A) does not express the attitude described by (A*).

Non-cognitivists could challenge this evidence by making further quasi-realist moves: they could say, for example, that the claim that

(1)   The way we endorse (A) is different from the way Bob and Kate's community endorses (L)

itself expresses an attitude of approval or disapproval, such as:

(1*)   Disapproval of thinking that (A) expresses the attitude described by (A*).

But I think they then face a different problem, which I will discuss in §34.

Non-cognitivists could also say that our feeling that something about the way we endorse (A) is missing from the way Bob and Kate's

---

[15] Though Blackburn does not discuss (A), he does discuss bivalence (1984, pp. 203–10, and 1993, pp. 23–30), and his discussion of bivalence suggests an interpretation of (A) as expressing the attitude described by (A*). Non-cognitivists also often say that just as inconsistent beliefs cannot both be true, conflicting attitudes of approval or disapproval cannot both be satisfied (see Stevenson 1963, p. 2, and Blackburn 1993, pp. 188–97). They can say that this explains why we have the attitude described by (A*).

community endorses (L) merely shows that *we think* that the way we endorse (A) is different from the way this community endorses (L), not that the way we endorse (A) is *actually* different from the way this community endorses (L). But they then need to explain why we mistakenly feel that something about the way we endorse (A) is missing from the way this community endorses (L). The most promising way for them to explain this, I think, is by saying that we have the attitude described by (1*) and that (1) expresses this attitude.

Alternatively, non-cognitivists could try to give a different quasi-realist explanation of how their view is compatible with (A). They could say that if someone thinks that conflicting normative judgements are both correct, this person both approves and disapproves of a single thing. And they could say that we endorse (A) because

(2)   A single person cannot knowingly both approve and disapprove of a single thing.

If this is why we endorse (A), non-cognitivism also seems compatible with (A).[16]

But is this really why we endorse (A)? Suppose that members of Bob and Kate's community take a like or dislike to be correct if and only if they have this like or dislike themselves. If (2) is true, it also seems true that

(3)   A single person cannot knowingly both like and dislike a single thing.[17]

Suppose that everyone in this community therefore endorses the claim that

---

[16] This explanation does, however, raise several further questions. First, is (2) true? Perhaps it is only true that a single person cannot *rationally* both approve and disapprove of a single thing. But that claim seems normative, in which case non-cognitivists must say that it itself expresses an attitude of approval or disapproval. Second, if (2) is true, why is it true? Perhaps (2) is true because conflicting attitudes of approval or disapproval cannot both be satisfied, as Stevenson 1963, p. 2, and Blackburn 1993, pp. 188–97, suggest. Third, if we endorse (A) because (2) is true, what kind of attitude does (A) express? Perhaps (A) expresses a commitment to having or not having certain non-cognitive attitudes in certain circumstances, as Blackburn 1993, pp. 188–97, suggests. This commitment seems to be a further non-cognitive attitude.

[17] Of course, a single person *can* knowingly both like and dislike a single thing *in different respects*: for example, Kate may like the smell of peanut butter but dislike its texture. Perhaps we should therefore add 'in a single respect' to (3). But then I think we should similarly add 'in a single respect' to (2).

(L)   When two people have conflicting likes or dislikes, at most one of these likes or dislikes is correct.

This imagined community then endorses (L) in exactly the same way in which, according to this explanation, we endorse (A). But as before, it is hard not to feel that *something* about the way we endorse (A) is missing from the way this community endorses (L). This is evidence that the way we endorse (A) is different from the way this imagined community endorses (L). In other words, it is evidence that we do not endorse (A) because (2) is true.

Non-cognitivists could also try to give a third quasi-realist explanation of how their view is compatible with (A). They could say that

(4)   The function of normative discourse is to coordinate attitudes of approval and disapproval.

They could say that we endorse (A) because this creates pressure on ourselves and others to have similar attitudes of approval and disapproval, which helps normative discourse to fulfil its function. And they could combine this with the first quasi-realist explanation: they could say that the truth of (4) explains why we do have the attitude described by (A*) but do not have the attitude described by (L*).[18]

But is this really why we endorse (A)? Suppose that Bob and Kate's community needs to coordinate its members' likes and dislikes: suppose, for example, that this community can make effective use of its limited agricultural resources only if its members have similar likes and dislikes. Suppose that, as a result of this,

(5)   The function of Bob and Kate's community's discourse about likes and dislikes is to coordinate likes and dislikes,

and suppose that everyone in this community therefore endorses the claim that

(L)   When two people have conflicting likes or dislikes, at most one of these likes or dislikes is correct.

This imagined community then endorses (L) in exactly the same way in which, according to this explanation, we endorse (A). But once again, it is

---

[18] For thoughts along these lines, see Björnsson 2015, and also Gibbard 1990, pp. 71–3, 107–8, 117, and Blackburn 1993, pp. 168–9.

hard not to feel that *something* about the way we endorse (A) is missing from the way this community endorses (L). This is evidence that the way we endorse (A) is different from the way this imagined community endorses (L). In other words, it is evidence that we do not endorse (A) because (4) is true.

As I have said, non-cognitivists could challenge this evidence by making further quasi-realist moves. I will now discuss these moves.

34. Disappearing Quasi-Realism

Once quasi-realism gets going, it is hard to stop. For example, as we have seen, non-cognitivists could say that that the claim that

(1)   The way we endorse (A) is different from the way Bob and Kate's community endorses (L)

itself expresses an attitude of approval or disapproval, such as:

(1*)   Disapproval of thinking that (A) expresses the attitude described by (A*).

In response, I could imagine another community. Suppose that Jack and Alice both belong to a community in which everyone has the attitude described by (L*), and suppose that, in this community's language, this attitude can be expressed by uttering (L). But now suppose that members of this community also have the following attitude:

(2*)   A dislike of thinking that (L) expresses the attitude described by (L*).

And suppose that, in this community's language, this attitude can be expressed by saying that

(2)   The way we endorse (L) is different from the way Bob and Kate's community endorses (L).

It is hard not to feel that *something* about the way we endorse (1) is missing from the way this imagined community endorses (2). This is evidence that the way we endorse (1) is different from the way this community endorses (2). But non-cognitivists could challenge this evidence as well. As before, they could say that the claim that

(3)   The way we endorse (1) is different from the way Jack and Alice's community endorses (2)

itself expresses an attitude of approval or disapproval, such as:

(3*)   Disapproval of thinking that (1) expresses the attitude described by (1*).

And they could keep making such moves in response to any other community I imagine.

They could also make certain other quasi-realist moves. I said in §32 that cognitivists can explain how their view is compatible with (A) by appealing to the claim that

(I)   When two people have mental states that represent the world in incompatible ways, at most one of these mental states is correct.

In response, non-cognitivists could endorse minimalism about representation: they could say that that the sentence ' "p" accurately represents the world' expresses the same attitude as the sentence 'p'.[19] They could then say that they can explain how their view is compatible with (A) by appealing to (I), just as cognitivists can.

Finally, I said in §31 that I take non-cognitivism to be the following view:

Normative judgements do not represent the world. These judgements ascribe normative properties to objects in the world, but whether these objects have these properties does not wholly depend on what the world is like.

Non-cognitivists could reject this description of their view. If they endorse minimalism about representation, they could say that normative judgements *do* represent the world and that whether objects have normative properties therefore *does* wholly depend on what the world is like.

---

[19]   Blackburn's remarks about 'Ramsey's ladder' may suggest that he endorses minimalism about representation (see 1998, pp. 78–9, 295–6, and 1999, p. 217). But he also writes that "moral opinion is not in the business of representing the world" (1999, p. 214), since a "representation *answers to* what is represented" and "ethical facts do not play this explanatory role" (1999, p. 216). See also Blackburn 1993, pp. 111–12, 175, 184–5, Rosen 1998, p. 396, and Dreier 2004, p. 29. Price 2011 and 2013 defends a global version of expressivism that incorporates minimalism about what he calls 'i-representation', though not about what he calls 'e-representation'. For discussion of this view, see Blackburn 2013.

Alternatively, they could appeal to Blackburn's interpretation of the claim that

(M)   What makes an action right or wrong is not that we approve or disapprove of this action

as expressing the following attitude:

(M*)   Disapproval of treating our own attitudes of approval or disapproval as reasons to approve or disapprove of an action.

They could say that if whether an object has a certain normative property does not wholly depend on what the world is like, it must instead depend on our attitudes. If so, my description of non-cognitivism contradicts (M). If non-cognitivists take (M) to express the attitude described by (M*), they could therefore reject my description of their view.

In response, I could try to describe the disagreement between cognitivists and non-cognitivists without making claims about representation. But non-cognitivists could then endorse minimalism about whatever else I appeal to when trying to describe this disagreement, or they could interpret whatever else I say when trying to describe this disagreement as incompatible with a claim that they take to express one of their own attitudes of approval or disapproval, such as (M).

Where do these quasi-realist moves lead? As has often been observed, they seem to make the difference between quasi-realism and realism disappear.[20] If non-cognitivists keep making such moves indefinitely, they will end up agreeing with cognitivists that

(4)   Normative judgements represent the world,

they will end up agreeing with realists that

(5)   There are normative properties,

and they will end up agreeing with everyone that

---

[20] See Wright 1985, Rosen 1998, and Dreier 2004. Even Blackburn himself suggests that quasi-realism makes it the case that there is "no point at which our use of ethical language supports realism rather than expressivism (or vice versa); if that is so, it is tempting to conclude that the debate is unreal" (1993, p. 4).

(S)   For all possible worlds W and W*, if the instantiation of descriptive properties in W and W* is exactly the same, then the instantiation of normative properties in W and W* is also exactly the same.

(G)   There are no descriptively specified conditions in which people's normative judgements are guaranteed to be correct.

(N)   Two predicates ascribe the same property if and only if they are necessarily coextensive.[21]

This may enable non-cognitivists to explain how their view is compatible with (A). But it also makes their view face the arguments I gave in chapters II to V: if non-cognitivists agree that (4), (5), (S), (G), and (N) are true, the arguments I gave in these chapters show not only that realism is false, but also that non-cognitivism is false.

Non-cognitivists could reply that their view does not give the same explanation of our normative practice as realism: they could say that whereas non-cognitivism takes this practice to be an expression of our non-cognitive attitudes, realism takes it to be a response to normative properties.[22] They could also reply that their view does not have the epistemological problems that realism has: they could say that since non-cognitivism takes our normative practice to be an expression of our non-cognitive attitudes, it does not need to explain how we can know which objects have which normative properties.[23] These replies may undermine the general claim that if non-cognitivists keep making quasi-realist moves, the difference between quasi-realism and realism disappears. But they do not undermine my specific claim that if non-cognitivists agree that (4), (5), (S), (G), and (N) are true, the arguments I gave in chapters II to V show not only that realism is false, but also that non-cognitivism is false. For these arguments did not appeal to the explanation of our normative practice or to epistemological problems for realism.

---

[21] You may think that non-cognitivists who make quasi-realist moves could reject (S), (G), or (N). In particular, you may think they could reject (N). But if so, I could distinguish cognitivism from non-cognitivism by appealing to the claim that non-cognitivists reject. For example, if they reject (N), I could say that whereas cognitivists take properties to be ways objects can be, non-cognitivists take properties to be shadows of concepts (see §6).

[22] See, for example, Blackburn 1993, pp. 7, 34, 175–6. See also Rosen 1998, p. 397, and Dreier 2004, pp. 37–9, 42.

[23] See Wright 1985, p. 314.

I therefore conclude that the quasi-realist explanations I discussed in §33 do not enable non-cognitivists to explain how their view is compatible with (A), unless they take their quasi-realist moves so far that they face my arguments against realism instead.

35. Hybrid Explanations

But non-cognitivists need not give up yet. They could also try to explain how their view is compatible with (A) by endorsing a hybrid view: a view that combines elements of non-cognitivism with elements of cognitivism.[24]

Consider first Michael Ridge's *ecumenical expressivism*, according to which a normative judgement consists of a 'normative perspective', which is "a set of relatively stable policies against accepting certain kinds of standards of deliberation", and the descriptive belief that an object is highly ranked by any standard of deliberation that is admissible relative to the normative perspective of the person who makes the judgement.[25] This view makes (A) true of some conflicting normative judgements. Suppose that Fred and Susan are both utilitarians, and suppose again that Fred thinks euthanasia is permissible but Susan thinks it is impermissible. If ecumenical expressivism is true, Fred then has the following attitudes:

A utilitarian normative perspective, and the descriptive belief that allowing people to have euthanasia is highly ranked by any standard of deliberation that is admissible relative to this perspective.

And Susan has the following attitudes:

A utilitarian normative perspective, and the descriptive belief that *not* allowing people to have euthanasia is highly ranked by any standard of deliberation that is admissible relative to this perspective.[26]

---

[24] See, for example, Copp 2001, Ridge 2006, 2007, 2009, and 2014, and Boisvert 2008. For discussion of these views, see Schroeder 2009, Ridge 2014, and the essays in Fletcher and Ridge 2015.

[25] Ridge 2014, pp. 115, 119–20. He calls this descriptive belief a 'representational' belief. The view defended by Ridge 2014 is a modification of his earlier view, according to which a normative judgement consists of an attitude of approval towards an action in so far as a certain prescriber would approve of this action and the descriptive belief that this prescriber would in fact approve of this action.

[26] Here and in what follows, I take the judgement that euthanasia is permissible to be equivalent to the judgement that it is right to allow people to have euthanasia, and I take the

The conflict between Fred's and Susan's normative judgements is then a conflict between their descriptive beliefs. Since these beliefs represent the world in incompatible ways, (A) is then true of these judgements.

But suppose next that Fred is a utilitarian and Susan is a Kantian. If ecumenical expressivism is true, Fred then has the following attitudes:

A utilitarian normative perspective, and the descriptive belief that allowing people to have euthanasia is highly ranked by any standard of deliberation that is admissible relative to this perspective.

And Susan has the following attitudes:

A *Kantian* normative perspective, and the descriptive belief that not allowing people to have euthanasia is highly ranked by any standard of deliberation that is admissible relative to this perspective.

The conflict between Fred's and Susan's normative judgements is then not a conflict between their descriptive beliefs, but between their normative perspectives. Since Ridge takes these perspectives to be policies that do not represent the world, (A) is then not true of these judgements, unless Ridge makes quasi-realist moves of the kind I discussed in §§33–34.[27]

Consider next Stephen Finlay's *end-relational theory*, according to which the claim that someone morally ought to perform an action expresses the descriptive belief that this action promotes one of the speaker's ends, and pragmatically conveys either the assumption or the demand that the audience share this end.[28] This view also makes

---

judgement that euthanasia is impermissible to be equivalent to the judgement that it is right to not allow people to have euthanasia.

[27] Ridge could also try to explain how his view is compatible with (A) by appealing to his account of disagreement. He writes that person A and person B "disagree in prescription about D's Φ-ing in C just in case in circumstances of honesty, full candor, and non-hypocrisy, A would advise Φ-ing in C and B would advise Ψ-ing in C, where Φ-ing and Ψ-ing are incompatible, in the sense of being impossible to combine without thereby having inconsistent beliefs" (2014, p. 190). But the fact that Φ-ing and Ψ-ing are incompatible in this sense does not ensure that at most one of these two conflicting pieces of advice is correct.

[28] More precisely, Finlay thinks that this end can either be explicitly introduced into the conversation, or be supplied by the subject of the 'ought' claim, or be an end of the person who is addressed by the 'ought' claim, or be "the shared, urgent concern of all the conversation's participants" (2009, p. 332). Finlay's view is a version of cognitivism, but it also resembles non-cognitivism, since it explains normativity in terms of ends: Finlay writes that if the end-relational theory is correct, moral uses of 'ought' "express demands and attitudes just as expressivists claim" (2009, p. 335), and that "the very nature of normativity can be comprehensively explained in terms of desire" (2007, p. 220). See also Finlay 2006, 2008, and 2014.

(A) true of some conflicting normative judgements. Suppose that Fred and Susan both have the end of minimizing suffering, and suppose that Fred thinks we ought to allow people to have euthanasia but Susan thinks we ought not to allow this. If the end-relational theory is true, Fred then has the following attitudes:

> The end of minimizing suffering and the descriptive belief that allowing people to have euthanasia promotes this end.

And Susan has the following attitudes:

> The end of minimizing suffering and the descriptive belief that *not* allowing people to have euthanasia promotes this end.

The conflict between Fred's and Susan's normative judgements is then a conflict between their descriptive beliefs. Since these beliefs represent the world in incompatible ways, (A) is then true of these judgements.

But suppose next that Fred has the end of minimizing suffering and Susan has the end of preventing the killing of human beings. If the end-relational theory is true, Fred then has the following attitudes:

> The end of minimizing suffering and the descriptive belief that allowing people to have euthanasia promotes this end.

And Susan has the following attitudes:

> The end of *preventing the killing of human beings* and the descriptive belief that not allowing people to have euthanasia promotes this end.

The conflict between Fred's and Susan's normative judgements is then not a conflict between their descriptive beliefs, but between their ends. Since these ends do not represent the world, (A) is then not true of these judgements, unless Finlay makes quasi-realist moves of the kind I discussed in §§33–34.

The end-relational theory can explain why Fred and Susan may nevertheless take (A) to be true of these judgements: because they may not realize that they have different ends. After some discussion, however, they will realize that this is the case. Finlay thinks that if they then continue to express their conflicting normative judgements, they are pragmatically conveying the *demand* that the other share their end.[29] But he thinks that

---

[29] As Finlay writes, speaking "in a way that supposes something to be true of your audience that is clearly controversial or false is a way of expressing a demand that it *be* true of them" (2009, p. 333).

if they were to discover that they do not share *any* fundamental end, they would stop expressing these judgements. He writes:

Were a person to come to accept fully that another does not share her funda-mental moral concerns, would she bother to address her moral claims to him? Would she have any expectation that by doing so she may succeed in influencing him? And would she bother to engage in a moral argument with him? I think it is clear that at least many of us would not, viewing moral discourse with the morally alien as a fruitless waste of time and effort.[30]

But even if many of us would take *expressing* our normative judgements to the morally alien to be a waste of time and effort, we would still take the morally alien's judgements to be *incorrect*.[31] More generally, I think we would still take (A) to be true of these judgements. This is evidence that the end-relational theory is false.[32]

I therefore conclude that non-cognitivists cannot explain how their view is compatible with (A) by endorsing a hybrid view, unless they combine such a view with quasi-realist moves of the kind I discussed in §§33–34.[33]

36. Can Non-Cognitivists Appeal to the Reduction Argument?

Non-cognitivists could also try to explain how their view is compatible with (A) by appealing to a non-cognitivist version of the reduction argument that has been given by Allan Gibbard.[34]

According to Gibbard, to judge that you ought to perform an action is to have a plan. Having a plan involves rejecting certain alternatives,

---

[30] Finlay 2008, p. 358.

[31] Or, at least, I would. As I said in §3, any philosophical argument has to start from what we currently think, and at this point a philosopher's 'we' means 'I and everyone who is like me'.

[32] For further discussion of the end-relational theory, see Joyce 2011, pp. 527–9, and Olson 2014, pp. 127–35. Finlay 2011 replies to Joyce.

[33] Another hybrid view is David Copp's *realist expressivism*, according to which moral judgements are beliefs that ascribe normative properties, and speakers who express these beliefs pragmatically convey that they have certain non-cognitive attitudes (see Copp 1995 and 2001). Since this view is a version of reductive realism, it is compatible with (A), but it faces the false guarantee and regress objections instead. The same seems to be true of the hybrid view defended by Boisvert 2008, who claims that the properties ascribed by moral predicates "are just whatever the correct moral theory says they are" and therefore seems to assume that a version of (P3) is true.

[34] See Gibbard 2003, pp. 88–111, and also Gibbard 2002a, 2002b, and 2006. For discussion, see Hawthorne 2002 and Majors 2005.

which he calls 'not okay to do', and rejecting rejecting other alternatives, which he calls 'okay to do'. Gibbard calls a consistent plan that covers any situation that anyone could ever be in a 'hyperplan'.[35] Since he thinks that we must identify acts in terms of their natural properties, he thinks that any hyperplan must have the following form:

In situation s_1, perform an act with natural property N_1, in situation s_2, perform an act with natural property N_2,...

Now consider the property of having either natural property N_1, or natural property N_2, or.... If we call this property 'N*', any hyperplan can be reformulated as follows:

In any possible situation, perform an act with natural property N*.

According to Gibbard, this shows that that anyone who has a hyperplan accepts that

(1)   There is a natural property that constitutes being okay to do.[36]

Gibbard calls a state of having both a hyperplan and a complete and consistent set of descriptive beliefs a 'hyperstate', and he calls us 'committed' to a claim if we would accept this claim in every hyperstate we could reach from our present plans and descriptive beliefs without changing our mind.[37] If he is right that anyone who has a hyperplan accepts (1), it follows that we would all accept (1) in every hyperstate we could reach without changing our mind. It therefore follows that we are all committed to (1).

Though Gibbard himself does not say this, non-cognitivists could say that this explains how their view is compatible with (A). For they could say that if we are all committed to (1), and if it is true that

(2)   The judgement that an action is okay to do is correct if and only if this action has the natural property that constitutes being okay to do,

then it follows that we are all committed to (A).

---

[35] See Gibbard 2003, p. 56.

[36] What Gibbard means by 'constitutes' is that for any alternative a open in any possible situation s, alternative a is okay to do in s just in case a in s has this natural property. He initially calls this property "prosaically factual", but he later argues that it is, in a broad sense, natural (2003, pp. 98–102).

[37] See Gibbard 2003, pp. 54, 90–1.

But suppose again that Fred thinks we ought to allow people to have euthanasia and Susan thinks we ought not to allow this. If plan-expressivism is true, Fred then has a plan to allow people to have euthanasia, and Susan has a plan to not allow people to have euthanasia. The hyperplans that Fred and Susan can reach from these plans without changing their minds are conflicting hyperplans, according to which different natural properties constitute being okay to do. Even if Gibbard is right that they are both committed to the claim that *there is* a natural property that constitutes being okay to do, they are therefore committed to *different* claims about *which* natural property constitutes being okay to do.[38] Like other non-cognitivists, Gibbard could respond with quasi-realist moves: he could say, for example, that the question which natural property constitutes the property of being okay to do is itself a question about what to do, which can be answered only by adopting a plan.[39] But he would then face the problems I discussed in §§33–34. I therefore conclude that non-cognitivists cannot explain how their view is compatible with (A) by appealing to this version of the reduction argument.

Are there other ways in which non-cognitivists could try to explain how their view is compatible with (A)? Perhaps there are. But I think that any other explanation they could propose will run into a variant of the problems I have discussed. I therefore think that non-cognitivism is incompatible with (A). We can call this the *symmetry objection* to non-cognitivism.

37. Non-Cognitivism and the Error Theory

Does the symmetry objection show that non-cognitivism is false? That depends on whether there is a defensible alternative to non-cognitivism that is compatible with (A) and with our other central thoughts about

[38] A similar objection to Gibbard's view is made by Schroeter and Schroeter 2005, who argue that Gibbard's view guarantees neither that all competent speakers use a certain normative predicate to ascribe the same natural property, nor that there is an independent standard of correctness for normative judgements to which speakers are answerable.

[39] As Gibbard 2002b writes: "Come to a full plan for life, and you will have come to a view on what property constitutes the thing to do. Will you have the answer right? ... [T]hat again is a question about how to live. It can be answered only in plan-laden terms" (p. 179). Gibbard also makes other quasi-realist moves: for example, he interprets (M) as an expression of a plan (2003, p. 183; see also 1990, pp. 164–6).

normative judgements and properties. I think there is such an alternative: the error theory.

When non-cognitivists attack cognitivism, they often ignore the error theory. Consider again Blackburn's interpretation of the claim that

(M)   What makes an action right or wrong is not that we approve or disapprove of this action.

Calling his own interpretation of (M) an 'internal reading' and the cognitivist interpretation of (M) an 'external reading', Blackburn writes:

There *would* be an external reading if realism were true. For in that case there would be a fact, a state of affairs ... whose rise and fall and dependency on others could be charted. But anti-realism acknowledges no such state of affairs and no such dependency.[40]

This ignores the fact that error theorists, who agree that there is no such state of affairs, can endorse the external reading of (M). Refuting realism is therefore not enough to refute this reading of (M). But in the argument that Blackburn elsewhere gives against the error theory, he takes his own internal reading of claims such as (M) for granted.[41]

The arguments I have given in chapters II to V show that there are no normative properties in the sense of ways objects can be.[42] Non-cognitivism and the error theory are both compatible with this conclusion. These views are therefore both compatible with the central thoughts about normative judgements and properties that played a role in these arguments. But unlike non-cognitivism, the error theory is also compatible with (A). For since the error theory is a version of cognitivism, it says that normative judgements are beliefs that represent the world.

Non-cognitivists may deny that the error theory is compatible with (A): they may say that if the error theory is true, all normative judgements are false and are therefore incorrect.[43] But (A) does not say that

---

[40] Blackburn 1993, p. 173.   [41] See Blackburn 1993, p. 153.

[42] Here and in what follows, I use the phrase 'properties in the sense of ways objects can be' to mean properties about which minimalism is false.

[43] I here assume that if a belief is false, it is incorrect. You may object that 'is incorrect' is a normative predicate. But I here take this predicate to be equivalent to the predicate 'is not correct', which I think is not normative (just as I think that the predicate 'is not wrong' is not normative, as I will explain in §48).

> When two people make conflicting normative judgements, one of these judgements is correct.

This claim is false, since both judgements may be incorrect. Instead, (A) only says that

> When two people make conflicting normative judgements, *at most* one of these judgements is correct.

Moreover, endorsing (A) does not commit us to thinking that *the world* is such that when two normative judgements conflict, it makes at most one of these judgements correct. It only commits us to thinking that *normative judgements* are such that when two of these judgements conflict, at most one of them is correct. That can be true even if the world does not make any normative judgement correct. Unlike non-cognitivism, therefore, the error theory is compatible with (A).

Non-cognitivists could now say that we also take the following claim to be true:

> (C)   Some normative judgements are correct.

They could say that (C) is also a central thought about normative judgements. And they could say that non-cognitivism and the error theory are therefore both incompatible with a central thought about these judgements: non-cognitivism is incompatible with (A), but the error theory is incompatible with (C).

I agree that (C) is a central thought about normative judgements in the sense that it is a thought we all have about these judgements. But as I said in §3, I take (A) to be a central thought about normative judgements not only in this sense, but also in the sense that (A) reflects the nature of these judgements. That is why I think that if a view about normative judgements is incompatible with (A), it is revisionary: it is not a view about what these judgements *currently* are, but a view about what these judgements should *become*. Is this also true of (C)? Does (C) also reflect the nature of normative judgements?

I think it does not. For if (A) reflects the nature of normative judgements, the symmetry objection shows that these judgements represent the world. And if mental states of a certain kind represent the world, the nature of these mental states does not guarantee that the world is ever as these mental states represent it to be. That is part of what it is for a mental state to represent the world: a mental state that represents the world can do so accurately, but can also do so inaccurately. If mental states of a certain kind represent the world, the nature of these states therefore does not guarantee that any of these states are correct. But if (C) reflected the nature of normative judgements, the nature of these judgements *would* guarantee that some of these judgements are correct. This means that

(1)   If (A) reflects the nature of normative judgements, (C) does not reflect the nature of these judgements.

I argued in §32 that (A) does reflect the nature of normative judgements. If so, it follows from (1) that (C) does not reflect the nature of these judgements. I therefore think that non-cognitivism's incompatibility with (A) makes non-cognitivism revisionary, but that the error theory's incompatibility with (C) does not make the error theory revisionary.

Non-cognitivists could also say that charity supports their view rather than the error theory, since charity requires that we interpret people's claims as mostly correct.[44] But charity does not require that we interpret people's claims *about a particular subject matter* as mostly correct: it does not require, for example, that we interpret religious believers' claims about God as mostly correct.[45] Instead, it requires that we interpret *all of a person's claims taken together* as mostly correct.[46] Moreover, charity also requires that we interpret people's claims as much as possible in accordance with their central thoughts about these claims. Since the error theory interprets normative claims in accordance with (S), (G), and (A), that is exactly what the error theory does.

Finally, non-cognitivists could say that moral judgement internalism supports their view rather than the error theory: they could say that

(2)   Necessarily, if a person makes a moral judgement, this person is motivated to act accordingly,

and they could say that this is evidence that moral judgements are motivating states rather than beliefs that represent the world.

---

[44] See Davidson 1984. Even Davidson thinks, however, that charity should allow for "explicable error" (1984, p. 196).

[45] See also Cuneo 2006, pp. 59–60.   [46] As Daly and Liggins 2010, p. 212, point out.

But people who are exhausted or depressed seem able to make moral judgements without being motivated to act accordingly.[47] Most philosophers who endorse moral judgement internalism therefore endorse a weaker version of this view: they think, for example, that

(3) *Normally*, if a person makes a moral judgement, this person is motivated to act accordingly,

or that

(4) Necessarily, if a person makes a moral judgement, either this person is motivated to act accordingly *or this person is practically irrational.*[48]

These versions of moral judgement internalism support only the claim that moral judgements are often accompanied by motivating states, not the claim that these judgements *are* motivating states. Moreover, even if (2) were true of moral judgements, this strong version of internalism does not seem true of other normative judgements, such as judgements about reasons for belief or judgements about epistemic rationality.[49]

I therefore conclude that the error theory is a defensible alternative to non-cognitivism that is compatible with (A) and with our other central thoughts about normative judgements. Since the error theory is a version of cognitivism, this means that the following view is true:

Normative judgements represent the world. Whether these judgements accurately represent the world wholly depends on what the world is like: it depends on whether objects in the world have the normative properties that these judgements ascribe to them.

In what follows, I will set aside minimalism and will simply say that normative judgements are beliefs.

---

[47] See, for example, Stocker 1979.

[48] The first version is endorsed by Dreier 1990, pp. 9–14, and the second is endorsed by Smith 1994a, pp. 60–3.

[49] For discussion of different versions of moral judgement internalism and the connection between this view and non-cognitivism, see Björnsson et al. 2015.

38. Revisionary Views

Non-cognitivists could also put forward a different revisionary version of their view. They could say that if the error theory is true, normative judgements are false beliefs that we should give up. And they could argue that we should replace these false beliefs with non-cognitive attitudes. Doing this would make non-cognitivism true, even though this view was not true before.[50] Reductive realists could similarly argue that we should replace these false beliefs with true beliefs that ascribe certain descriptive properties. Doing this would make reductive realism true, even though this view was not true before. Before I can discuss these revisionary versions of non-cognitivism and reductive realism, I need to discuss whether we can believe the error theory. I will therefore return to these views in §74.

39. Preview

You may think that there is an alternative to realism and non-cognitivism that avoids my objections. In the next chapter, I will argue that there is not.

---

[50] Köhler and Ridge 2013 defend non-cognitivism in this way. Boghossian 2006, p. 19, argues that relativism must also be defended in this way.

VII

Further Views

Is there is an alternative to realism and non-cognitivism that avoids my objections?

40. Cognitivist Expressivism

One such view may seem to be Terry Horgan and Mark Timmons's *cognitivist expressivism*, according to which normative judgements are beliefs that do not represent the world.[1] Since this view says that normative judgements are beliefs, Horgan and Timmons take it to be a version of cognitivism. But like non-cognitivism, cognitivist expressivism denies that normative judgements represent the world. It therefore faces the symmetry objection just as much as non-cognitivism does. This view does make it clear, however, that 'non-cognitivism' is a misleading name. The disagreement between cognitivists and non-cognitivists is not about whether normative judgements are beliefs, but about whether these judgements represent the world. It would therefore perhaps be clearer to call cognitivism 'representationalism' and non-cognitivism 'non-representationalism'.

41. Descriptive Fictionalism

Another view that may seem to avoid my objections is Mark Kalderon's *descriptive fictionalism*, according to which normative sentences represent

---

[1] See Timmons 1999 and Horgan and Timmons 2000, 2006a, and 2006b. Timmons 1999 calls this view 'assertoric non-descriptivism'. Horgan and Timmons 2000 call it 'nondescriptivist cognitivism'.

the world but normative judgements do not.[2] By divorcing sentences from judgements in this way, Kalderon avoids certain problems for non-cognitivism, such as problems with sentences that contain unasserted normative clauses.[3] But the claim that

(A) When two people make conflicting normative judgements, at most one of these judgements is correct

is about judgements rather than about sentences. Since descriptive fictionalism denies that normative judgements represent the world, this view also faces the symmetry objection.

Kalderon could try to avoid this objection by switching to a different version of fictionalism: instead of taking normative judgements to be non-cognitive attitudes, he could take them to be beliefs about the content of a fiction.[4] He could then say, for example, that the sentence

Euthanasia is permissible

expresses the belief that

In our moral fiction, euthanasia is permissible.

This would make (A) true of some conflicting normative judgements. Suppose again that Fred thinks euthanasia is permissible but Susan thinks it is impermissible. If Fred and Susan are both utilitarians, their conflicting normative judgements would then perhaps represent the content of a single moral fiction in incompatible ways, in which case at most one of these judgements would be correct.[5] But if Fred is a utilitarian and Susan is a Kantian, it is unclear how their conflicting normative judgements could represent the content of a single moral fiction in incompatible ways. This problem is similar to the problem for hybrid views that I discussed in §35.

---

[2] See Kalderon 2005, pp. 112, 126–9. He calls this view 'hermeneutic fictionalism'. Some philosophers defend fictionalism as a revisionary alternative to the error theory, which I will discuss in §74, but Kalderon defends it as a view about what our normative judgements currently are.

[3] As Eklund 2009 argues, however, Kalderon also needs to give an account of the judgements that such sentences express.

[4] Alternatively, he could say that normative judgements are attitudes of *make-believe* towards a certain fiction. See Kalderon 2005, pp. 121–9, and Eklund 2015, §2.3 and §2.4.

[5] At least, if this fiction is sufficiently determinate.

42. Constructivism

Kantian views may also seem to avoid my objections. When discussing J. L. Mackie's moral error theory, Bernard Williams writes:

> Consider another picture of what it would be for a demand to be 'objectively valid'. It is Kant's own picture. According to this, a demand will be inescapable in the required sense if it is one that a rational agent must accept if he is to be a rational agent.... [This] conception deploys an intelligible and adequate sense of objectivity. It seems to have little to do with those demands being part of the fabric of the world.[6]

This picture has been elaborated in two different ways. The first is *Kantian constructivism*, according to which

(1)   What makes a moral judgement correct is that this judgement would be the outcome of a rational construction procedure.

If this view is restricted to moral judgements, it may be defensible.[7] But if we generalize it to all normative judgements, it says that

(2)   What makes a *normative* judgement correct is that this judgement would be the outcome of a rational construction procedure.

And then this view runs into a problem. If (2) is true, whether

Judgement J is correct

depends on whether

Judgement J would be the outcome of a rational construction procedure.

Since the term term 'rational' is a normative term, the claim that judgement J would be the outcome of a rational construction procedure itself expresses a normative judgement. This means that if (2) is true, whether

---

[6] Williams 1985b, pp. 174–5.

[7] Views along these lines are defended by Rawls 1971 and 1993 about judgements about justice and by Scanlon 1998 about a subset of moral judgements, though Rawls does not appeal only to rationality and Scanlon appeals to reasonableness. Rawls and Scanlon do not say that the construction procedure *itself* is rational, but instead that the procedure involves rational people or reasonable rejection.

Judgement J would be the outcome of a rational construction procedure

depends on whether

The judgement *that judgement J would be the outcome of a rational construction procedure* would be the outcome of this rational construction procedure,

which, in turn, depends on whether

The judgement *that the judgement* that judgement J would be the outcome of a rational construction procedure *would be the outcome of this rational deliberation procedure* would be the outcome of this rational construction procedure,

and so on. This is the start of an infinite regress.

As I said in §22, some infinite regresses are benign, since the direction of determination in these regresses is from the first claim to the last. But if (2) were true, the direction of determination would be the other way around: the truth of the last claim would make the next-to-last claim true, the truth of the next-to-last claim would make the second-to-last claim true, and so on. Since the infinity of the regress would ensure that there is no last claim, this would make it indeterminate whether any of these claims are true. Like versions of reductive realism that assume that (P2) is true, this generalized version of Kantian constructivism therefore faces the regress objection.[8]

Constructivists could avoid this objection by switching to a non-Kantian version of their view. They could, for example, endorse Sharon Street's *Humean constructivism*, according to which

The fact that R is a reason for person P to do A is constituted by the fact that the judgement that R is a reason for P to do A withstands scrutiny from the standpoint of P's own judgements about reasons.[9]

---

[8] For a related objection to constructivism, which combines a version of the regress objection with a version of the symmetry objection, see Hussain 2012. See also Enoch 2009.

[9] See Street 2008, pp. 223–4, and also Street 2010, p. 373, and 2012, pp. 40–1. She writes that her view "reduces facts about reasons to facts about what we *judge* or *take* to be reasons, with the latter understood in a way that is prior to and independent of the former" (2008, p. 242).

If we generalize this view to all normative judgements, it seems to assume that

(3)   What makes a normative judgement correct is that this judgement would withstand scrutiny from the standpoint of the normative judgements of the person it is about.[10]

According to Street, a normative judgement withstands such scrutiny if and only if this judgement is not "mistaken as determined by the standards of correctness that are constitutively set by [this person's] normative judgments in combination with the non-normative facts".[11] For example, suppose that

(4)   Fred thinks that there is a reason for him to become a doctor

and that

(5)   Fred can only become a doctor if he studies medicine.

Street's view seems to be that (4) and (5) together make it correct for Fred to think that there is a reason for him to study medicine, in the following sense: if he thinks that there is *no* reason for him to study medicine, either (4) is false or he does not realize that (5) is true.[12] The property of withstanding scrutiny is therefore a descriptive property, which means that Humean constructivism avoids the regress objection.[13]

But it runs into a different objection instead. For (3) entails that

(6)   If people's normative judgements withstand scrutiny from the standpoint of the normative judgements of the people these judgements are about, they are guaranteed to be correct.

Suppose again that Fred is a deeply depraved person, and suppose that Susan's judgement that there is a reason for Fred to maximize other people's suffering withstands scrutiny from the standpoint of Fred's normative judgements. Is Susan's judgement then guaranteed to be correct? I think our answer to this question is 'No'. This shows that instead of endorsing (6), we think that

---

[10] I say 'seems to assume' because many normative judgements are not about a person. It is unclear to me what Street's view assumes about such judgements.

[11] Street 2008, p. 230.   [12] Street 2008, pp. 227–9.

[13] As Street 2008, p. 232, puts it, her view "smuggles no substantive normative assumptions into its definiens".

(~6) If people's normative judgements withstand scrutiny from the standpoint of the normative judgements of the people these judgements are about, they are *not* guaranteed to be correct.

It therefore shows that like versions of reductive realism that assume that (P1) is true, Humean constructivism faces the false guarantee objection.[14]

43. Constitutivism

A second way to elaborate the Kantian picture is *Kantian constitutivism*, according to which

(1) What makes a normative judgement correct is that this judgement is implied by a norm that is constitutive of being an agent.[15]

What is it for a norm to be constitutive of being an agent? This could mean that being an agent involves *accepting* this norm: in other words, that being an agent involves implicitly making a certain normative judgement. Alternatively, it could mean that being an agent involves *being subject to* this norm: in other words, that being an agent involves being such that a certain normative judgement is true of you.

Suppose first that Kantian constitutivists say that being an agent involves implicitly making a certain normative judgement. They could take this judgement to be a version of Kant's categorical imperative, such as:

---

[14] Street 2009 argues that examples of what she calls 'ideally coherent eccentrics', such as Gibbard's coherent anorexic (1990, p. 165) and Parfit's man with future Tuesday indifference (1984, p. 123–4), are not good counterexamples to her view. These examples involve prudential reasons and rationality, where Street's view seems most plausible. But when dealing with ideally coherent *immoral* eccentrics, like Gibbard's coherent Caligula (1999, p. 145), her view seems much less plausible: it does not seem sufficient to say, as Street does, that "we loathe" this Caligula and "have every normative reason to lock him up", that when we say he has most reason to stop torturing people we are "speaking falsely but with good reason", and that he is like an alien creature (Street 2009, p. 293).

[15] See, for example, Korsgaard 1996, 2008, and 2009. For discussion, see Gibbard 1999, Enoch 2006 and 2011b, Hussain and Shah 2006 and 2013, and Street 2010 and 2012. The distinction between constructivism and constitutivism is not entirely sharp: Korsgaard's view also incorporates constructivist elements, and Street's view also incorporates constitutivist elements. For discussion of constructivism and constitutivism, see the essays in Lenman and Shemmer 2012 and Bagnoli 2013. For discussion of the relation between Kantian constitutivism and the error theory, see Shah 2010.

(2)   It is permissible for us to do A if and only if we can will the maxim behind A to be a universal law.[16]

But suppose that Bob is a thoroughgoing utilitarian: he rejects (2), he never says anything that presupposes or entails (2), and he regularly acts in ways that (2) does not permit. Kantian constitutivists could then insist that Bob nevertheless implicitly endorses (2). But this is hard to square with what he says and does. Alternatively, they could deny that Bob is an agent. But this is hard to square with the fact that he acts and talks much as other people do. The only difference between Bob and other people, or at least the Kantians among them, is that he does not share their first-order moral view.

Moreover, even if Kantian constitutivists could defensibly deny that Bob is an agent, they cannot deny that he is what David Enoch calls a *schmagent*: a being who is very similar to agents but who does not implicitly endorse (2).[17] Being a schmagent may involve implicitly making a different normative judgement, such as:

(3)   It is permissible for us to do A if and only if A maximizes happiness.

Kantian constitutivists may be tempted to say that we should be agents rather than schmagents. But Bob can similarly say that we should be schmagents rather than agents. Kantian constitutivists may say that we should be agents because (2) is supported by sound arguments. But Bob can similarly say that we should be schmagents because (3) is supported by sound arguments. Moreover, as I said in §23, arguments for a first-order normative claim such as (2) or (3) must either have premises that are together normative or rely on a suppressed normative bridge principle.[18] What makes these premises or this bridge principle correct? Since Kantian constitutivists reject realism, they cannot say that these premises or this bridge principle are correct because the objects to which they ascribe normative properties really have these properties.[19] And it is unclear what they can say instead.

---

[16] See, for example, Korsgaard 2008, pp. 12–13.   [17] See Enoch 2006 and 2011b.

[18] I will say more about this when I discuss Hume's law in §48. By a 'normative bridge principle' I mean a claim that posits a necessary connection between certain descriptive properties and certain normative properties.

[19] Korsgaard writes, for example, that moral reflection "is reflection about what to do, not reflection about what is to be found in the normative part of the world" (1996, p. 116), and she rejects the view that moral requirements must be given "some sort of ontological

To avoid these problems, Kantian constitutivists could switch to a different version of their view: they could say that being an agent involves being such that a certain normative judgement is true of you.[20] As before, they could take this judgement to be a version of the categorical imperative, such as (2). But as before, being a schmagent may involve being such that (3) is true of you. Kantian constitutivists could say that (2) is true of us and (3) is false of us because it is in fact true that

(4)   We are agents rather than schmagents.

But what is it for (4) to be true? This seems to be that (4) accurately represents the world. And the only difference between agents and schmagents is that (2) is true of agents and (3) is true of schmagents. If Kantian constitutivists say that (4) accurately represents the world, they are therefore in effect saying that the judgement that

(2)   It is permissible for us to do A if and only if we can will the maxim behind A to be a universal law

accurately represents the world, and that the judgement that

(3)   It is permissible for us to do A if and only if A maximizes happiness

fails to accurately represent the world. They are then in effect realists about at least one normative judgement. Depending on which kind of realism they endorse, their view then faces either the reduction argument or the false guarantee and regress objections.

44. Quietism

A final alternative to realism and non-cognitivism that may seem to avoid my objections is *quietism*.[21] This is not a well-defined view, but a

---

foundation, by positing the existence of certain normative facts or entities to which moral requirements somehow refer" (2008, pp. 29–30).

[20] Alternatively, they may say that being an agent involves being such that a certain normative judgement is *correct* of you. This makes no difference to what follows.

[21] Versions of quietism are defended by Dworkin 1996 and 2011, Nagel 1997, Scanlon 1998, pp. 62–3, 2003, and 2014, Kramer 2009, and Parfit 2011b, pp. 485–7. Scanlon 2002, pp. 146–7, attributes a version of quietism to Rawls (see Rawls 1993, pp. 116–18), though Rawls also appeals to the Kantian view I discussed in §42. For discussion of quietism,

set of related claims about normative properties and truth. One of these claims is made by Thomas Nagel, who suggests that

(1)   There are normative truths, but there are no normative properties in the sense of ways objects can be.[22]

But quietists cannot avoid my objections by endorsing (1). If normative judgements represent the world, they ascribe normative properties in the sense of ways objects can be. Since (1) denies that there are normative properties in this sense but does say that there are normative truths, (1) can only be true if normative judgements do not represent the world. If quietists endorse (1), their view therefore faces the symmetry objection just as much as non-cognitivism does. Of course, they could try to avoid this objection by endorsing minimalism about representation. But as we saw in §34, they would then face my arguments against realism instead.

Quietists also make several other claims. For example, T.M. Scanlon claims that

(2)   Whether a normative claim is true or false depends only on standards that are internal to normative discourse,[23]

and Ronald Dworkin claims that

(3)   Views about the nature of normative judgements and properties, such as realism, non-cognitivism, and the error theory, themselves express normative judgements.[24]

These claims may sound suggestive, but I do not see how they enable quietists to avoid my objections. Moreover, I will argue in §54 that though (3) may be true of realism, it is not true of the error theory.

Finally, Derek Parfit thinks that there are different senses of the verb 'to exist', and suggests that

see McPherson 2011 and Enoch 2011a, pp. 121–33. A related view is defended by Cuneo and Shafer-Landau 2014. For discussion, see Evers and Streumer 2016. Another related view, according to which there are normative truths but normative properties are 'irreal', is defended by Skorupski 2010. As Olson 2012 points out, however, since Skorupski's criterion for calling a property 'real' or 'irreal' is whether this property has or lacks causal efficacy, his view may be closer to non-reductive realism.

[22] See Nagel 1986, pp. 139–40, and also Nagel 1997, p. 101.
[23] See Scanlon 2014, p. 19. See also Nagel 1997, p. 101–3.
[24] See Dworkin 1996, pp. 97–112, and 2011, pp. 23–68.

(4)   The sense in which normative properties exist is different from the sense in which other properties exist.[25]

Quietists may think that this enables them to avoid the reduction argument, by enabling them to explain why normative properties are an exception to (N). But they then need to explain what these different senses are, and why the sense in which normative properties exist makes these properties an exception to (N). It is hard to see how they can explain this. And if they cannot explain this, they are in effect merely asserting that normative properties are an exception to (N). I therefore think that quietists cannot avoid my objections by endorsing (1), (2), (3), or (4).

More generally, I think that none of the views I have discussed in this chapter avoids my objections to realism and non-cognitivism. Defenders of these views face the same choices as everyone else. They must tell us whether normative judgements represent the world. If they say that these judgements do not represent the world, their view runs into the symmetry objection. If they say that these judgements do represent the world, they must tell us whether the properties that these judgements ascribe are identical to descriptive properties. If they say that these properties are not identical to descriptive properties, their view runs into the reduction argument. And if they say that these properties are identical to descriptive properties, their view runs into the false guarantee and regress objections. There is no way around this.

45. What Makes a Judgement or Property Normative?

I said in §1 that

(1)   A mental state is a normative judgement if and only if it can be expressed with a sentence that conceptually entails that something satisfies a normative predicate,

and that

---

[25] See Parfit 2011b, pp. 469, 485–7.

(2)   A property is normative if and only if it can be ascribed with a
normative predicate.

I also said that these claims are compatible with different views about
what *makes* a judgement or property normative. I can now explain this.

Non-cognitivists take the primary things that are normative to be
judgements. For example, Allan Gibbard writes that there is "a special
normative element in talk of what it makes sense to do, and that element
resides in a special state of mind".[26] Other non-cognitivists make similar
claims.[27] As we have seen, non-cognitivists who accept minimalism also
take there to be normative properties. But they think that what makes
these properties normative is that they can be ascribed with normative
predicates, and that what makes these predicates normative is that they
can be used to express normative judgements. So non-cognitivists think
that normativity comes from judgements, and extends to properties via
the predicates that are used to express these judgements. That is why
Blackburn says that normative judgements are attitudes that we "spread
on the world".[28]

By contrast, non-reductive realists take the primary things that are
normative to be properties. Many of them take there to be a single
fundamental normative property, such as the property of being a reason,
which makes other properties normative by partly constituting these
other properties.[29] They think that what makes predicates normative is
that they ascribe normative properties, and that what makes judgements
normative is that they apply normative predicates and thereby ascribe
normative properties. So non-reductive realists think that normativity
comes from properties, and extends to judgements via the predicates that
ascribe these properties and express these judgements.

Since (1) and (2) do not say whether normativity extends from
judgements to properties or the other way around, these claims are
compatible with both of these views about what makes a judgement or
property normative. Moreover, both non-cognitivists and non-reductive

---

[26]   Gibbard 1990, p. 9; see also Gibbard 2003, pp. 6–7.

[27]   See, for example, Blackburn 1984, p. 182, 1998, pp. 49–50, and 1999, p. 213.

[28]   Blackburn 1984, p. 189; see also Blackburn 1993, p. 152.

[29]   For example, many non-reductive realists think that what makes the property of being
good normative is that it is partly constituted by the property of being a reason, since what it
is for something to be good is that there are reasons to respond to it in certain ways. A view
along these lines is proposed by Scanlon 1998, pp. 97–8.

realists should accept (1) and (2). For non-cognitivists think that normativity extends from judgements to properties via normative predicates, and non-reductive realists think that normativity extends from
properties to judgements via normative predicates. And normativity can
only extend from judgements to properties or from properties to judgements in these ways if (1) and (2) are true.

What about reductive realists? Since they are realists, you may think
that they also take the primary things that are normative to be properties.
But as I said in §17, if reductive realism is true, the difference between
normative and descriptive properties is a difference in language that is
not matched by a difference in the nature of these properties. Reductive
realists therefore cannot say that normativity extends from properties
to judgements. They could instead say that the primary things that are
normative are predicates, or the concepts that these predicates express.[30]
Or they could follow non-cognitivists in saying that the primary things
that are normative are judgements. In either case, like non-cognitivists and
non-reductive realists, they should accept (1) and (2). The same is true of
the other views I have discussed. This supports both the taxonomy I gave
in §1 and the use I made of (1) and (2) in my arguments.[31]

46. Conclusion

We now seem able to draw a more general conclusion. As we have seen,
the reduction argument shows that

(1)   If there are normative properties, these properties are identical to
descriptive properties,

---

[30] As Ridge 2014, p. 101, suggests, certain forms of cognitivism "in effect locate normativity in the *way* in which one judges the relevant contents. ... On this model, there are no
irreducibly normative states of affairs. Instead, there are *distinctively normative ways of
cognizing* certain descriptive states of affairs". Ridge here has in mind hybrid forms
of cognitivism, such as the view defended by Copp 2001. See also Dreier 1990, pp. 18–19.

[31] A different claim that some non-cognitivists and realists make is that what makes a
judgement or a concept normative is the role it plays in regulating our attitudes, our
practices, or our reasoning (see Ridge 2014, pp. 18–21, and Wedgwood 2002, p. 268, and
2007, p. 155). Realists could make a similar claim about what makes a property normative.
But this is compatible with my claim that both non-cognitivists and realists should accept
(1) and (2). And non-cognitivists and realists will then still disagree about which things are
primarily normative: judgements, properties, or predicates or concepts.

and the false guarantee and regress objections show that

(2) If there are normative properties, these properties are not identical to descriptive properties.

These claims together entail that normative properties do not exist. But the symmetry objection shows that

(3) Normative judgements are beliefs that ascribe normative properties.

These three claims together entail that the error theory is true: they together entail that normative judgements are beliefs that ascribe normative properties, but that these properties do not exist. You may therefore be inclined to reconsider what I have said so far. Can this really be the truth?

VIII

The Error Theory

Can the error theory be true? To answer this question, we should find out to which judgements the theory applies, what the theory entails, and whether what the theory entails can be true.

47. Which Properties Are Normative?

Some philosophers have a very broad conception of normativity. For example, Joshua Gert writes that he understands

the normative widely, so that it includes – amongst many other things – the beautiful, the disgusting, the funny, the rational, the moral, the good and the bad in various forms, harm and benefit, health and disease, function and purpose, and truth and falsity.[1]

My conception of normativity is narrower: the only properties that I take to be normative are rightness, wrongness, permissibility, goodness, badness, rationality, being a reason, and properties that are equivalent to or incorporate one of these properties.[2]

I endorse this narrower conception partly because the other properties that Gert lists simply do not strike me as normative. Of course, that a painting is beautiful can be a reason to look at it and can make it wrong to destroy it, and being a reason and being wrong are normative properties. But that does not mean that beauty is *itself* a normative

---

[1] Gert 2012, p. 1.
[2] I assume that this goodness and badness are not attributive (as they are in the predicates 'is a good knife' and 'is a bad knife'), that rationality is more than just consistency and probabilistic coherence, and that 'being a reason' means counting in favour. Properties that I take to be equivalent to or incorporate one of these properties are, for example, being obligatory, which I take to be equivalent to being right, and being such that we ought to do it, which I take to be equivalent to either being right or being such that there is most reason for us to do it.

property. I think that similar claims apply to disgust, funniness, harm, benefit, health, disease, function, purpose, truth, and falsity.[3]

But I also have a theoretical reason to endorse this narrower conception. As I said in §3, I take the following claims to be central thoughts about normative judgements:

(G)   There are no descriptively specified conditions in which people's normative judgements are guaranteed to be correct.

(A)   When two people make conflicting normative judgements, at most one of these judgements is correct.

I take these claims to be true of judgements that ascribe rightness, wrongness, permissibility, goodness, badness, rationality, being a reason, or a property that is equivalent to or incorporates one of these properties. But I do not take them to be true of judgements that ascribe beauty, disgust, funniness, harm, benefit, health, disease, function, purpose, truth, or falsity. I take (A) to be false of judgements that ascribe beauty, disgust, or funniness: when two people make conflicting judgements about what is beautiful, disgusting, or funny, it does not seem to me that at most one of these judgements is correct. And I take (G) to be false of judgements that ascribe harm, benefit, health, disease, function, purpose, truth, or falsity: it seems to me that there may well be descriptively specified conditions in which such judgements are guaranteed to be correct. Moreover, I think that the fact that (G) and (A) are true of judgements that ascribe rightness, wrongness, permissibility, goodness, badness, rationality, and being a reason marks an important similarity between these judgements. It is no coincidence, I think, that philosophical discussion of normativity has focused mostly on these judgements.

Which conception of normativity you endorse does not matter to my arguments: if your conception is broader than mine, you can replace the phrase 'normative property' in what follows with either the phrase

rightness, wrongness, permissibility, goodness, badness, rationality, being a reason, or property that is equivalent to or incorporates one of these properties,

---

[3] I assume here that this truth is the truth of descriptive beliefs, not of normative judgements.

or with the phrase

> property that can be ascribed with a judgement of which (G) and (A) are true.

You can then regard me as defending an error theory about this narrower class of normative properties.

48. Which Beliefs Ascribe Normative Properties?

I have argued that normative judgements are beliefs that ascribe normative properties. Which beliefs ascribe such properties? As I said in §1, the clearest examples are beliefs that apply a normative predicate to an object, such as:

> Murder is wrong.
>
> Euthanasia is permissible.
>
> Keeping your promises is right.

But the error theory also applies to many other beliefs, such as:

> There is a reason for you to quit smoking.
>
> You ought to keep your promises.
>
> Some actions are wrong.
>
> Either murder is wrong or euthanasia is permissible.

For these beliefs also conceptually entail that something has a normative property, which means that they can only be true if this property exists.[4] Do these beliefs *ascribe* this property? Only if we say that

> A belief ascribes a property if and only if it conceptually entails that something has this property.

That is how I will use the term 'ascribe' in what follows. But the error theory applies to these beliefs whether or not we use this term in this way.

---

[4] As I said in §1, the first belief entails that a consideration satisfies the predicate 'is a reason for you to quit smoking', the second entails that you satisfy the predicate 'is such that he or she ought to keep his or her promises', the third entails that an action satisfies the predicate 'is wrong', and the fourth entails that an action satisfies either the predicate 'is wrong' or the predicate 'is permissible'.

Consider next the following beliefs:

Euthanasia is not wrong.

If murder is wrong, so is euthanasia.

These beliefs do not ascribe normative properties: the first merely says that euthanasia lacks the property of being wrong, and the second merely says that euthanasia has the property of being wrong if murder also has this property. Why may these beliefs nevertheless seem to be normative judgements? Because expressing the first belief conversationally implicates that

Euthanasia is permissible,

and because expressing the second belief conversationally implicates that

Euthanasia is wrong.[5]

The belief that euthanasia is permissible and the belief that euthanasia is wrong do ascribe normative properties. The error theory therefore does apply to these beliefs. But it does not apply to the belief that euthanasia is not wrong or to the belief that if murder is wrong, so is euthanasia.[6]

Consider next the following beliefs:

Either it is raining or murder is wrong.

Either it is both raining and not raining or murder is wrong.

Since the first belief does not conceptually entail that anything is wrong, it does not ascribe a normative property. But the second belief does: since it is conceptually impossible that it is both raining and not raining, this belief conceptually entails that murder is wrong. The error theory therefore does not apply to the first belief, but does apply to the second belief.

Now consider the following argument:

It is not raining.

Either it is raining or murder is wrong.

Therefore, murder is wrong.[7]

---

[5] See also Olson 2014, p. 14.

[6] You may object that the predicate 'is not wrong' has the same meaning as the predicate 'is permissible'. But I think it does not. I will return to this in §54.

[7] See Prior 1960, pp. 201–2. For discussion, see, among others, Karmo 1988, Maitzen 1998 and 2010, the essays in Pigden 2010, and Brown 2014 and 2015.

If what I have said is true, this argument has descriptive premises and a normative conclusion. But according to Hume's law, descriptive premises cannot entail a normative conclusion. What I have said may therefore seem to violate Hume's law. As Campbell Brown suggests, however, we should take this law to say that premises that are *together* descriptive cannot entail a normative conclusion.[8] The premises of this argument together say that

It is not raining and either it is raining or murder is wrong.

Since this claim conceptually entails that murder is wrong, these premises are together normative.[9]

Consider next the following argument:

It is both raining and not raining.

Therefore, either it is both raining and not raining or murder is wrong.

If what I have said is true, this argument has a descriptive premise and a normative conclusion. Does what I have said therefore violate Hume's law? It does, but only because any descriptive contradiction violates Hume's law: since a contradiction entails everything, it also entails all normative judgements. If you take this to be a problem, you should not reject what I have said but should instead deny that a contradiction entails everything.[10]

49. Judgements About Standards

Consider next the following beliefs:

Etiquette requires that male guests at formal dinners wear a tie.

According to the rules of chess, you ought to move your bishop diagonally.

This is a good knife.

These beliefs say that something is required by a certain standard, that you ought to do something according to certain rules, and that an object

---

[8] Brown 2015, pp. 3–4.

[9] Similar claims apply to the following argument: everything Fred says is true; Fred says that murder is wrong; therefore, murder is wrong (see Karmo 1988, p. 253). This argument's premises are also together normative.

[10] See also Brown 2015, p. 4.

is a good object of a certain kind. We can call them *judgements about standards*. Are they normative judgements?

Consider first the belief that

Etiquette requires that male guests at formal dinners wear a tie.

Since what etiquette requires is wholly determined by social conventions, there are descriptively specified conditions in which people's beliefs about what etiquette requires are guaranteed to be correct: namely, conditions in which people have full descriptive information about these conventions. This means that (G) is false of this belief. I therefore do not take it to be a normative judgement.

Consider next the judgement that

According to the rules of chess, you ought to move your bishop diagonally.

Since what you ought to do according to the rules of chess is wholly determined by what these rules say, there are descriptively specified conditions in which people's beliefs about what you ought to do according to these rules are guaranteed to be correct: namely, conditions in which people have full descriptive information about what these rules say. This means that (G) is false of this belief as well. I therefore do not take this belief to be a normative judgement either.

Finally, consider the belief that

This is a good knife.

Since whether an object is a good knife is wholly determined by the extent to which it can be used for cutting, there are descriptively specified conditions in which people's beliefs about whether an object is a good knife are guaranteed to be correct: namely, conditions in which people have full descriptive information about the extent to which this object can be used for cutting. This means that (G) is false of this belief too. I therefore do not take this belief to be a normative judgement either.

Why may these beliefs nevertheless seem to be normative judgements? Because they may conversationally implicate such a judgement. Suppose you are organizing a formal dinner and I show up in an old T-shirt. If you say to me in a stern tone of voice that

Etiquette requires that male guests at formal dinners wear a tie,

you are conversationally implicating that

Bart ought to wear a tie.

The belief that Bart ought to wear a tie is a normative judgement. The error theory therefore does apply to this belief. But it does not apply to the belief that etiquette requires that male guests at formal dinners wear a tie.

If your conception of normativity is broader than mine, you may want to extend the term 'normative judgement' to judgements about standards. But you should agree that the error theory does not apply to these judgements. Since (G) is false of judgements about standards, reductive realism is true of them instead.

50. Instrumental Normative Judgements

Consider next the following beliefs:

If you want to be a doctor, you ought to study medicine.

If you want to stay alive, there is a reason for you to quit smoking.

If you want to be a philosopher, it is rational for you to avoid contradicting yourself.

We can call such beliefs *instrumental normative judgements*. It is often suggested that the error theory does not apply to these judgements.[11]

But I think it does. There are two different accounts of instrumental normative judgements. According to the *wide-scope account*, these judgements ascribe a normative property to avoiding a combination of attitudes, actions, or absences of attitudes or actions.[12] If so, their contents are equivalent to the following claims:

You ought to avoid the following combination: wanting to be a doctor and not studying medicine.

There is a reason for you to avoid the following combination: wanting to stay alive and not quitting smoking.

---

[11] See Mackie 1977, pp. 27–9, and Joyce 2001, pp. 35, 121–3.

[12] An account of this kind is proposed by Broome 1999. For discussion, see, among many others, Schroeder 2004 and Way 2010.

It is rational for you to avoid the following combination: wanting to be a philosopher and contradicting yourself.

If this account is correct, these judgements ascribe normative properties, which means that the error theory applies to them.

According to the *narrow-scope account*, instrumental normative judgements say that someone's having a desire gives rise to something's having a normative property.[13] If so, their contents conceptually entail the following claims:

Necessarily, if you want to be a doctor, you ought to study medicine.

Necessarily, if you want to stay alive, there is a reason for you to quit smoking.

Necessarily, if you want to be a philosopher, it is rational for you to avoid contradicting yourself.[14]

If this account is correct, these judgements conceptually entail that there is a possible world in which something has a normative property, which means that they can be true only if this property exists. Do these judgements then *ascribe* this property? Only if we say that

A belief ascribes a property if and only if it conceptually entails that *there is a possible world in which* something has this property.

That is how I will use the term 'ascribe' in what follows. But if the narrow-scope account is correct, the error theory applies to these beliefs whether or not we use this term in this way.

If the narrow-scope account is correct, instrumental normative judgements belong to a wider class of beliefs about necessary connections between descriptive and normative properties. Some other examples of such beliefs are:

Necessarily, if an action maximizes happiness, this action is right.

Necessarily, if a consideration increases the probability that a belief is true, this consideration is a reason for this belief.

---

[13] Joyce 2001, pp. 121–3, appeals to the narrow-scope account to argue that the error theory does not apply to instrumental normative judgements. For discussion, see Bedke 2010 and Olson 2014, pp. 152–3.

[14] You may think that if the narrow-scope account is correct, the contents of these judgements merely entail material conditionals. But this does not capture the idea that someone's having a desire *gives rise to* something's having a normative property.

Necessarily, if a state of affairs contains happiness, this state of affairs is to that extent intrinsically good.[15]

Such beliefs also conceptually entail that there is a possible world in which something has a normative property, which means that they can be true only if this property exists. The error theory therefore applies to these beliefs as well.

You may think that the error theory does not apply to instrumental normative judgements because (G) may not seem true of these judgements. It may seem, for example, that

(1)   If people would make certain instrumental normative judgements after considering all relevant descriptive information, these judgements are guaranteed to be correct.

But suppose that Bob is deeply attached to homeopathy. Suppose that whenever he is confronted with evidence against the effectiveness of homeopathy, he endorses ad hoc hypotheses to explain away this evidence. And suppose that, after considering all relevant descriptive information, he would think that if you want to be a doctor, you ought to study homeopathy. Is Bob's judgement then guaranteed to be correct?

I think our answer to this question is 'No'. This shows that instead of endorsing (1), we think that

(~1)   If people would make certain instrumental normative judgements after considering all relevant descriptive information, these judgements are *not* guaranteed to be correct.

And I think we will have similar thoughts about other descriptively specified conditions in which people make instrumental normative judgements. This suggests that we do take (G) to be true of these judgements.[16]

Why may (G) nevertheless seem false of instrumental normative judgements? One reason for this is that it is easy to conflate the belief that

---

[15] That instrumental normative judgements belong to this wider class of beliefs is also noted by Bedke 2010 and Olson 2014, p. 153.

[16] As Gibbard writes, the "puzzles of instrumental rationality lie not just in the facts", where by 'facts' he means descriptive facts (1990, p. 17). He supports this claim by appealing to the prisoner's dilemma and a Russian roulette example. Bedke 2010, pp. 48–9, makes a similar point by appealing to the disagreement between what he calls 'present aim instrumentalists' and 'complete life instrumentalists'.

(2)   If you want to be a doctor, you ought to study medicine

with the descriptive belief that

(3)   You can become a doctor only if you study medicine.

But if the wide-scope account is correct, (2) says that you ought to avoid the following combination: wanting to be a doctor and not studying medicine. By contrast, (3) entails that you ought to avoid this combination only if we make an additional assumption: for example, if we assume that

(4)   You ought to avoid the following combination: having an end and not taking the necessary means to this end.

And if the narrow-scope account is correct, (2) and the claim that

(5)   You want to be a doctor

together entail that you ought to study medicine. By contrast, (3) and (5) entail that you ought to study medicine only if we make an additional assumption: for example, if we assume that

(6)   You ought to do what you want to do.

This shows that if either the wide-scope or the narrow-scope account is correct, (2) is not equivalent to (3). More generally, it shows that instrumental normative judgements are not equivalent to descriptive beliefs about necessary or efficient means. I therefore conclude that the error theory does apply to instrumental normative judgements.

51. Judgements About Reasons for Belief

Consider next the following belief:

(1)   There is a reason to believe that the Earth has existed for billions of years.

You may think that the error theory does not apply to this belief, since (G) may not seem true of judgements about reasons for belief. It may seem, for example, that

(2)   If people would make certain judgements about reasons for belief after considering all relevant descriptive information, these judgements are guaranteed to be correct.

But suppose that Fred is deeply religious. Suppose that whenever he is confronted with evidence against creationism, he endorses ad hoc hypotheses to explain away this evidence. And suppose that, after considering all relevant descriptive information, he would think that there is no reason to believe that the Earth has existed for billions of years. Is Fred's judgement then guaranteed to be correct?

As before, I think our answer to this question is 'No'. This shows that instead of endorsing (2), we think that

> (~2)   If people would make certain judgements about reasons for belief after considering all relevant descriptive information, these judgements are *not* guaranteed to be correct.

And I think we will have similar thoughts about other descriptively specified conditions in which people make judgements about reasons for belief. This suggests that we do take (G) to be true of these judgements.

Why may (G) nevertheless seem false of judgements about reasons for belief? I think there are three reasons for this. First, it is easy to conflate (1) with the descriptive belief that

> (3)   There is evidence that the Earth has existed for billions of years.

But (3) is a descriptive belief only if it uses the term 'evidence' to mean what Thomas Kelly calls 'indicator evidence': if it uses this term to mean a consideration that indicates that a belief is true, either by logically implying the content of this belief or by making it more likely that this content is true.[17] And reasons for belief are not the same thing as indicator evidence. A consideration can be a reason to believe a necessary truth without either logically implying this truth or making this truth more likely to hold.[18] There can be indicator evidence for trivial beliefs there is no reason for us to have, since forming these beliefs would be

[17] See Kelly 2008, §3, and Kelly 2007, p. 470.
[18] You may object that a necessary truth is logically implied by any proposition. But it is clearly not the case that any proposition is indicator evidence for any necessary truth. If we want to say that a consideration can be evidence for a proposition by logically implying this proposition, we should therefore impose some kind of relevance constraint on this implication. And it will then no longer be the case that a necessary truth is logically implied by any proposition.

a waste of our cognitive resources.[19] And there can perhaps also be practical reasons to have a belief for which there is no indicator evidence. Of course, we often take indicator evidence to be a reason for a belief in the sense that we take it to count in favour of this belief. But we then make a normative judgement about this evidence and this belief.[20]

Another reason why (G) may seem false of judgements about reasons for belief is that (1) may seem equivalent to the belief that

(4)   If you want to have true beliefs about the age of the Earth, there is a reason for you to believe that the Earth has existed for billions of years.[21]

But suppose that a geologist confronts Fred with overwhelming evidence that the Earth has existed for billions of years. Can Fred then make it the case that there is no reason for him to believe this by giving up his desire to have true beliefs about the age of the Earth? He clearly cannot: as Kelly writes, "one cannot immunize against the possibility of acquiring reasons for belief by not caring about the relevant subject matter".[22] This means that (1) is not equivalent to (4). Moreover, if (1) were equivalent to (4), this would not matter, since I have already argued that we take (G) to be true of instrumental normative judgements such as (4).

Finally, (G) may seem false of judgements about reasons for belief because these judgements may seem to be about what Jonas Olson calls 'the standard of being a responsible believer'.[23] Olson more generally

---

[19]   See Harman 1986, p. 12. Kelly 2003, p. 625, claims that when I "stumble upon strong evidence" for a trivial belief, there is a reason for me to have this belief. But if so, it remains true that there can be indicator evidence for trivial beliefs that there is no reason for us to have, if forming these beliefs would be a waste of our cognitive resources and we are not currently attending to this indicator evidence.

[20]   See also Scanlon 1998, p. 60 and 2014, p. 35, and Shah 2011, pp. 98–9.

[21]   Foley 1987 defends a view along these lines: he writes that "the epistemic goal is concerned with *now* believing those propositions that are true and *now* not believing those propositions that are false", and that if "a person has this goal and if on careful reflection he would believe Y to be an effective means to this goal, then, all else being equal, it is rational (in an epistemic sense) for him to bring about Y" (p. 8). But as Kelly 2003, pp. 623–5, points out, we do not seem to have a general desire to have true beliefs: at most, we have desires to have true beliefs about particular subject matters, such as the age of the Earth. See also Olson 2014, pp. 158–9.

[22]   Kelly 2003, p. 628. See also Kelly 2007, pp. 466–7, and Cuneo 2007, p. 59.

[23]   Olson 2014, p. 164. Olson takes the term 'reason for belief' to be ambiguous, and takes this to be one disambiguation of this term.

suggests that sentences about reasons can express judgements about standards: for example, he thinks that the sentence

(5) There is a reason for male guests at formal dinners to wear a tie

can express the belief that

(6) Etiquette requires that male guests at formal dinners wear a tie.[24]

If so, the sentence

(1) There is a reason to believe that the Earth has existed for billions of years

can similarly express the belief that

(7) The standard of being a responsible believer requires that you believe that the Earth has existed for billions of years.

I think, however, that sentences such as (5) and (1) never express judgements about standards. For (6) entails (5) only if we make an additional assumption: if we assume, for example, that

(8) There is a reason to do what etiquette requires.

Similarly, (7) entails (1) only if we make an additional assumption: if we assume, for example, that

(9) There is a reason to believe what the standard of being a responsible believer requires.

If you and I both endorse (8), I can conversationally implicate (5) by uttering (6). Similarly, if you and I both endorse (9), I can conversationally implicate (1) by uttering (7). But that does not mean that (5) and (1) are equivalent to (6) and (7). In other words, it does not mean that sentences about reasons can express judgements about standards.

I therefore conclude that the error theory does apply to judgements about reasons for belief. This means that the theory applies to all normative judgements: it applies to judgements that ascribe right-ness, wrongness, permissibility, goodness, badness, rationality, being a

---

[24] Olson 2014, p. 121. Joyce 2001, pp. 39–40, makes similar claims. But Joyce does not make such claims about reasons for belief, and stresses that only those who endorse etiquette would say without qualification that there is a reason to do what etiquette requires.

reason, or a property that is equivalent to or incorporates one of these properties. This does not include judgements about standards, but it does include instrumental normative judgements and judgements about reasons for belief.

52. Moral Error Theories

Most error theorists do not take their theory to apply this widely. J. L. Mackie takes his moral error theory to apply only to categorical moral judgements: judgements that entail reasons for action that are, as Mackie puts it, "not contingent upon any present desire of the agent to whose satisfaction the recommended action would contribute as a means".[25] Richard Joyce makes similar claims about his moral error theory.[26] And Jonas Olson takes his error theory to apply only to judgements that entail what he calls 'irreducibly normative reasons', which he takes to exclude many instrumental normative judgements and judgements about reasons for belief.[27]

Why do Mackie, Joyce, and Olson not take their error theories to apply to all normative judgements? One reason for this is that Joyce and Olson think that certain sentences about reasons can express judgements about standards, in which case Joyce calls these reasons 'institutional' and Olson calls them 'reducible'.[28] They therefore take there to be judgements about reasons to which their error theories do not apply. As I have said, I think that these sentences never express judgements about standards. But like Joyce and Olson's error theories, the error theory I defend does not apply to judgements about standards.

A more important reason why Mackie, Joyce, and Olson do not take their error theories to apply to all normative judgements is that their arguments differ from mine. Mackie's first argument for his moral error theory is the *argument from relativity*. According to this argument, the best explanation of the fact that members of different societies make

---

[25]   Mackie 1977, p. 29.   [26]   Joyce 2001, pp. 35, 121–3, and 2007, pp. 52–3.

[27]   Olson 2014, pp. 153–4, 158–9. Moral error theories are also defended by Hinckfuss 1987, Garner 1990, 1994, and 2007, and Burgess 2007. Loeb 2008 defends a closely related irrealist view that he calls 'moral incoherentism', according to which "both objectivity and its denial ... are central and persistent features of our moral thought and talk", which means that "no adequate, coherent moral semantics can be found" (p. 365).

[28]   See Joyce 2001, p. 40, and Olson 2014, p. 121.

different moral judgements is that these judgements "reflect people's adherence to and participation in different ways of life".[29] Since this explanation does not appeal to moral properties, Mackie takes it to indicate that such properties do not exist. His second argument is the *argument from queerness*. According to this argument, if something had a moral property, it "would be sought by anyone who was acquainted with it, not because . . . this person, or any person, is so constituted that he desires this end, but because the end has to-be-pursuedness somehow built into it".[30] Since this would make moral properties utterly different from all other properties, Mackie also takes it to indicate that such properties do not exist.

Joyce's and Olson's arguments for their error theories are both versions of the argument from queerness. Joyce's version starts with a defence of the following two claims:

(3)   If we morally ought to perform an action, we ought to perform this action regardless of what our desires or interests are.

(4)   If we morally ought to perform an action, there is a reason for us to perform this action.

These claims together entail that

(5)   If we morally ought to perform an action, there is a reason for us to perform this action regardless of what our desires or interests are.[31]

According to Joyce, if someone tells me that there is a reason for me to perform an action that I have no desire to perform and that is not in my interest, I can intelligibly answer 'Why?' or 'So what?'. I am then what

---

[29]   Mackie 1977, p. 36.

[30]   Mackie 1977, p. 40. This is the metaphysical part of the argument from queerness. When outlining this part of the argument, Mackie also writes: "What is the connection between the natural fact that an action is a piece of deliberate cruelty . . . and the moral fact that it is wrong? It cannot be an entailment, a logical or semantic necessity. Yet it is not merely that the two features occur together. The wrongness must somehow be 'consequential' or 'supervenient': it is wrong because it is a piece of deliberate cruelty. But just what *in the world* is signified by this 'because'?" (1977, p. 41). The argument from queerness also has an epistemological part, according to which if we had knowledge about moral properties, "it would have to be by some special faculty of moral perception or intuition, utterly different from our ordinary ways of knowing everything else" (1977, p. 38). For discussion, see, among others, Brink 1984, Garner 1990, Joyce 2001, Shepski 2008, and Olson 2014.

[31]   Joyce 2001, p. 77.

Joyce calls 'alienated' from this reason.[32] He argues that a consideration is a reason for me to perform an action only if I cannot be alienated from it in this way. And he therefore concludes that the consequent of (5) is false. If so, it follows that its antecedent is false as well: in other words, it follows that there are no actions that we morally ought to perform.

Olson's version starts with a defence of the following claim:

(6)   If we morally ought to perform an action, there is an irreducibly normative reason for us to perform this action.

By an 'irreducibly normative reason' Olson means a reason that is "not reducible, for example, to facts about what would promote the satisfaction of [our] desires, or to facts about [our] roles or engagement in rule-governed activities".[33] Like Mackie, he argues that such reasons are queer and that the best explanation of why we make judgements about them does not appeal to their existence.[34] And he therefore concludes that the consequent of (6) is false. If so, it follows that its antecedent is false as well: in other words, as before, it follows that there are no actions that we morally ought to perform.

Olson thinks that the reduction argument that I gave in chapters II and III is also a version of the argument from queerness.[35] But the reduction argument does not say that normative properties have to-be-pursuedness built into them, or that we cannot be alienated from them, or that such properties are queer. Instead, it says that if there were irreducibly normative properties, they would be the only properties of which it is not true that

---

[32] Joyce 2001, pp. 80–5. Joyce also writes that if we morally ought to do something, this gives us "'real' reasons' – reasons that cannot legitimately be ignored" and that are "not available for legitimate questioning" (2001, p. 51). And he writes that though he is "willing to attribute to ordinary moral thought a presupposition about non-institutional desire-transcendent reasons", this is "an extremely inchoate presupposition" (2011, p. 525).

[33] Olson 2014, p. 122. He defends (6) partly by arguing against Finlay's end-relational theory (Olson 2014, pp. 126–35).

[34] Olson 2014, pp. 117–26, 135–8, 141–8. Olson says that "most moral error theorists maintain that moral properties are necessarily uninstantiated", but denies that this means that moral properties do not exist (p. 12 n. 17). As I said in §6, I think that necessarily uninstantiated properties do not exist, since they are not ways objects can be. But I take this disagreement to be merely terminological.

[35] Olson 2014, p. 92 n. 38.

(N)   Two predicates ascribe the same property if and only if they are necessarily coextensive.

Olson suggests that the reduction argument is problematic because it "generalises beyond the moral and the normative" and because whether (N) is true depends on "more general issues in metaphysics".[36] But I take the argument's generality to be a strength: what gives the argument its force, I think, is that (N) is true of all other properties, which makes it hard to deny that (N) is true of normative properties as well.

I also think that Mackie, Joyce, and Olson underestimate the generality of their own arguments. Consider first judgements about prudential reasons. Suppose that Bob is a smoker, and suppose that we tell him:

The fact that smoking harms your health is a reason for you to quit smoking.

If Bob does not care about his health, he can intelligibly answer 'Why?' or 'So what?'. This suggests the he could be alienated from this reason as well. Joyce could reply that Bob's reasons depend on his desires *and interests*, and that it is in Bob's interest to remain healthy. But then we should doubt Joyce's claim that a consideration is a reason for a person to perform an action only if this person cannot intelligibly answer 'Why?' or 'So what?'. This suggests that Joyce's argument also applies to certain prudential reasons.[37]

Consider next instrumental normative judgements. Suppose that Fred finds himself with a desire to do something that he thinks is wrong, such as a desire to push a man in front of an approaching train. And suppose that we tell him:

If you want to push this man in front of this train, there is a reason for you to stand close to him and give him a firm push.

If Fred thinks that it is wrong to push the man in front of the train, he can intelligibly answer 'So what? It is wrong to do this, so I am not interested in your advice'. It therefore seems that he could be alienated

---

[36]   Olson 2014, p. 100. Olson calls (N) 'Hume's dictum' (p. 92).

[37]   Joyce 2007, p. 53, claims that his moral error theory does not apply to prudential 'oughts', which suggests that he thinks it does not apply to prudential reasons either.

from this reason too. This suggests that Joyce's argument also applies to certain instrumental normative judgements.[38]

Finally, consider judgements about reasons for belief. I argued in §51 that these judgements are neither descriptive beliefs about evidence, nor instrumental normative judgements, nor judgements about the standard of being a responsible believer. Instead, these judgements ascribe normative properties just like moral judgements do. This suggests that if Mackie is right that moral properties have to-be-pursuedness built into them, the property of being a reason for belief similarly has to-be-believedness built into it. And it suggests that if Joyce is right that we cannot be alienated from our moral reasons, we similarly cannot be alienated from our reasons for belief. It therefore suggests that, contrary to what Mackie and Joyce think, their arguments also apply to judgements about reasons for belief.[39]

Olson comes closest to seeing the generality of his own argument: he rightly notes that "a plausible moral error theory must be an error theory about all irreducible normativity".[40] But he does not take his argument to apply to all instrumental normative judgements, since he thinks that the contents of many of these judgements "reduce to empirical claims about agents' desires and (actual or believed) efficient means of bringing about the satisfaction of these desires".[41] And he thinks that his argument only applies to judgements about reasons for belief if we use the term 'reason for belief' to mean *epistemic* reason for belief, and not if we use this term to express an instrumental normative judgement or a judgement about the standard of being a responsible believer.[42] But I argued in §§50–51 that instrumental normative judgements are not descriptive beliefs about necessary or efficient means, and that judgements about reasons for belief are neither instrumental normative judgements nor judgements

---

[38] Bedke 2010 also argues that the argument from queerness applies to instrumental normative judgements. See also Scanlon 2014, pp. 16–17 n. 1.

[39] For further discussion of whether arguments for moral error theories apply to judgements about reasons for belief, see, among others, Cuneo 2007, Heathwood 2009, Bedke 2010, Rowland 2013, and Cowie 2014.

[40] Olson 2014, p. 3.   [41] Olson 2014, p. 153.

[42] Olson 2014, pp. 156–9, 162, 164. Husi 2011 similarly distinguishes between normativity in the 'norm-involving' sense and normativity in the 'authoritative' sense (pp. 425, 438), and argues that we can hold on to normativity in the first sense while rejecting it in the second sense. Unlike Olson, however, Husi applies this strategy to all reasons, not just to reasons for belief.

about the standard of being a responsible believer.[43] This suggests that, contrary to what Olson claims, his argument does apply to these judgements.

53. What the Error Theory Entails

Normally, if a belief ascribes a property to an object that this object does not have, this belief is false. This suggests that the error theory entails that all normative judgements are false. But some philosophers deny that the error theory entails this. Suppose I believe that the present king of France is bald. According to P. F. Strawson, this belief presupposes that there is a present king of France, in the sense that the truth of the sentence

There is a present king of France

is a necessary condition for the sentence

The present king of France is bald

to be either true or false.[44] Since there is no present king of France, Strawson thinks that the belief that the present king of France is bald is neither true nor false. According to Joyce, the belief that stealing is wrong similarly presupposes that there is a property of wrongness. If so, and if there is no property of wrongness, this belief is also neither true nor false.[45] The error theory then entails that all normative judgements are neither true nor false.

But I doubt this. If I believe that the desk at which I wrote this book is both red and blue all over, my belief ascribes a non-existent property to my desk. But this belief is clearly false, since my desk is in fact not both red and blue all over. More generally, if a belief ascribes a property to a non-existent object, it fails to pick out an object that has or lacks this property. Strawson may be right that such beliefs are neither true nor false. But if a belief ascribes a non-existent property to an existing object,

---

[43] Moreover, I think Olson should agree that his argument applies to reasons for belief. As I argue in Streumer 2016a, his objections to Finlay's end-relational theory can be extended to judgements about reasons for belief, in which case they show that these judgements are not beliefs about standards.

[44] See Strawson 1950 and 1952, pp. 174–5. Strawson defends this view about statements rather than about beliefs.

[45] See Joyce 2001, pp. 6–7.

it *does* pick out an object that has or lacks this property. More precisely, it picks out an object that lacks this property, since this property does not exist. We should therefore treat such beliefs the way we treat other beliefs that ascribe a property to an object that this object lacks: we should take such beliefs to be false.[46]

In response, Joyce could say that the claim that

(1)   Stealing is wrong

expresses the same belief as the claim that

(2)   Wrongness is had by stealing.

If there is no property of wrongness, (2) ascribes a second-order property to a non-existent property. If Strawson is right, this means that (2) is neither true nor false. And Joyce could say that if (1) and (2) express the same belief, the belief that stealing is wrong is therefore also neither true nor false.[47]

But I doubt that (1) and (2) express the same belief. And if they did, it would be an open question whether this belief ascribes the property of wrongness to stealing or the second-order property of being had by stealing to wrongness. It seems more natural to regard it as ascribing the property of wrongness to stealing. If so, and if there is no property of wrongness, this belief is false. I therefore take the error theory to entail that all normative judgements are false.

54. Can It Be True That All Normative Judgements Are False?

Some philosophers think that it cannot be true that all normative judgements are false. Consider the judgement that stealing is wrong. If this judgement is false, it follows that

(1)   Stealing is not wrong.

---

[46] See also Olson 2014, pp. 12–13. Of course, normative judgements can also ascribe a normative property to a non-existent object: for example, I may believe that the present king of France ought to make his presence felt more strongly. If Strawson is right, such normative judgements are neither true nor false.

[47] See Joyce 2001, pp. 6–7, and 2015, §4. As Joyce notes, the idea that sentences of the form '*a* is F' can be reformulated as 'F-ness is had by *a*', and that this throws into doubt the distinction between objects and properties, is due to Ramsey 1925. See also MacBride 2005.

And we may think that (1) has the same meaning as the claim that

(2)   Stealing is permissible.

But (2) expresses a normative judgement, since it ascribes the normative property of being permissible to stealing. This suggests that the claim that all normative judgements are false is inconsistent. And if this claim is inconsistent, the error theory cannot be true.[48]

In response, I could deny that (2) ascribes a normative property: I could say that (2) merely says that stealing lacks the property of being wrong.[49] But then the error theory would entail that everything is permissible.[50] Moreover, this response leaves it unclear why the judgement that stealing is wrong *does* ascribe a normative property. For if (1) has the same meaning as (2), it seems that the claim that

(3)   Stealing is wrong

similarly has the same meaning as the claim that

(4)   Stealing is not permissible,

which merely says that stealing lacks the property of being permissible.

Fortunately, there is a better response. As Charles Pigden and Jonas Olson have suggested, we should deny that the claim that

(1)   Stealing is not wrong

has the same meaning as the claim that

(2)   Stealing is permissible.

For whereas (1) merely says that stealing lacks the normative property of being wrong, (2) says that stealing has the normative property of being permissible. Of course, as I said in §48, claims like (1) do conversationally implicate claims like (2). But we can cancel this implicature by saying that we do not take stealing to be permissible.[51]

---

[48] For discussions of this problem, see Boghossian 2006, pp. 27–8, Sinnott-Armstrong 2006, pp. 32–7, Pigden 2007, pp. 450–4, Dworkin 2011, pp. 42–4, and Olson 2014, pp. 11–15.

[49] Pigden 2007, pp. 451–2, considers a solution along these lines but rejects it.

[50] See Olson 2014, p. 12.

[51] See Pigden 2007, pp. 452–4, and Olson 2014, pp. 14–15. As Williams 1985a, p. 62, writes: "If there is a system of rules, then no doubt if the rules are silent on a certain matter…

Similarly, we should deny that the claim that

(4)   Stealing is not permissible

has the same meaning as the claim that

(3)   Stealing is wrong.

For whereas (4) merely says that stealing lacks the normative property of being permissible, (3) says that stealing has the normative property of being wrong. As before, claims like (4) do conversationally implicate claims like (3). But we can cancel this implicature by saying that we do not take stealing to be wrong.

You may object that the relation between these claims seems closer than conversational implicature. For the claim that stealing is wrong has the same meaning as the claim that

(5)   Stealing is impermissible.

But I have just denied that the claim that stealing is wrong has the same meaning as the claim that

(4)   Stealing is not permissible.

This entails that the claim that stealing is *im*permissible does not have the same meaning as the claim that stealing is *not* permissible. Is this defensible? You may think that it is not. But I can avoid this problem by rephrasing what the error theory entails. I can say that the theory entails that the following claims are true:

(1*)   Stealing does not have the property of being wrong.

(4*)   Stealing does not have the property of being permissible.

I can then say that *if* (1) has the same meaning as (2), then the meaning of (1) must be different from the meaning of (1*), and that *if* (4) has the same meaning as (3), then the meaning of (4) must be different from the meaning of (4*). For (1*) and (4*) explicitly say that an object lacks a certain normative property without ascribing any other normative property to this object.

that fact can naturally be taken to mean permission. . . . But if there is no law, then silence is not meaningful, permissive, silence: it is simply silence."

You may also have a different reason for thinking that what the error theory entails cannot be true. As I said in §44, some quietists think that

(6)   Views about the nature of normative judgements and properties, such as realism, non-cognitivism, and the error theory, themselves express normative judgements.

If (6) is true and if the error theory entails that all normative judgements are false, it follows that the error theory entails its own falsity.[52]

But is (6) true? I said in §1 that

A mental state is a normative judgement if and only if it can be expressed with a sentence that conceptually entails that something satisfies a normative predicate.

If so, the sentence 'Realism is true' expresses a normative judgement, since it conceptually entails that something satisfies a normative predicate. Of course, it does not entail that a *specific* object satisfies a *specific* normative predicate. To avoid having to say that it expresses a normative judgement, we could therefore say that

A mental state is a normative judgement if and only if it can be expressed with a sentence that conceptually entails that a specific object satisfies a specific normative predicate.[53]

But then the sentence 'Either murder is wrong or euthanasia is permissible' would not express a normative judgement either.[54] Since I am inclined to think that this sentence does express a normative judgement, I am inclined to agree with quietists that the sentence 'Realism is true' expresses a normative judgement as well.

But that does not mean that the sentence 'The error theory is true' expresses a normative judgement. For instead of entailing that something satisfies a normative predicate, this sentence entails that nothing satisfies any normative predicate whatsoever. Moreover, it also does not mean that the sentence 'Realism is false' expresses a normative

---

[52] See Dworkin 2011, pp. 40–4.

[53] See Maitzen 1998, p. 361–2 and 2010, p. 295. Maitzen claims that the sentence "Some ethical sentences, standardly construed, are true" is non-ethical, and uses this sentence to give a purported counterexample to Hume's law (1998, p. 354; see also 2010, p. 293). If he is right, the sentence "Realism is true" can be used in a similar way.

[54] As Maitzen 2010, p. 296, notes.

judgement. For unlike the sentence 'Realism is true', this sentence does not entail that anything satisfies a normative predicate. Quietists who endorse (6) may object that if a sentence expresses a normative judgement, its negation must express a normative judgement as well. But we have already seen that this is false: whereas the sentence 'Murder is wrong' expresses a normative judgement, the sentence 'Murder is not wrong' does not. I therefore think that what the error theory entails can be true.

55. Conclusion

I conclude that the error theory applies to all normative judgements, that the theory entails that all normative judgements are false, and that it can be true that all normative judgements are false. But you may still be strongly inclined to reject the error theory. So am I.

IX

Believing the Error Theory

We are strongly inclined to reject the error theory. But perhaps the fault does not lie with the theory. Perhaps it lies with us.

56. My Inability to Believe the Error Theory

Few theories are so hard to believe that no philosopher has ever defended them. But as far as I know, no other philosopher has ever defended an error theory about all normative judgements. This suggests that such a theory is very hard to believe.

Is it impossible to believe? That depends partly on how we use the term 'belief'. I will use this term in such a way that at least two conditions have to be met for a person to believe that p. The first is that

(B1) A person believes that p only if this person is very confident that p.

We can distinguish *full* from *partial* belief: we fully believe that p if we are very confident that p, and we partly believe that p if we are only somewhat confident that p. I will use the term 'belief' to mean full belief.[1]

The second condition is that

(B2) A person believes that p only if this person adequately understands p.

Suppose I do not understand the general theory of relativity. If (B2) is true, I then do not believe this theory. Suppose next that a physicist tells me that the general theory of relativity is true. I may then come to believe

---

[1] I will be neutral about whether beliefs are binary or come in degrees: if they are binary I use the term 'belief' simply to mean belief, and if they come in degrees I use the term 'belief' to mean a high degree of belief.

that this theory is true. But if (B2) is true, I do not thereby come to believe the theory itself. I come to believe the theory itself only if I adequately understand it. On the other hand, if I *do* adequately understand the general theory of relativity, I cannot come to believe that this theory is true without thereby coming to believe the theory itself.

We can also distinguish *explicit* from *implicit* belief: we explicitly believe that *p* if we currently think that *p*, and we implicitly believe that *p* if our current thoughts commit us to *p*, for example, by presupposing or entailing *p*. And we can distinguish *occurrent* from *dispositional* belief: we have an occurrent belief that *p* if we currently think that *p*, and we have a dispositional belief that *p* if we are disposed to think that *p* in certain circumstances, for example, when someone asks us whether it is the case that *p*.[2] I will use the term 'belief' to mean explicit and occurrent belief.

Since our concept of a belief is not entirely precise, there are different correct ways to use the term 'belief'.[3] If we want to set the bar low, we can say that a person believes that *p* even if this person is only somewhat confident that *p* or does not adequately understand *p*. If we want to set the bar higher, we can say that a person believes that *p* only if conditions (B1) and (B2) are met. And if we want to set the bar even higher, we can add further conditions: for example, we can say that a person believes that *p* only if this belief is stable and influences his or her actions. As I have said, I will set the bar at meeting conditions (B1) and (B2). But I take (B1) and (B2) to be partly stipulative: I take them to pick out *a* correct way to use the term 'belief', not *the* correct way.

If this is how we use the term 'belief', can we believe the error theory? My own experience suggests that we cannot. When I consider the

---

[2] For these distinctions, see, for example, Harman 1986, pp. 13–14. I here take explicit belief to be identical to occurrent belief, but Harman does not: he writes that "one believes something explicitly if one's belief in that thing involves an explicit mental representation whose content is the content of that belief" (p. 13), and that "a belief is occurrent if it is either currently before one's consciousness or in some other way currently operative in guiding what one is thinking or doing" (p. 14).

[3] As Stevenson 2002, p. 106, writes, our concept of a belief "may well be vague in certain respects", and "may even be a family resemblance concept . . . with some of its extension left indeterminate by preceding usage". Stevenson distinguishes six different ways to use the term 'belief'; mine corresponds most closely to what he calls 'linguistic reasoned beliefs' (pp. 116–17, 120).

symmetry objection, I find myself forming the belief that normative properties exist. This belief is not fully explicit, but I am committed to it by my own normative judgements in combination with the belief that these judgements are beliefs that ascribe normative properties. When I focus on the nature of normative properties, however, my implicit belief that such properties exist weakens. When I consider the reduction argument, I find myself forming the belief that either reductive realism is true or normative judgements are not beliefs after all. As before, this belief is not fully explicit, but I am committed to it by my own normative judgements in combination with the belief that there are no irreducibly normative properties. When I consider the false guarantee and regress objections, I find myself forming the belief that either non-reductive realism is true or normative judgements are not beliefs after all. As before, this belief is not fully explicit, but I am committed to it by my own normative judgements in combination with the belief that if there are normative properties they are not identical to descriptive properties. I never succeed in putting these arguments together and thereby coming to believe the error theory. Instead, I come to believe different parts of the theory at different times, while implicitly forming other beliefs that conflict with the theory.

This suggests that the error theory is what Roy Sorensen calls a 'belief blindspot' to me: a consistent proposition that I cannot believe.[4] The error theory consists of two parts: the claim that

(1) Normative judgements are beliefs that ascribe normative properties,

and the claim that

(2) Normative properties do not exist.

I can believe each part of the theory individually, but only if I do not believe the other part at the same time. This suggests that (1) and (2) are what Sorensen calls 'semi-blindspots' to me: neither claim is by itself a belief blindspot, but believing (1) prevents me from believing (2), and believing (2) prevents me from believing (1). And it suggests that the

---

[4] Sorensen 1988, pp. 52–3.

conjunction of (1) and (2) is what Sorensen calls a 'holistic blindspot' to me: a belief blindspot that consists of semi-blindspots.[5]

If anyone is in a good position to come to believe the error theory, I am. I understand the error theory, I have carefully considered the arguments I gave in chapters II to VII, and when I consider each argument individually I believe that it is sound. But no matter how hard I try, I do not come to believe the error theory. I take this to be evidence that I cannot believe the error theory. More generally, since I am in a better position to come to believe this theory than almost anyone else, I take it to be evidence that *we* cannot believe the error theory.

You may think that if *you* believed that these arguments are sound, you *would* come to believe the error theory. But it is hard to be certain about this unless you actually believe that all of these arguments are sound. And I do not know anyone else who believes this. Philosophers generally endorse the majority of the arguments I gave in chapters II to VII: non-reductive realists generally endorse the false guarantee and regress objections and the symmetry objection, reductive realists generally endorse the reduction argument and the symmetry objection, and non-cognitivists generally endorse the reduction argument and the false guarantee and regress objections. But they never put these arguments together and come to believe the error theory. I think this is evidence that we cannot believe this theory.

57. Why We Cannot Believe the Error Theory

But this evidence does not explain why we cannot believe the error theory. Why are we unable to put these arguments together and come to believe this theory?

I think the explanation is that if we use the term 'belief' in accordance with (B1) and (B2), two further conditions also have to be met for a person to believe that p. The first of these is that

(B3)   A person believes that p only if this person believes what he or she believes to be entailed by p.

---

[5] Sorensen 1988, p. 93. Sorensen himself does not make these claims about the error theory.

To see this, suppose that Bob says:

> I believe that Socrates was a man, and I believe that this entails that Socrates was a human being, but I do not believe that Socrates was a human being.

Bob may then be insincere, or may be considering whether to give up one of these beliefs, or may fail to adequately understand what he is saying. If he is insincere, he does not believe what he says he believes. If he is considering whether to give up one of these beliefs, he is no longer very confident about at least one of the things he says he believes, which means that he fails to meet condition (B1). But he may also be neither insincere nor considering whether to give up one of these beliefs. In that case, however, he is too confused to adequately understand what he is saying, which means that he fails to meet condition (B2). In none of these cases does Bob believe what he says he believes. This suggests that if we use the term 'belief' in accordance with conditions (B1) and (B2), condition (B3) has to be met as well.

If you doubt this, this may be because you conflate (B3) with a different claim. Suppose again that Bob says:

> I believe that Socrates was a man, and I believe that this entails that Socrates was a human being, but I do not believe that Socrates was a human being.

If Bob is only somewhat confident about at least one of these things, he can believe what he says he believes. This shows that the following claims are false:

(1) A person *partly* believes that p only if this person believes what he or she believes to be entailed by p.

(2) A person believes that p only if this person believes what he or she *partly* believes to be entailed by p.

But it does not show that (B3) is false, since (B3) uses the term 'belief' to mean full belief.

Suppose next that Bob says:

> I believe that Socrates was a man, but I do not believe that Socrates was a human being.

He can then perhaps also believe what he says he believes.[6] This is certainly possible in more complicated cases in which the entailment is not obvious. That shows that the following claim is false:

(3)   A person believes that p only if this person believes what is *actually* entailed by p.

But it does not show that (B3) is false, since (B3) is about what a person *believes* to be entailed by p.[7]

Finally, suppose that Bob is taking part in a lottery with a thousand tickets. He could then say:

> I believe that the first ticket will not win, I believe that the second ticket will not win...and I believe that the thousandth ticket will not win. I believe that this entails that no ticket will win. But I also believe that one of the tickets will win.

As long as he is not completely confident about each of these claims, he can then believe what he says he believes. This shows that the following claim is false:

(4)   A person believes that p_1, believes that p_2,...and believes that p_n only if this person believes what he or she believes to be entailed by the conjunction of p_1, p_2,...and p_n.

But it does not show that (B3) is false, since (B3) is about a single belief.[8]

The second further condition that I think has to be met if we use the term 'belief' in accordance with (B1) and (B2) is that

(B4)   A person believes that p only if this person does not believe that there is no reason to believe that p.

---

[6] At least, if being a man does not conceptually entail being a human being. If it does, Bob fails to adequately understanding what he is saying.

[7] Contrary to what Forcehimes and Talisse 2016, p. 853, suggest, I do not think that "unless one believes *all* of the entailments of one's belief that p, one does not understand one's belief, and hence cannot qualify as a full believer in p". As they point out, if that were so, we would have hardly any beliefs.

[8] In a draft of Streumer 2013a, I put forward a version of (B3) according to which we cannot fail to believe what we believe to be entailed by our own *beliefs*. Olson 2014, pp. 169–70, rejects this version of (B3) (which I there called '(B1)') by appealing to the preface paradox. The present version of (B3) and the version I put forward in Streumer 2013a cannot be rejected in this way.

To see this, suppose that Kate says:

> I believe that Socrates was a man, but I believe that there is no reason to believe this.

As before, Kate may then be insincere, or may be considering whether to give up one of these beliefs, or may fail to adequately understand what she is saying. If she is considering whether to give up one of these beliefs, she is no longer very confident about at least one of the things she says she believes, which means that she fails to meet condition (B1). But she may also be neither insincere nor considering whether to give up one of these beliefs. In that case, however, she is too confused to adequately understand what she is saying, which means that she fails to meet condition (B2). In none of these cases does Kate believe what she says she believes. This suggests that if we use the term 'belief' in accordance with conditions (B1) and (B2), condition (B4) has to be met as well.

As before, if you doubt this, this may be because you conflate (B4) with a different claim. Suppose again that Kate says:

> I believe that Socrates was a man, but I believe that there is no reason to believe this.

If Kate is only somewhat confident about at least one of these things, she can believe what she says she believes. This shows that the following claims are false:

(5) A person *partly* believes that p only if this person does not believe that there is no reason to believe that p.

(6) A person believes that p only if this person does not even *partly* believe that there is no reason to believe that p.

But it does not show that (B4) is false, since (B4) uses the term 'belief' to mean full belief.

Suppose next that Kate says:

> I believe that Socrates was a man, but I do not know what reason there is to believe this.

Or suppose that Kate believes that Socrates was a man but does not have any beliefs about whether there is a reason to believe this. She can then also believe what she says she believes. This shows that the following claims are false:

(7)   A person believes that p only if this person knows *what* reason there is to believe that p.

(8)   A person believes that p only if this person believes *that there is* a reason to believe that p.

But it does not show that (B4) is false, since (B4) requires only that a person does *not* believe that there is *no* reason to believe that p.

Suppose next that Kate says:

I believe that Socrates was a man, but I do not believe that there is any consideration that stands in an irreducibly normative favouring relation to this belief.

Kate can then also believe what she says she believes. This shows that the following claim is false:

(9)   A person believes that p only if this person does not believe that there is no consideration that stands in an *irreducibly normative favouring relation* to this belief.

But it does not show that (B4) is false, since (B4) does not say that a person believes that p only if this person accepts non-reductive realism about reasons for belief. For all (B4) says, this person may accept a different view about such reasons, or may have no view about them at all.

Suppose next that Kate says:

I am going to watch TV tonight, but I believe that there is no reason to do this.

Kate can then do what she says she will do while believing what she says she believes. This shows that the following claim is false:

(10)   A person *performs an action* only if this person does not believe that there is no reason to perform this action.

But it does not show that (B4) is false, since (B4) is only about reasons for belief. We can perform actions for no reason at all because our actions are controlled by our will. By contrast, our beliefs are not controlled by our will. To the extent that we control them, we do this by making judgements about reasons for belief to which they are responsive.[9]

Suppose next that Kate says:

I will accept for the sake of argument that the law of non-contradiction is false, but I believe that there is no reason to accept this.

Since acceptance is controlled by our will, Kate can then accept what she says she accepts.[10] This shows that the following claim is false:

(11)   A person *accepts* that p only if this person does not believe that there is no reason to accept that p.

But it does not show that (B4) is false, since (B4) is about believing that p, not about accepting that p.

I therefore think that if we use the term 'belief' in accordance with (B1) and (B2), conditions (B3) and (B4) also have to be met for a person to believe that p. And I think that this explains why we cannot believe the error theory. For the error theory says that normative judgements are beliefs that ascribe normative properties, but that normative properties do not exist. Since judgements about reasons for belief are normative judgements, the property of being a reason for belief is a normative property. The error theory therefore entails that there is no reason to believe this theory. And anyone who understands the theory well enough to believe it knows that it entails this. Therefore, given that

(B3)   A person believes that p only if this person believes what he or she believes to be entailed by p,

anyone who believes the error theory believes that there is no reason to believe this theory. But given that

(B4)   A person believes that p only if this person does not believe that there is no reason to believe that p,

that is impossible. I think this explains why we cannot believe the error theory.

There is probably also a deeper explanation of why it is the case that if we use the term 'belief' in accordance with (B1) and (B2), conditions

---

[9]   See Owens 2000 and 2002.
[10]   See, for example, Lehrer 1990, pp. 148–9.

(B3) and (B4) have to be met as well. This explanation may appeal to the nature of the mental state that this use of the term 'belief' picks out. And it may ultimately appeal, at least in part, to the way human beings have evolved in their environment over a long period of time. There are probably also deeper explanations of why we take (S), (G), and (A) to be true, which may also appeal, at least in part, to the way human beings have evolved in their environment over a long period of time. But I will not try to give such explanations.

I am sometimes asked how I know that I do not believe the error theory. Could it not be the case that I believe this theory without realizing that I believe it? To explain how I know that I do not believe this theory, I can again appeal to (B3). I know that the error theory entails that all normative judgements are false. Given that

(B3)   A person believes that *p* only if this person believes what he believes to be entailed by *p*,

if I believed the error theory, I would believe that all normative judgements are false. I would then be inclined to give up my normative judgements. But I am in fact not at all inclined to give up these judgements. That is how I know that I do not believe the error theory.

58. Are There Counterexamples to (B4)?

You may have an objection to my explanation of why we cannot believe the error theory. In this section and the next two sections, I will discuss several objections. If you already accept my explanation, you can skip these sections and continue with §61.

Many philosophers think that there are counterexamples to (B4). One purported counterexample is constituted by religious beliefs. Suppose that Susan says:

I believe that God exists, but I believe that there is no evidence for this belief.

She can then perhaps believe what she says she believes. But she may take there to be other reasons to believe that God exists: she may think that she will be denied entry to heaven if God exists but she fails to believe this, as Pascal thought, or that believing that God exists enables her to become her true self, as Kierkegaard seems to have thought. For this example to be a counterexample to (B4), Susan should instead say:

> I believe that God exists, but I believe that there is no reason to believe this.

She may then seem to believe what she says she believes. But I think that if we use the term 'belief' in accordance with (B1) and (B2), Susan does not really believe this. She may instead use the term 'reason for belief' to mean evidence, or she may use the term 'belief' to mean acceptance, or she may merely mean to say that she does not know what reason there is to believe that God exists.

Hallvard Lillehammer and Niklas Möller disagree. They write:

> Given some of the things that are at stake in matters of faith it is hardly surprising that someone's level of confidence in a religious proposition can vary independently of reasons they take to exist in favour of its truth.[11]

But I do not deny this. I claim only that we cannot be *very confident* in a religious proposition while believing that there is *no reason whatsoever* to believe it. They continue:

> To think otherwise is to confuse the (hopeful) belief that God exists with the belief that He has provided us with reasons to believe in His existence. Whether He either could or should provide us with such reasons is a matter of theological dispute.[12]

But I do not deny this either. I claim only that we cannot believe that God exists while at the same time believing that *there is* no reason to believe that he exists, not even a reason that he has not revealed to us. If Susan thinks that God has not revealed such a reason to us, she does not believe that there is no reason to believe that God exists, but only that we do not know what this reason is.

A second purported counterexample to (B4) is constituted by self-evident beliefs. Suppose that Susan takes it to be self-evident that $1+1=2$, and suppose that she says:

> I believe that $1+1=2$, but I believe that there is no reason to believe this.

---

[11] Lillehammer and Möller 2015, p. 455.
[12] Lillehammer and Möller 2015, p. 455.

She may then also seem to believe what she says she believes. But *p* is self-evident if and only if adequately understanding *p* gives us sufficient reason to believe that *p*. I therefore think that if Susan takes it to be self-evident that 1+1=2, she does not really believe that there is no reason to believe that 1+1=2.[13]

A third purported counterexample to (B4) is constituted by compulsive or deluded beliefs. Suppose that Susan suffers from the Capgras delusion, which makes her think that her family members have been replaced by robots, and suppose that she says:

> I believe that my husband has been replaced by a robot, but I believe that there is no reason to believe this.

She may then also seem to believe what she says she believes. But if we use the term 'belief' in accordance with (B1) and (B2), even people with a compulsive or deluded belief do not seem to believe that there is no reason whatsoever for this belief. For example, people who suffer from the Capgras delusion have brain damage that gives them certain abnormal experiences, and they mistakenly assume that the best explanation for these experiences is that their family members have been replaced by robots.[14] They therefore seem to take there to be reasons for their deluded beliefs. Moreover, if some people with compulsive or deluded beliefs believe that there are no reasons for these beliefs, I could revise (B4) to:

(B4*) A person believes that *p* only if this person does not believe that there is no reason to believe that *p*, unless the belief that *p* is compulsive or deluded.

Since a belief in the error theory is not compulsive or deluded in the relevant sense, this revision would not undermine my explanation of why we cannot believe the error theory.

A fourth purported counterexample to (B4) is constituted by certain philosophical beliefs. Suppose that a lecture on scepticism convinces

---

[13] Bergamaschi Ganapini 2016, p. 528, makes the related claim that (B4) is false of beliefs in what Wittgenstein calls 'hinge propositions' and of the beliefs that foundationalists take to be basic. But when Wittgenstein calls certain propositions 'hinge propositions' and foundationalists take certain beliefs to be basic, I think they only mean that we can be justified in having such beliefs without basing them on other beliefs, not that we can have such beliefs while believing that there are no reasons for them.

[14] See Bortolotti 2010, p. 120.

Susan that there is no reason to believe that her senses are reliable, and suppose that she says:

> I believe that my senses are reliable, but I believe that there is no reason to believe this.[15]

She may then also seem to believe what she says she believes. But I think that if we use the term 'belief' in accordance with (B1) and (B2), Susan does not really believe this. As before, she may instead use the term 'reason for belief' to mean evidence, or she may use the term 'belief' to mean acceptance, or she may merely mean to say that she does not know what reason there is to believe that her senses are reliable. Alternatively, she may have different beliefs at different times: during the lecture she may be very confident that there is no reason to believe that her senses are reliable while being only somewhat confident that her senses are reliable, and after the lecture she may again be very confident that her senses are reliable while being only somewhat confident that there is no reason to believe this.[16]

Alexander Hyun and Eric Sampson disagree. They think that Susan

may be convinced by skeptical arguments that she has no reason to believe that her senses are reliable and, at the same time, believe that they are, either because (i) nature has constituted her so that she cannot help but believe that they are reliable; (ii) she thinks that she could not possibly give reasons in their defense; (iii) she is convinced that her life will go much better if she believes that they are reliable; or (iv) all of the above.[17]

But suppose first that (i) is true: suppose that Susan cannot help but believe that her senses are reliable. In that case, her belief that her senses are reliable is in effect compulsive. And as I have said, if compulsive beliefs constitute a counterexample to (B4), my explanation of why we cannot believe the error theory can instead appeal to (B4*).[18] Suppose

---

[15] See Hyun and Sampson 2014, pp. 634–5. They also list several other philosophical beliefs that they take to be counterexamples to (B4): the belief that my reason is reliable, the belief that I am not a brain in a vat, the belief that there are other minds, and the belief that my inductive reasoning is reliable. Lillehammer and Möller 2015, pp. 455–6, also give the last example. My claims about the belief that my senses are reliable apply to these other purported counterexamples as well.

[16] As Lillehammer and Möller 2015, p. 456, note. See also Forcehimes and Talisse 2016, p. 851.

[17] Hyun and Sampson 2014, p. 634.

[18] See also Forcehimes and Talisse 2016, pp. 851–2.

next that (ii) is true: suppose that Susan thinks that she could not possibly give reasons to believe that her senses are reliable. In that case, Susan does not really believe that *there is* no reason to believe that her senses are reliable, but only that she cannot say what reason there is to believe this. As I said in §57, that does not show that (B4) is false. Finally, suppose that (iii) is true: suppose that Susan is convinced that her life will go much better if she believes that her senses are reliable. She then does seem to take there to be a reason to believe that her senses are reliable: namely, that her life will go much better if she believes this.[19]

Some philosophers think that a belief in the error theory itself constitutes a counterexample to (B4): they think that since someone who believes the error theory believes that there are no reasons at all, such a person can have a belief while believing that there is no reason for this belief. This sounds suggestive, but I am not sure what to make of it. Of course, it is true that

(1)   If we believed the error theory, (B4) would be false of us.

But the mere fact that (B4) *would* be false of us *if* we believed the error theory does not show that (B4) is *actually* false of us. Merely pointing out that (1) is true is therefore not enough to show that we can believe the error theory.[20]

It is also true that

(2)   We can believe that there are no considerations that stand in an irreducibly normative favouring relation to our beliefs.

But as I said in §57, that does not show that (B4) is false, since (B4) does not say that a person believes that *p* only if this person accepts nonreductive realism about reasons for belief. Of course, to believe an error

---

[19] Hyun and Sampson take this reason to be 'explanatory' rather than 'justificatory': they take it to be a consideration that explains Susan's belief but that does not count in favour of her belief (2014, p. 634). But if Susan *herself* does not take this reason to be justificatory, and if she also believes that there is no other justificatory reason for her belief that her senses are reliable, then I think she does not really believe that her senses are reliable.

[20] Forcehimes and Talisse 2016 argue that if we believed the error theory, (B3) would also be false of us: they think that anyone "who fully believes entailments lack any reason-giving force can fail to believe what she fully believes to be entailed by one of her full beliefs" (p. 854). But I do not think that (B3) is true of us because we believe that entailments have reason-giving force. Instead, I think that (B3) is true in virtue of what it is to believe that *p*, and in virtue of what it is to believe that *p* entails *q*.

theory about all normative judgements, we must believe that judgements about reasons for belief ascribe a normative relation, since otherwise there would be normative judgements about which we would not believe the error theory. But that is required for it to be true that we believe the error theory. It is *not* required by (B4).[21]

Jonas Olson gives a more specific version of this example. He writes:

> I can...base my belief that the error theory is true on the argument from queerness, without judging that this argument favours my attitude of believing that the error theory is true. I can thus maintain that while there are arguments on which I base my belief that the error theory is true, there are no irreducibly normative reasons for the attitude of believing that the error theory is true. Hence we can indeed believe the error theory.[22]

Olson is here replying to my earlier defence of (B4), in which I wrote that "reasons for belief are considerations that we *base* our beliefs on, and we cannot base a belief on a consideration without making at least an implicit normative judgement".[23] In response, he points out that children and non-human animals form beliefs on the basis of perception "although they presumably lack the relevant normative thoughts". I agree. I therefore withdraw my earlier claim that basing a belief on a consideration involves making an implicit normative judgement.[24]

But that does not undermine my explanation of why we cannot believe the error theory. For though Olson is right that

(3)   We can base a belief on a consideration *without* believing that this consideration is *a* reason for this belief,

this does not mean that

[21]   Moreover, for it to be true that we believe the error theory, we do not need to believe that judgements about reasons for belief ascribe an *irreducibly* normative relation. We only need to believe that these judgements ascribe a *normative* relation.

[22]   Olson 2014, pp. 171–2. See also Bergamaschi Ganapini 2016, pp. 528–9. Olson himself may seem to be a real-life counterexample to (B4), since he may seem to believe the error theory while believing that there are no reasons for belief. But Olson actually does not believe that there are no reasons for belief: as I explained in §52, he thinks that judgements about reasons for belief can be instrumental normative judgements or judgements about the standard of being a responsible believer, in which case he thinks his error theory does not apply to them.

[23]   Streumer 2013a, p. 198. I there called this claim '(B2)'.

[24]   Even to young children, however, which beliefs they form on the basis of their perceptual inputs will not seem arbitrary. This may indicate that they do make implicit normative judgements when basing their beliefs on these inputs.

(4)   We can base a belief on a consideration *while* believing that this
consideration is *no* reason for this belief.

If I perceive that the desk at which I wrote this book is white, I will
normally form the belief that this desk is white on the basis of this
perceptual input without making a normative judgement. But suppose
I believe that I have taken a powerful drug that makes red objects look
white to me. In that case, my perceptual input will not change: the desk at
which I wrote this book will still look white to me. But I will now believe
that this input is no reason to believe that this desk is white. And if
I believe that this perceptual input is no reason for this belief, I will be
unable to form the belief that this desk is white on the basis of this
input.[25]

Similar claims apply to any other consideration that we can base our
beliefs on. Suppose I believe that men are not human beings. I will then
be unable to form the belief that Socrates is a human being on the basis of
the consideration that Socrates is a man, since I will then believe that this
consideration is no reason for this belief. Or suppose I believe that only
evidence can be a reason for a belief. I will then be unable to form the
belief that God exists on the basis of the consideration that I will be
denied entry to heaven if I fail to believe this, since I will then believe that
this consideration is no reason for this belief. Even if Olson is right that
(3) is true, this therefore does not show that (B4) is false.[26]

---

[25] Owens 2000, p. 13, writes that "responsiveness to reasons does not require actual
reflection on reasons: I can form a rational belief in *p* based on evidence *e* without forming
either the belief that I have that evidence, or the belief that *e* suffices to justify *p*". But he also
suggests that forming a belief that *p* based on evidence *e* *does* require *not* positively believing
that I do *not* have this evidence. I think it similarly requires not positively believing that *e* is
no reason to believe *p*.

[26] For further discussion, see Bergamaschi Ganapini 2016 and Streumer 2016b. You may
object that if I do not believe that a consideration is a reason for a belief, I may nevertheless
think that this consideration stands in some other positive normative relation to this belief:
for example, that it justifies this belief, that it supports this belief, or that it makes it the case
that I ought to have this belief. This shows that (4) should be generalized to: we can base a
belief on a consideration *while* believing that this consideration *stands in no positive
normative relation* to this belief. Since the error theory entails that these other positive
normative relations also do not exist, this does not affect my arguments.

59. Rationality and the Nature of Belief

Other philosophers make more general objections to my explanation. For example, Lillehammer and Möller claim that (B4) is true only of rational beliefs.[27] A similar claim could be made about (B3).

I agree that if a belief meets conditions (B3) and (B4), this belief is rational in a certain sense: it is closed under believed entailment, since the person who has this belief believes what he or she believes to be entailed by this belief, and it is not believed to be unsupported, since the person who has this belief does not believe that there is no reason for this belief. But that is no objection to my explanation. For as Lillehammer and Möller say, being closed under believed entailment and not being believed to be unsupported are descriptive properties, which means that being rational in this sense is also a descriptive property. Since I have argued that if we use the term 'belief' in accordance with (B1) and (B2), conditions (B3) and (B4) also have to be met, I take this descriptive property to be partly constitutive of the mental state that this use of the term 'belief' picks out. If you deny that this property is partly constitutive of belief, you are setting the bar for believing that p lower than I have done: you may think, for example, that a person can believe that p even if he or she is only somewhat confident that p, or even if he or she does not adequately understand p.

Another general objection to my explanation is that (B3) and (B4) are incompatible with certain views about the nature of belief. But I do not think they are. Consider first the view that

(1) To believe that p is to be such that others can predict your behaviour by ascribing this belief to you, along with other mental states, and assuming that you are rational.[28]

This view does not entail that (B3) and (B4) are true, but neither does it entail that (B3) and (B4) are false. Moreover, meeting conditions (B3) and (B4) may be part of what makes a belief rational. In that case, when others assume that you are rational, they are assuming that your beliefs meet conditions (B3) and (B4).

---

[27] See Lillehammer and Möller 2015, p. 456.
[28] A view along these lines is defended by Davidson 1980 and Dennett 1987.

Similar claims apply to the other main views about the nature of belief, according to which

(2) To believe that p is to have in your mind a representation that p.

(3) To believe that p is to have a mental state that stands in certain relations to your behaviour and to your other mental states.

(4) To believe that p is to have certain dispositions, such as a disposition to assert p in certain circumstances.[29]

These views also do not entail that (B3) and (B4) are true, but neither do they entail that (B3) and (B4) are false. Moreover, just as meeting conditions (B3) and (B4) may be part of what makes a belief rational, meeting these conditions may also be part of what makes a mental state represent the world, or may play a role in the relations to behaviour and to other mental states that make a mental state a belief, or may be a manifestation of the dispositions that make a mental state a belief. Of course, certain versions of these views may be incompatible with (B3) and (B4). But as I said in §56, I take my use of the term 'belief' to be partly stipulative: I take (B1) and (B2) to pick out *a* correct way to use the term 'belief', not *the* correct way. I therefore think that if a view about the nature of belief is incompatible with (B3) or (B4), it does not use the term 'belief' the way I do when I say that we cannot believe the error theory.

60. Is There a Way in Which We Can Come to Believe the Error Theory?

You may also think that there is a specific way in which we can come to believe the error theory. One way in which we may seem able to do this is that

(1) We can believe that judgements about reasons for belief are not normative judgements, and we can then come to believe an error theory about all judgements that we take to be normative.

I agree that we can do what (1) describes. But if I am right that judgements about reasons for belief are normative judgements, we would then not believe an error theory about all judgements that are

---

[29] Views along these lines are defended, respectively, by Dretske 1988, Lewis 1980, and Schwitzgebel 2002.

actually normative. Instead, we would merely believe an error theory about all judgements that *we take to be* normative. And when I say that we cannot believe the error theory, I mean that we cannot believe an error theory about all judgements that are actually normative.

A second way in which we may seem able to come to believe the error theory is that

(2) We can endorse a revisionary view about reasons for belief, and we can then replace our judgements about reasons for belief with certain descriptive beliefs, such as judgements about the standard of being a responsible believer.

But as I will explain in §74, this is not as easy to do as it may seem. Moreover, if I am right that judgements about reasons for belief are normative judgements, we would then not believe an error theory about all judgements that are *currently* normative. Instead, we would merely believe an error theory about all judgements that would *then* be normative: we would believe an error theory about all judgements that are normative after we have replaced some of our normative judgements with descriptive beliefs. And when I say that we cannot believe the error theory, I mean that we cannot believe an error theory about all judgements that are currently normative.

A third way in which we may seem able to come to believe the error theory is that

(3) We can come to believe an error theory about all normative judgements without thereby coming to believe that there is no reason to believe this theory.

Hyun and Sampson think that we can do this, and so do Andrew Forcehimes and Robert Talisse. Both illustrate (3) with an example. Hyun and Sampson's example is as follows:

A person might fully believe that there are no animals in the room, and hence understand this claim well enough to be in a position to believe it, but fail to believe (and hence to know) that this claim entails that there are no falcons in the room. Perhaps her thoughts simply do not turn to falcons in a way that would give rise to beliefs about them.[30]

---

[30] Hyun and Sampson 2014, p. 635.

And Forcehimes and Talisse's example is as follows:

I am an arthritis-denier. I know what is typically claimed about arthritis – how it stiffens the joints, commonly occurs in wrists, fingers, and ankles, and so forth. But, because I think the elderly made up arthritis to trick the young into doing work for them, I hold that (i) when people make arthritis diagnoses they ascribe arthritis properties, and (ii) arthritis properties do not exist. Next suppose, on account of my red, swollen toe, I go to the doctor. She tells me that I have a bad case of gout. I believe her. When I arrive home, I give my partner the bad news. To my surprise, my partner explains that gout is a form of arthritis.[31]

I agree that we can believe that there are no animals in the room without believing that there are no falcons in the room, and I agree that we can believe that arthritis does not exist without believing that gout does not exist. But does this show that we can do what (3) describes? Suppose that Fred is trying to believe the error theory. In other words, suppose he is trying to believe that

(4)   Normative judgements are beliefs that ascribe normative prop-
       erties, but these properties do not exist.

As I have said, when I say that we cannot believe the error theory, I mean that we cannot believe an error theory about all judgements that are *actually* normative. And I argued in §51 that these judgements include judgements about reasons for belief. To come to believe the error theory, Fred must therefore come to believe that

(5)   Judgements about reasons for belief are beliefs that ascribe the
       property of being a reason for belief, but this property does not
       exist.

This means that he cannot come to believe the error theory in the way Forcehimes and Talisse's example suggests: he cannot come to believe the error theory by failing to realize that this theory applies to judge-ments about reasons for belief.

To believe (5), Fred must believe both of its conjuncts. He must therefore believe both that

---

[31] Forcehimes and Talisse 2016, p. 852. Bergamaschi Ganapini 2016, p. 532, suggests that we can come to believe the error theory without believing that there is no reason to believe this theory "by temporarily ignoring that this is entailed by [our] belief about normative judgements in general". My reply in what follows also applies to this suggestion.

(6)   Judgements about reasons for belief are beliefs that ascribe the property of being a reason for belief

and that

(7)   The property of being a reason for belief does not exist.

If (5) is true, believing (7) is equivalent to believing that

(8)   There are no reasons for belief.

This means that in order to believe the error theory, Fred must believe (8). And, of course, (8) entails that

(9)   There is no reason to believe the error theory.

Now suppose that Fred is trying to believe the error theory. Can he do this while temporarily ignoring the entailment from (8) to (9)? Perhaps he could if he was not explicitly thinking about the error theory. But when he is trying to believe the error theory, he *is* explicitly thinking about this theory. I therefore think that Fred also cannot come to believe the error theory in the way Hyun and Sampson's example suggests: he also cannot come to believe the error theory by failing to connect (8) to the error theory.

You may think that there must be *some* way in which we can come to believe the error theory, since we can imagine a possible world in which people believe this theory. As Hyun and Sampson describe it, in this world,

the error theory is taught to school children from an early age. On Sunday mornings, everyone gathers in large buildings in their communities where they hear readings from *Ethics: Inventing Right and Wrong*, recite the error-theory creed, and sing hymns about J. L. Mackie. In this way, children and young adults are instructed with the teachings of the error theory. There is no opposition. No one has ever heard of a different meta-ethical theory.[32]

But reciting the 'error-theory creed' and singing hymns about Mackie is not enough to believe the error theory. Do these people make normative judgements about which (S), (G), and (A) are true? Are their judgements about reasons for belief normative the way ours are? And if we use the

---

[32] Hyun and Sampson 2014, p. 633. They add that they "offer these considerations in a Moorean spirit, not as a decisive refutation of Streumer's view".

term 'belief' in accordance with (B1) and (B2), do these people then nevertheless believe the error theory? It is hard to say, but I think they do not. I think that what Hyun and Sampson are describing is merely a world in which people *seem* to believe the error theory. That is shown, I think, by my explanation of why we cannot believe the error theory, together with my replies to the objections I have discussed.

61. Can We Believe That We Cannot Believe the Error Theory?

It is hard to believe that there are philosophical theories that we can understand but that we cannot believe. Are there any other examples? The Churchlands' eliminativist materialism, which I will discuss in §77, may be one.[33] But whether or not there are other examples of such theories, I think we can believe that we cannot believe the error theory. I myself believe this. I am convinced by the arguments I gave in chapters II to VII when I consider each argument individually, but I am unable to put these arguments together and come to believe the error theory. This highly unusual situation has convinced me that I cannot believe the error theory. And if I can believe this, so can you.

62. Why Our Inability to Believe the Error Theory Is Not a Problem for This Theory

You may think that our inability to believe the error theory is a problem for this theory. But I do not think it is. It is clearly not a problem for a theory if we *do not* believe it. So why would it be a problem for a theory if we *cannot* believe it? Just as a theory can be true if we do not believe it, a theory can also be true if we cannot believe it. Of course, if we cannot believe a theory, we cannot sincerely say that this theory is true. But that does not show that this theory is false.

You may object that since I defend the error theory while claiming that we cannot believe this theory, I am committed to the truth of the following claim:

---

[33] See Paul Churchland 1981 and 1988 and Patricia Churchland 1986.

(1)   The error theory is true, but I do not believe that it is true.

This claim is Moore-paradoxical: just as we cannot sincerely say 'It is raining, but I do not believe that it is raining', we cannot sincerely assert (1). You may think that this is a problem for my defence of the error theory.[34]

I agree that we cannot sincerely assert (1). But I have so far defended the error theory without asserting that this theory is true. And if I have made assertions that entailed or presupposed that this theory is true, I was, to this extent, insincere. That would not show that my arguments are unsound or that the error theory is false. Instead, it would merely show that I have insincerely put forward sound arguments and have insincerely told you the truth.

You may also object that since philosophy should bring our beliefs into reflective equilibrium, we should not defend philosophical theories that we cannot believe. David Lewis expresses the thought behind this objection in a forceful way when he writes:

If our official theories disagree with what we cannot help thinking outside the philosophy room, then no real equilibrium has been reached. Unless we are doubleplusgood doublethinkers, it will not last. And it should not last, for it is safe to say that in such a case we will believe a great deal that is false.[35]

And Lewis also writes that we should endorse

a simple maxim of honesty: never put forward a philosophical theory that you yourself cannot believe in your least philosophical and most commonsensical moments.[36]

These claims may seem sensible, but I think they are false. There is no reason why the truth could not be beyond our grasp. If it is, we should not believe falsehoods for the sake of reaching reflective equilibrium. We should instead try to come as close as possible to believing the truth. It would be dishonest to try to do anything else.

---

[34] Hájek 2007 presents a version of this objection to several philosophical views, such as eliminativism about belief, scepticism about higher-order beliefs, and relativism about truth, though he does not take it to be a refutation of these views.

[35] Lewis 1983, p. x.

[36] Lewis 1986, p. 135. See also Sorensen 1988, p. 214. For discussion of the relation between error theories and reflective equilibrium, see McPherson 2009, pp. 17–21, and Daly and Liggins 2010, pp. 215–16.

63. Coming Close to Believing the Error Theory

Though we cannot believe the error theory, I think we can come close to believing this theory. There are at least five ways in which we can do this. Why this matters will become clear in §72 and §76.

First, we can be very confident that the error theory is true while failing to adequately understand the theory. Since I do understand the error theory, I myself cannot come close to believing the theory in this way. Now that you have read this far, I hope you cannot do this either. But other people may be able to do this.

Second, we can be somewhat but not very confident that the error theory is true. We can do this because (B3) and (B4) are not true of partial beliefs. Suppose that Kate says:

> I believe that Socrates was a man, and I believe that this entails that Socrates was a human being, but I do not believe that Socrates was a human being.

Or suppose that she says:

> I believe that Socrates was a man, but I believe that there is no reason to believe this.

As I said in §57, Kate can then partly believe what she says she believes. But she will only be able to do this if these partial beliefs are very weak: if she is *far* from confident that Socrates was a man and that this entails that Socrates was a human being, and if she is *far* from confident that Socrates was a man but that there is no reason to believe this. This means that any partial belief in the error theory must be correspondingly weak.

Third, we can believe a more limited error theory, such as a moral error theory. As long as we believe that the arguments for this more limited error theory do not apply to judgements about reasons for belief, we will be able to believe this theory. I therefore do not doubt that Mackie believed his moral error theory and that Joyce believes his moral error theory. But since I think that the arguments I gave in chapters II to VII apply to all normative judgements, I cannot come close to believing the error theory in this way.

Fourth, we can believe that there are sound arguments that together seem to show that the error theory is true. That is what I believe about the arguments I gave in chapters II to VII. What does this mean? It does not mean believing that

> There are *seemingly* sound arguments for the error theory.

In other words, it does not mean believing that there are arguments for the error theory that seem sound, but that may on closer inspection turn out to be unsound. Instead, it means believing that

> There are *sound* arguments that together *seem* to show that the error theory is true.

This belief is somewhat similar to the beliefs we have when appearances are deceptive. When we put a stick in the water, this stick seems bent, but we do not believe that it is actually bent. When we are travelling in the desert, there may seem to be an oasis in the distance, but we may not believe that there is actually an oasis in the distance. In a similar way, when I consider the arguments I gave in chapters II to VII, these arguments together seem to show that the error theory is true, but I do not believe that they actually show this. Instead of failing to believe this because I take these arguments to be unsound, however, I fail to believe this because I cannot believe what these arguments seem to show.

You may object that if I really believed that these arguments are sound, I would believe that they *show* that the error theory is true. But I know that the claim that

> There are sound arguments that together show that the error theory is true

entails that the error theory is true. Given that

> (B3)   A person believes that *p* only if this person believes what he or she believes to be entailed by *p*,

it follows that I cannot believe that there are sound arguments that together show that the error theory is true. But I can believe that there are sound arguments that seem to show this.

Finally, we can believe different parts of the error theory at different times, while implicitly changing some of our other beliefs. When we consider arguments for the claim that

> (1)   Normative judgements are beliefs that ascribe normative properties,

we can believe (1), while at the same time failing to believe that

(2) Normative properties do not exist,

and instead implicitly believing that normative properties do exist. And when we consider arguments for (2), we can believe (2), while at this time failing to believe (1) and instead implicitly believing that normative judgements are non-cognitive attitudes rather than beliefs that ascribe normative properties. As I explained in §56, something like this happens to me when I consider the arguments I gave in chapters II to VII.

You may wonder why I take this to be a way to come close to believing the error theory, since it involves forming implicit beliefs that are incompatible with this theory.[37] I have three answers to this question. First, whereas my belief in (1) and my belief in (2) are explicit, the other beliefs I form while coming to believe (1) or (2) are merely implicit. Second, whereas my belief in (1) and my belief in (2) are based on what I take to be sound arguments, the other beliefs I form while coming to believe (1) or (2) are not based on arguments. Instead, I form these other beliefs merely to enable myself to believe (1) or (2). Third, I know that the reason why I am temporarily giving up my belief in either (1) or (2) is not that I am convinced that this part of the error theory is false, but is instead that this is the only way in which I can come to believe the other part of the theory. That is why I take this to be a way to come close to believing the error theory.

64. Conclusion

I have argued that we cannot believe the error theory, both by presenting evidence that we cannot believe this theory and by proposing an explanation of why we cannot believe this theory. I will next argue that this means that there is no reason for us to believe the error theory.

---

[37] See Bergamaschi Ganapini 2016, p. 531.

X

Reason to Believe
the Error Theory

I have often heard the following argument:

> If the error theory is true, there are no normative properties. The property of being a reason for belief is a normative property. This means that there is no reason to believe the error theory.[1]

But this argument does not show that there is no reason to believe the error theory. All it shows is that

(1)   *If the error theory is true,* there is no reason to believe this theory.

And the belief that (1) is true can only make us believe that there is no reason to believe the error theory if we already believe the error theory, which I have argued we cannot do.[2] If you take this argument to show that there is no reason to believe the error theory, this may be because you are combining (1) with the assumption that

(2)   If a theory is false, there is no reason to believe this theory.

But this assumption is not true: there can be reasons to believe a theory that is in fact false but that we do not know is false. And we do not know that the error theory is false.[3]

---

[1] This argument is usually presented as part of an objection to the error theory, which I will discuss in §72. See Stratton-Lake 2002, p. xxv, and Cuneo 2007, pp. 117–18.

[2] Sorensen 1988, p. 78, calls conditionals with antecedents that we cannot believe 'antecedental blindspots'. As he notes, such blindspots resist modus ponens.

[3] You may object that if a theory is false, it follows that the evidence for this theory is misleading, which means that there is no reason to believe this theory. But if that were true there could never be a reason to believe a theory that is in fact false.

Though this argument fails, I do think that there is no reason for us to believe the error theory. This can be shown in a different way.

65. Reasons and Ability

To show that there is no reason for us to believe the error theory, I will give three arguments for the claim that

(R)   There can be a reason for a person to perform an action only if this person can perform this action.

I will then argue that if these arguments show that (R) is true, similar arguments show that

(RB)   There can be a reason for a person to have a belief only if this person can have this belief.

Since we cannot believe the error theory, I will conclude that there is no reason for us to believe this theory. I will reach this conclusion in this roundabout way because it is easier to show that (R) is true than that (RB) is true.

There are different uses of the term 'can'. (R) could mean, for example, that

(R1)   There can be a reason for a person to perform an action only if this person would perform this action if he or she tried to perform it.

But (R) could also mean that

(R2)   There can be a reason for a person to perform an action only if there is a possible world in which this person performs this action,

or (R) could mean that

(R3)   There can be a reason for a person to perform an action only if there is a historically and nomologically accessible possible world in which this person performs this action,

where a possible world is historically and nomologically accessible if and only if it has the same past and laws of nature as the actual world.

I argued in chapter IX that if we use the term 'belief' in accordance with (B1) and (B2), the following conditions also have to be met for a person to believe that *p*:

(B3)   A person believes that *p* only if this person believes what he or she believes to be entailed by *p*.

(B4)   A person believes that *p* only if this person does not believe that there is no reason to believe that *p*.

I take (B3) and (B4) to be necessary truths about the nature of the mental state that this use of the term 'belief' picks out. I therefore think that if we use this term in accordance with (B1) and (B2), there is no possible world in which we believe the error theory. If so, I can show that there is no reason to believe the error theory by defending the weakest version of (R): (R2). But my arguments will in fact support the disjunction of (R1) and (R3). Since this disjunction entails (R2), they will also support (R2).

66. The Argument from Crazy Reasons

My first argument is what we can call the *argument from crazy reasons*. Suppose that Fred is a normal human being, and consider the following claims:

(1)   There is a reason for Fred to travel back in time to prevent the Crusades, slavery, and the two world wars.

(2)   There is a reason for Fred to travel to the other side of the world within thirty seconds to prevent an imminent plane crash.

(3)   There is a reason for Fred to develop medicines against all known diseases by the end of the week.

There clearly are no such crazy reasons. (R) explains why not: because Fred cannot perform the actions that (1), (2), and (3) say there are reasons for him to perform.

If you reject (R), you could propose different restrictions on the existence of reasons in order to ensure that there are no such crazy reasons. You could, for example, propose the following restrictions:

There can be a reason for a person to perform an action only if this person does not have to travel back in time in order to perform this action.

There can be a reason for a person to perform an action only if this person does not have to travel to the other side of the world within thirty seconds in order to perform this action.

There can be a reason for a person to perform an action only if this person does not have to do something that even the best scientists cannot do in order to perform this action.

But you will then face two problems. The first is that I could keep making further claims about crazy reasons, thereby forcing you to keep proposing further restrictions. (R) is clearly a simpler and less ad hoc explanation of the non-existence of crazy reasons than such an ever-expanding list of restrictions. The second problem is that for each restriction you propose, I can ask:

Why can there be a reason for a person to perform an action only if this person does not have to travel back in time in order to perform this action?

Why can there be a reason for a person to perform an action only if this person does not have to travel to the other side of the world within thirty seconds in order to perform this action?

Why can there be a reason for a person to perform an action only if this person does not have to do something that even the best scientists cannot do in order to perform this action?

To which the obvious answers seem to be:

Because a person *cannot* travel back in time.

Because a person *cannot* travel to the other side of the world within thirty seconds.

Because a person *cannot* do something that even the best scientists cannot do.

In other words, (R) seems to be what explains and unifies this ever-expanding list of restrictions. I therefore think that instead of endorsing such an ever-expanding list, we should endorse (R).

Some opponents of (R) think that claims like (1), (2), and (3) can be true. For example, Roger Crisp thinks that there can be reasons to perform "actions which cannot in an ordinary sense be performed, such as my flying several metres through the air to avoid a charging tiger".[4] He defends this view in two ways. First, he suggests that we think that 'ought' implies 'can' because of "the close relation between 'ought' and emotional responses such as guilt or blame", and he claims that "the notion of a reason is quite comprehensible independently of the emotions".[5] But the argument from crazy reasons does not appeal to guilt or blame, and neither will my next two arguments for (R). Second, he admits that his reason to fly several metres through the air "is of course largely irrelevant to deliberation", but he claims that this does not matter, since there can be reasons of which we are unaware that are similarly irrelevant to deliberation.[6] I will come back to this in §68.

Other opponents of (R) agree that claims like (1), (2), and (3) *seem* false, but think that this appearance is misleading. As we saw in §23, according to Mark Schroeder, for any proposition R, person X, and action A,

> For R to be a reason for X to do A is for there to be some *p* such that X has a desire whose object is *p*, and the truth of R is part of what explains why X's doing A promotes *p*.[7]

This view entails that there can be some very crazy reasons. For example, it entails that it can be the case that

(4)   There is a reason for you to eat your car,

if there is some *p* such that you have a desire whose object is *p*, and if the proposition that is a reason for you to eat your car is part of what explains why your eating your car promotes *p*.[8] Though some people can apparently eat cars, Schroeder's view implies that (4) can be true of you even if you are not one of these people.[9]

Schroeder admits that (4) seems false, but he suggests that this is because (4) conversationally implicates that your reason to eat your car is weighty. He thinks we can cancel this implicature by saying what this reason is and by adding that it has very little weight: for example, by saying that

---

[4] Crisp 2006, p. 43.
[5] Crisp 2006, pp. 42–3.   [6] Crisp 2006, pp. 39, 43.
[7] Schroeder 2007, p. 59.   [8] See Schroeder 2007, pp. 92–7.
[9] The French entertainer Michel Lotito is said to have eaten a Cessna 150 airplane by cutting it up into very small pieces. He could presumably have eaten a car as well.

(4*)   The fact that your car contains your recommended daily intake of iron is a reason for you to eat your car, but this reason has very little weight.

If so, similar claims apply to (1), (2), and (3): we could then cancel (1)'s implicature that Fred's reason to travel back in time is weighty by saying, for example, that

(1*)   The fact that the Crusades, slavery, and the two world wars caused an enormous amount of suffering is a reason for Fred to travel back in time to prevent these events, but this reason has very little weight.

I agree that (1*) sounds less crazy than (1). But this difference seems too small to ensure that (1*) is not crazy. Schroeder may think he needs to accept claims such as (4) because they are entailed by his view. But he could easily prevent his view from entailing these claims by taking A to range only over the actions that person X can perform.[10]

67. The Argument from Tables and Chairs

My second argument for (R) is what we can call the *argument from tables and chairs*. There are no reasons for tables and chairs to perform any action whatsoever, since inanimate objects cannot perform actions. When a person cannot perform an action, this person is in the same position with regard to *this* action that a table or a chair is in with regard to *all* actions. This suggests that just as there are no reasons for tables and chairs to perform any action whatsoever, there is no reason for this person to perform this action. In other words, it suggests that (R) is true.

If you reject (R), you could propose a different explanation of why there are no reasons for tables and chairs to perform any action whatsoever. You could say that what explains this is not that

(1)   There can be a reason for an entity to perform an action only if this entity can perform this action,

---

[10] On the other hand, if Schroeder took A to range only over the actions that person X can perform, this would not fully solve what he calls the 'too many reasons problem' (2007, pp. 84–7). He would still need to solve this problem by saying that the claim that there is a reason for X to do A conversationally implicates that this reason is weighty.

but is instead that

(2)   There can be a reason for an entity to perform an action only if entities of this kind can perform actions.[11]

But suppose that Kate cannot perform any action whatsoever. If (2) were true but (1) were false, there could then be reasons for her to perform very many actions. For Kate is a person, and persons are entities of a kind that can perform actions. But Kate *herself* cannot perform any of these actions. What makes it true that she is an entity of a kind that can perform actions is only that *other people* can perform these actions. Why would whether there are reasons for Kate to perform these actions depend on whether other people can perform them? I think this should depend on whether Kate herself can perform these actions. I therefore think that we should endorse (1) rather than (2).

You could also say that what explains why there are no reasons for tables and chairs to perform any action whatsoever is that

(3)   There can be a reason for an entity to perform an action only if this entity can have beliefs about reasons.

But suppose that Kate is irreversibly paralyzed. If (3) were true but (1) were false, there could then be reasons for her to perform very many actions. For though Kate is irreversibly paralyzed, she can still have beliefs about reasons. But she cannot actually *perform* these actions. Why would whether there are reasons for her to perform these actions depend only on whether she can have beliefs about reasons? I think this should also depend on whether Kate can actually perform these actions. I therefore think that we should endorse (1) rather than (4). And since (1) entails (R), I think we should endorse (R).[12]

---

[11]   I here use the term 'entity' to cover both inanimate objects and people.

[12]   Heuer 2010, p. 240, claims that the argument from tables and chairs is ultimately "just the argument [from crazy reasons] under a different guise". But whereas the argument from crazy reasons says that there are no reasons of a certain kind and suggests that (R) is the best explanation of the non-existence of these reasons, the argument from tables and chairs says that there is a difference between people and inanimate objects and suggests that (R) is the best explanation of this difference.

68. The Argument from Deliberation

My third argument for (R) is what we can call the *argument from deliberation*. Suppose that (R) were false. In that case, when you engage in rational deliberation about what to do, you would need to take into account not only reasons to perform actions that you can perform, but also reasons to perform actions that you cannot perform. Since the Crusades, slavery, and the two world wars caused an enormous amount of suffering, you would then almost always have to conclude that there is most reason for you to travel back in time and prevent the Crusades, slavery, and the two world wars. And you would then have to try to act on this conclusion: you would have to try to travel back in time to prevent the Crusades, slavery, and the two world wars. If (R) were false, rational deliberation would therefore almost always result in your trying to perform actions that you cannot perform. But rational deliberation clearly should not have such pointless results. This suggests that (R) is true.[13]

If you reject (R), you could propose a different restriction on rational deliberation that prevents it from having such results. You could, for example, propose one of the following restrictions:

(1)   When judging which reasons there are for or against performing an action, a person should take into account only reasons to perform actions that he or she can perform.

(2)   When judging which action there is most reason to perform, a person should take into account only reasons to perform actions that he or she can perform.

(3)   A person should try to perform an action only if he or she can perform this action.

But if (1), (2), or (3) were true, the only reasons that could make a difference to the result of rational deliberation would be reasons to perform actions that we can perform.[14] In that case, why should we think that there

---

[13] You may think that this argument assumes that consequentialism is correct. But the argument merely assumes that rational deliberation should take into account the amount of suffering that an action would prevent, and that the larger this amount of suffering is, the more likely it should be that rational deliberation results in your trying to perform this action. That is true according to any defensible moral view.

[14] Alternatively, you may make the more general claim that the less likely it is that a person will successfully perform an action, the less likely it should be that rational

are also reasons to perform actions that we cannot perform? Part of what makes a consideration a reason is that we should take it into account in rational deliberation. If a consideration cannot make a difference to the result of rational deliberation, it therefore does not seem to be a reason at all.

As we saw in §66, Roger Crisp denies this. He admits that reasons to perform actions that we cannot perform are "largely irrelevant to deliberation", but he claims that this does not matter, since there can be reasons of which we are unaware that are similarly irrelevant to deliberation.[15] But reasons of which we are unaware merely *do not* make a difference to the result of rational deliberation. Since these reasons *would* make a difference to this result if we were aware of them, we should not deny that they exist. By contrast, if (1), (2), or (3) were true, reasons to perform actions that we cannot perform *could not* make a difference to the result of rational deliberation. This suggests that such reasons do not exist.

Of course, rational deliberation should sometimes result in your trying to perform an action that you cannot perform: if you do not know that you cannot perform this action and you have the justified belief that there is most reason for you to perform it.[16] For example, if you do not know that you cannot save a drowning man and you have the justified belief that there is most reason for you to rescue him, then rational deliberation should result in your trying to rescue this man. But that is compatible with (R). By contrast, if (R) were false, rational deliberation would not merely sometimes but *almost always* result in your trying to perform actions that you cannot perform. I therefore think that we should endorse (R).

69. Are There Counterexamples to (R)?

Some philosophers take there to be counterexamples to (R). I will now discuss several of these examples. If you already accept (R), you can skip this section and continue with §70.

deliberation results in this person's trying to perform this action. Like (1), (2), and (3), this claim also entails that the only reasons that can make a difference to the result of rational deliberation are reasons to perform actions that we can perform.

[15] Crisp 2006, pp. 39, 43.
[16] Kearns and Star 2009, p. 236, give an example of this kind.

Two purported counterexamples have been given by Ulrike Heuer. In Heuer's first example, someone cannot perform an action at a certain time, but can perform this action at a later time after gaining a new ability. She writes:

> I cannot play the piano, say. Is there, therefore, no reason for me to do it? If there was no reason to play the piano for someone who can't play it already, there would presumably be no reason to learn to play it either. Reasons for learning something require that there is a reason for doing what (as yet) one cannot do.[17]

But this example merely shows that (R) should be indexed to time.[18] If we take 't_1' and 't_2' to refer to any two subsequent points in time, we should take (R) to say that

(R*) There can be a reason at t_1 for a person to perform an action at t_2 only if this person can at t_1 perform this action at t_2.

What does this mean? If we interpret (R) as (R1), it means that

(R1*) There can be a reason at t_1 for a person to perform an action at t_2 only if this person would perform this action at t_2 if he or she tried to perform a certain series of actions between t_1 and t_2.

And if we interpret (R) as (R2), it means that

(R2*) There can be a reason at t_1 for a person to perform an action at t_2 only if there is at t_1 a historically and nomologically accessible possible world in which this person performs this action at t_2.

Suppose that it would take me two years to learn to play the piano. In that case, there can be a reason for me today to play the piano in two years' time, since I can start taking lessons today that will enable me to play the piano in two years' time. And this reason can give rise to a reason for me to start taking lessons today. This example therefore does not refute (R).

---

[17] Heuer 2010, p. 237.
[18] It has often been pointed out that the claim that 'ought' implies 'can' should similarly be indexed to time. See Zimmerman 1996, Streumer 2003, and Vranas 2007, p. 171.

In Heuer's second example, there is a reason at t_1 for a person to perform an action at t_2, but this person then makes it impossible for him- or herself to perform this action at t_2. She writes:

> A person, call her Lilly, has a reason to attend a meeting which she dreads, but she can make it impossible that she will attend by, say, locking herself into a room and throwing the key away. Is it now true that she doesn't have a reason to go to the meeting? After all, she can't. If so, it would be unclear why she has a reason not to disable herself, or to overcome the self-inflicted obstacle once it exists.[19]

Suppose that this meeting starts at 10.00 and finishes at 10.30, and suppose that Lilly locks herself in at 9.00. In that case, (R) says that after 9.00 it is no longer true that there is a reason for Lilly to attend the meeting. But if you reject (R), you cannot defensibly say that it *never* ceases to be true that there is a reason for her to attend the meeting.[20] Instead, you will presumably say that this ceases to be true at 10.30, since after 10.30 she can only attend the meeting by changing the past. But Lilly locked herself in and threw away the key at 9.00, which means that it is *already true after 9.00* that she can only attend the meeting by changing the past. This suggests that the time at which it ceases to be true that there is a reason for her to attend the meeting is 9.00 rather than 10.30, exactly as (R) says.

Heuer objects that if there is no longer a reason for Lilly to attend the meeting once she has locked herself in, it is "unclear why she has a reason not to disable herself".[21] But I think this is clear: if a consideration is a reason for a person to perform an action, this very same consideration is also a reason for this person not to make it impossible for him- or herself to perform this action. For example, suppose that the fact that an important decision would be taken at the meeting was a reason for Lilly to attend the meeting. If so, this fact was also a reason for her not

---

[19] Heuer 2010, p. 237. Such examples have also been put forward as counterexamples to the claim that 'ought' implies 'can'. See, for example, White 1975, p. 149, and Sinnott-Armstrong 1984. For responses, see Zimmerman 1996, pp. 97–100, Haji 2002, pp. 47–9, Streumer 2003, Howard-Snyder 2006, pp. 235–6, and Vranas 2007, pp. 175–82.

[20] See Vranas 2007, pp. 176–7, and p. 201 n. 10. Of course, if you reject (R), you could dig in your heels and say that this never ceases to be true. But that is very implausible. Does it remain true hundreds of years from now, after Lilly has died, that there is a reason for her to attend this meeting?

[21] Heuer 2010, p. 237.

to make it impossible for herself to attend the meeting. More generally, (R) allows that after 9.00 the following claims are still true:

There was a reason for Lilly to attend the meeting.

There was a reason for Lilly not to lock herself in.

Because there were reasons for Lilly to attend the meeting and not to lock herself in, she is blameworthy for not having attended the meeting.

Since (R) allows that these claims are still true, and since any defensible view has to say that there is *some* time at which it ceases to be true that there is a reason for Lilly to attend the meeting, this example does not refute (R) either.

So-called Frankfurt cases can also be regarded as counterexamples to (R).[22] Suppose that Black is a powerful neurosurgeon who has implanted a device in Susan's brain that enables him to manipulate her decisions, without her being aware of this. Black wants Susan to kill Fred. But Black can accurately predict what she will decide to do, and he predicts that she will all by herself decide to kill Fred, without Black having to intervene. Susan subsequently does kill Fred in this way. Since Black did not intervene, it then seems that Susan is blameworthy for having killed Fred. But she could not have avoided killing him. For if Black had predicted that she was not going to decide to kill Fred, he would have used the device in her brain to make her decide to kill him. Such examples therefore seem to show that

(1)   A person can be blameworthy for having performed an action even if this person could not have avoided performing this action.[23]

Moreover, it is often thought that

(2)   A person can be blameworthy for having performed an action only if there was a reason for this person not to perform this action.

---

[22] Such examples were first given by Frankfurt 1969. For an overview of the literature about them, see Fischer 2011.

[23] This is the negation of what Copp 1997 calls the 'blameworthiness reading' of the principle of alternate possibilities.

If (2) is true and if Susan is blameworthy for having killed Fred, this entails that there was a reason for Susan not to kill Fred. And that contradicts (R): since Susan could not have avoided killing Fred, (R) says that there was no reason for her not to kill him. This may seem to show that we should reject (R).[24]

But I think we should reject (1) instead. Since Susan would not have been blameworthy for having killed Fred if Black had made her decide to kill him, I think that what she is blameworthy for is not simply *having killed Fred*, but is instead *having killed Fred all by herself*.[25] And she *could* have avoided killing Fred all by herself, by not deciding all by herself to kill him and thereby forcing Black to use the device in her brain to make her decide to kill him. I therefore think that this example does not show that (1) is true. You may object that it makes no sense to say that Susan is responsible for having killed Fred all by herself without thereby being responsible for having killed Fred.[26] If 'responsible' means causally responsible, that is true, since we cannot cause X in a particular way without thereby causing X. But (1) is a claim about blameworthiness, and we *can* be blameworthy for having done X in a particular way without thereby being blameworthy for having done X. For example, suppose I promise to read your book closely but I actually only read it superficially. I am then not blameworthy for having read your book, but I am blameworthy for having read your book superficially. In the same way, Susan can be blameworthy for having killed Fred all by herself without thereby being blameworthy for having killed Fred. I therefore think that Frankfurt cases do not refute (R) either.

---

[24] Widerker 1991 and Copp 1997, p. 445, show that (1), the claim that 'ought' implies 'can', and a claim that is analogous to (2) are an inconsistent triad. The same is true of (1), (2), and (R). For discussion, see Haji 2002, pp. 36–58.

[25] This point is made by Naylor 1984, though she puts it in terms of responsibility rather than blameworthiness. Copp 1997, p. 444, similarly denies that the person in a Frankfurt example is blameworthy for the action he or she performs, and adds that this person "may deserve blame for something else", such as "permitting herself to be the kind of person" who would perform an action of this kind.

[26] See Kane 1998, pp. 41–2, and Kane 2005, p. 85.

70. Extending the Arguments to Reasons for Belief

I conclude that (R) is true. And I think that if my arguments show that (R) is true, similar arguments show that

(RB)   There can be a reason for a person to have a belief only if this person can have this belief.

For if (R) is the simplest and least ad hoc explanation of the non-existence of crazy reasons for action, (RB) is likewise the simplest and least ad hoc explanation of the non-existence of crazy reasons for belief, such as reasons for people with limited mathematical abilities to believe complex mathematical theorems. If a generalized version of (R) is the best explanation of the fact that there are no reasons for tables and chairs to perform any action whatsoever, a generalized version of (RB) is likewise the best explanation of the fact that that are no reasons for tables and chairs to have any belief whatsoever. And if (R) is the best explanation of the fact that rational practical deliberation should not result in your pointlessly trying to perform actions that you cannot perform, (RB) is likewise the best explanation of the fact that rational epistemic deliberation should not result in your pointlessly trying to form beliefs that you cannot form.

If you endorse (R) but reject (RB), this may be because you think that beliefs are not controlled by our will. I agree that they are not controlled by our will. But 'can' in (RB) need not mean 'can merely by trying to do so': in other words, (RB) need not mean that

(RB1)   There can be a reason for a person to have a belief only if this person would have this belief if he or she tried to have it.

Instead, we can interpret (RB) as saying that

(RB2)   There can be a reason for a person to have a belief only if there is a historically and nomologically accessible possible world in which this person has this belief,

or perhaps as saying that

(RB3)   There can be a reason for a person to have a belief only if this person would have this belief if he or she was aware of sufficient evidence for this belief.

You may object to (RB3) that Bob could be so irrational that he would not believe that p if he was aware of sufficient evidence for this belief, even though it may be true that Bob *can* believe that p. This objection may show that we should not interpret (RB) as (RB3). But in a similar way, Bob could be so weak-willed that he would not perform an action if he tried to perform this action, even though it may be true that Bob *can* perform this action. This objection therefore does not drive a wedge between reasons for action and reasons for belief. Instead, it identifies a problem for conditional analyses of 'can' of the kind that (R1) and (RB3) incorporate.

You may also endorse (R) but reject (RB) because you take reasons for belief to be evidence for this belief, and because a consideration can be evidence for a belief regardless of whether anyone can have this belief. I agree that a consideration can be indicator evidence for a belief regardless of whether anyone can have this belief. But as I said in §51, reasons for belief are not the same thing as indicator evidence. Indicator evidence often counts in favour of having a belief, but not if this belief is trivial and forming it would be a waste of our cognitive resources. Similarly, if (RB) is true, indicator evidence does not count in favour of a belief if we cannot have this belief.

71. Conclusion

I conclude that

(RB)   There can be a reason for a person to have a belief only if this person can have this belief.

And since I have already argued that we cannot believe the error theory, I conclude that there is therefore no reason for us to believe this theory.

XI

Objections, Rejection, Revision

I have argued that we cannot believe the error theory and that there is therefore no reason for us to believe this theory. You may think that this undermines the error theory. But I think it does not. Instead, I think it makes the theory more likely to be true.

72. Objections to the Error Theory

One way in which our inability to believe the error theory makes this theory more likely to be true is by undermining objections to the theory. These objections are usually presented as objections to moral error theories. But they do not refute the error theory about all normative judgements that I defend.

One objection, which has been made in most detail by Terence Cuneo, is what we can call

> *The objection from self-defeat or toothlessness.* Either error theorists say that there are reasons to believe the theory, or they say that there is no reason to believe the theory. If they say that there are reasons to believe the theory, their view is self-defeating. For the property of being a reason is a normative property, which does not exist if the error theory is true. But if error theorists say that there is no reason to believe the theory, their view is polemically toothless. For if there is no reason to believe the error theory, it is not a rational mistake to reject this theory.[1]

---

[1] See Cuneo 2007, pp. 117–18. Before making this objection, Cuneo argues that the arguments for a moral error theory also apply to judgements about reasons for belief. The

I argued in chapter X that there is no reason to believe the error theory, but not because the property of being a reason does not exist if the error theory is true. As I have said, that only shows that

(1)   *If the error theory is true*, there is no reason to believe this theory,

and the belief that (1) is true can only make us believe that there is no reason to believe the error theory if we already believe this theory, which I have argued we cannot do. Instead, I argued that there is no reason for us to believe the error theory because we cannot believe this theory.

But that does not make the error theory polemically toothless. For I showed in §63 that we can come close to believing this theory: we can have a weak partial belief in the error theory, we can believe that there are sound arguments that together seem to show that the error theory is true, and we can believe different parts of the error theory at different times while implicitly changing some of our other beliefs. Since we can come close to believing the error theory in these ways, there can be reasons for us to come close to believing the theory in these ways, and it can be a rational mistake if we do not come close to believing the theory in these ways.

Cuneo could reply that since there are no reasons if the error theory is true, there is also no reason to come close to believing the error theory if this theory is true. But as before, that only shows that

(2)   *If the error theory is true*, there is no reason to come close to believing this theory,

and the belief that (2) is true will only make us believe that there is no reason to come close to believing the error theory if we already believe this theory, which I have argued we cannot do.[2]

---

first part of this objection is also made by Stratton-Lake 2002, p. xxv. See also Gibbard 2003, p. 195, and Parfit 2011b, pp. 293, 522, 619.

[2] If we come close to believing the error theory by having a partial belief in the error theory, the belief that (2) is true can make us have a partial belief that there is no reason to come close to believing this theory. But as I explained in §63, any partial belief in the error theory must be very weak. To the extent that this partial belief can make us have a partial belief that there is no reason to come close to believing this theory, that partial belief must be correspondingly weak. It therefore will not stop us from coming close to believing the error theory.

Cuneo could also reply that since I believe both (2) and the negation of the consequent of (2), I should believe the negation of the antecedent of (2): in other words, I should believe that the error theory is false. But I know that what makes it the case that I believe both (2) and the negation of the consequent of (2) is not that the error theory is *actually* false, but is instead that my inability to believe the error theory enables me to believe claims that are incompatible with this theory, such as the negation of the consequent of (2). This shows neither that the error theory is false nor that I should believe that it is false. If my arguments are sound, it is therefore not the error theory but Cuneo's objection to it that is polemically toothless.[3]

A second objection to the error theory, which is suggested by Nishi Shah's work, is what we can call

> *The objection from the normativity of belief.* Beliefs are normative, in the sense that a mental state M is a belief if and only if
>
> (3)   There is a reason for us to have M if and only if there is evidence that the content of M is true.
>
> If the error theory is true, there are no reasons, which means that there are no mental states of which (3) is true. This means that if the error theory is true, there are no beliefs. The error theory therefore contradicts itself, since it says that normative judgements are beliefs.[4]

I doubt that beliefs are normative in this sense. But if they are, I can avoid this objection by reformulating the error theory. We can call a mental state M a *quasi-belief* if and only if

> (3*)   *We take there to be* a reason for us to have M if and only if *we take there to be* evidence that the content of M is true.[5]

---

[3] Cuneo also writes that, if the error theory is true, there cannot be arguments for anything, since "the premises of an argument are offered in support of its conclusion in the sense of... being offered as a *reason* for accepting that conclusion" (2007, p. 121). But premises can be indicator evidence for a conclusion without being reasons to believe this conclusion, in the sense of counting in favour of believing it. See also Olson 2014, pp. 160–3.

[4] See Shah 2010, pp. 363–5 and 2011, and Evans and Shah 2012. Shah endorses a different version of (3), but this does not matter to my reply. This objection is also mentioned by Cuneo 2007, pp. 121–2, and discussed by Olson 2014, pp. 166–8.

[5] In (3*), our *taking* there to be a reason and our *taking* there to be evidence are themselves quasi-beliefs. It may be objected that this makes (3*) circular. But (3*) is not meant to be a definition of quasi-beliefs.

The error theory can then say that normative judgements are quasi-beliefs that ascribe normative properties.[6] If it is reformulated in this way, the theory does not contradict itself, since it does not entail that there are no quasi-beliefs.

Of course, it then remains the case that

(4)   If the error theory is true, there are no beliefs.

But if my arguments are sound, this cannot make us think that there are no beliefs, since we cannot take the antecedent of (4) to be true. Moreover, whenever (3*) is true of a mental state M, *we take* (3) to be true of this mental state.[7] We therefore cannot notice the difference between beliefs and quasi-beliefs. And since we cannot notice this difference, if my arguments show that we cannot believe an error theory according to which normative judgements are beliefs, they also show that we cannot quasi-believe an error theory according to which normative judgements are quasi-beliefs.[8]

A third objection to the error theory, which has been made in most detail by Ronald Dworkin and Thomas Nagel, is what we can call

The normative objection. The error theory has deeply implausible normative implications. For example, it entails that torturing children for fun is not wrong. But the claim that torturing children for fun is wrong is much more plausible than any philosophical theory could ever be. This shows that we should reject the error theory.[9]

This objection assumes that

---

[6] You may object that this makes the truth of the error theory depend on whether we take (3) to be true, since (3*) in effect says that we take (3) to be true. But philosophers who think that beliefs are normative in this sense take (3) to be a conceptual truth about belief. If so, those who have the concept of a belief implicitly take (3) to be true.

[7] As before, our *taking* the antecedent of (4) to be true and our *taking* (3) to be true are themselves quasi-beliefs.

[8] You may object that I have not shown that (B3) and (B4) are true of quasi-beliefs. But if we cannot notice the difference between beliefs and quasi-beliefs, the reasons I have given to take (B3) and (B4) to be true of beliefs are also reasons to take (B3) and (B4) to be true of quasi-beliefs.

[9] See Dworkin 1996, pp. 117–18, and, more cautiously, Nagel 1997, p. 115. See also Gibbard 2003, p. 195, and Huemer 2005, pp. 115–17. Parfit 2011b, p. 522, makes a similar objection to scepticism about reasons for belief. For a different response to Dworkin and Nagel's objection, see Olson 2014, pp. 141–8.

(5)   If a claim C and a philosophical theory T cannot both be true, and if C is much more plausible than T, this shows that we should reject T.[10]

When we call a claim 'plausible', we may mean that we are confident that this claim is true. If so, (5) is equivalent to the following claim:

(5*)   If a claim C and a philosophical theory T cannot both be true, and if we are much more confident that C is true than that T is true, this shows that we should reject T.

This claim may be true when C is a particular moral claim and T is a moral error theory. But (5*) is false when C is a particular normative claim and T is the error theory about all normative judgements that I defend. For in that case, what explains why we are much more confident that C is true than that T is true is not that C is *actually* true, but is instead that we cannot believe T.[11] This shows neither that T is false nor that we should reject T.[12]

Alternatively, when we call a claim 'plausible', we may mean that there is reason to believe this claim. If so, (5) is equivalent to the following claim:

---

[10] (5) is closely related to the claim that if a claim C is much more plausible than the premises of an argument that aims to show that C is false, we should not give up our belief in C in response to this argument. This claim is suggested by Moore 1925 and 1939, and a version of it is endorsed by Dworkin 1996, p. 117. For discussion of such claims, see Kelly 2005. For discussion of arguments against the error theory that rely on such claims, see McPherson 2009.

[11] Dworkin writes: "Of course I do not mean that our convictions are right just because we find them irresistible, or that our inability to think anything else is a reason or ground or argument supporting our judgment. . . . I mean that . . . we can do no better for any claim, including the most sophisticated skeptical argument or thesis, than to see whether, after the best thought we find appropriate, we think it so" (1996, p. 118). This ignores the possibility that what explains why we are much more confident that C is true than that T is true is not that C is *actually* true, but is instead that we cannot believe T.

[12] In Streumer 2013a, I formulated (5*) as follows: If a claim C and a philosophical theory T cannot both be true, and if C seems much more clearly true to us than T, we should reject T. Hyun and Sampson 2014 object that since C may seem very clearly true to us even if we cannot believe C, "the mere fact (supposing that it is a fact) that we cannot believe the error theory is not sufficient to explain why the error theory does not seem very clearly true to us" (p. 638). My current formulation of (5*) avoids this objection.

(5**) If a claim C and a philosophical theory T cannot both be true, and if there is much more reason to believe C than there is to believe T, this shows that we should reject T.[13]

As before, this claim may be true when C is a particular moral claim and T is a moral error theory. But (5**) is false when C is a particular normative claim and T is the error theory about all normative judgements that I defend. For in that case, what explains why there is much more reason to believe C than to believe T is not that C is more likely to be *true* than T, but is instead that we cannot believe T and that there is therefore no reason for us to believe T.[14] As before, this shows neither that T is false nor that we should reject T.

Finally, when we call a claim 'plausible', we may mean that there is evidence for this claim. If so, (5) is equivalent to the following claim:

(5***) If a claim C and a philosophical theory T cannot both be true, and if there is much stronger evidence that C is true than there is that T is true, this shows that we should reject T.

This claim is clearly true.[15] But I think the arguments I have given in chapters II to VII together constitute strong evidence that the error theory I defend is true. Is there stronger evidence that any particular normative claim is true? Only, I think, if we assume that

(6) Our confidence that a certain claim is true is *itself* evidence that this claim is true.

Some philosophers defend a version of (6).[16] But we cannot reject T by relying on the conjunction of (5***) and (6) when C is a particular normative claim and T is the error theory about all normative judgements that I defend. For in that case, part of what explains our confidence that C is true is that we cannot believe T: if we

---

[13] A closely related claim is endorsed by Kelly 2005, p. 194.

[14] You may object that if the error theory is true, there is likewise no reason to believe C. But since we cannot believe the error theory, we cannot come to believe in this way that there is no reason to believe C.

[15] At least, if we *can* reject T. But it is clear that we can reject the error theory.

[16] See, for example, Chisholm 1989, p. 63. Almost all philosophers who endorse a version of (6), including Chisholm, weaken this claim in various ways. For discussion, see Christensen 1994 and Vahid 2004.

had been able to believe T, we would have been much less confident that C is true.[17]

You may think that these responses to Dworkin and Nagel's objection ignore the deeper worry behind this objection: they ignore the worry that error theories are malignant views that threaten to undermine our normative judgements, including our deepest and most important moral convictions.[18] But since we cannot believe the error theory about all normative judgements that I defend, this theory cannot undermine any of our normative judgements at all, let alone undermine our deepest and most important moral convictions. I therefore think that this error theory is benign rather than malignant.

You may reply that we can have a partial belief in the error theory I defend, and that this partial belief may weaken our confidence in our normative judgements. But I argued in §63 that any partial belief in this error theory must be very weak. This weak partial belief may lower our confidence in our normative judgements somewhat, but it will be too weak to make us give up these judgements. Moreover, as I will explain in §76, this partial belief will not affect *which* normative judgements we make, since it will lower our confidence in all possible normative judgements to the same extent. It is therefore no threat to our deepest and most important moral convictions.

You may also reply that coming close to believing the error theory I defend may make us believe a moral error theory. As Hyun and Sampson write,

a way to come close to believing the error theory is to believe those theses that are parts of the error theory, and surely *moral error theory* is a part of the error theory. So if there are reasons to come close to believing the error theory, then

---

[17] Rowland 2013, p. 23, presents a more complicated version of the normative objection. He first argues that we know that *p* only if there is a reason to believe that *p*. If so, the error theory entails the following two claims: (i) I do not know that there is thought when I am thinking, and (ii) no one knows anything. Rowland then argues that if (5) is true, it follows that we should reject (ii), since the negation of (i) is much more plausible than (ii). And he then says that if the error theory entails (ii), and if we should reject (ii), it follows that we should reject the error theory. But I think this follows only if the negation of (ii) is much more plausible *than the error theory*. I therefore think that my response to Dworkin and Nagel's version of the normative objection also applies to the last step of Rowland's version.

[18] The way Dworkin and Nagel introduce the objection suggests that this is at least one worry behind it. See Dworkin 1996, pp. 87–8, and Nagel 1997, pp. 5–6.

there are reasons to believe moral error theory, and as a result our deepest and most important moral convictions are indeed threatened.[19]

As I explained in §63, we can believe different parts of the error theory at different times: when we consider arguments for the claim that

(7) Normative judgements are beliefs that ascribe normative properties,

we can believe (7), while at the same time failing to believe that

(8) Normative properties do not exist.

And when we consider arguments for (8), we can believe (8), while at this time failing to believe (7). But the arguments I gave in chapters II to VII will make us believe a moral error theory only if we mistakenly think that these arguments fail to apply to judgements about reasons for belief. To ensure that coming close to believing the error theory I defend does not undermine our moral convictions, we should therefore keep in mind that these arguments do apply to judgements about reasons for belief.

A fourth objection to the error theory, which has been made by Crispin Wright and Simon Blackburn, is what we can call

The objection from bad faith. The error theory entails that all normative judgements are false. Normally, if we believe that one of our beliefs is false, we give up this belief. But error theorists do not give up their normative judgements. This makes them guilty of a form of bad faith.[20]

This objection may have some force against moral error theorists, but it has no force against me. Like everyone else, I cannot believe the error theory about all normative judgements that I defend. And to be in bad faith is to close one's eyes to the truth not because one *cannot* believe

---

[19] Hyun and Sampson 2014, p. 640.

[20] Wright writes that a moral error theory "relegates moral discourse to bad faith.... [A]s soon as philosophy has taught us that the world is unsuited to confer truth on any of our claims about what is right, or wrong, or obligatory, and so on, the reasonable response ought surely to be to forgo making any such claims" (1995, p. 184; see also Wright 1992, pp. 9–10, 86–7). Blackburn writes that if "a vocabulary embodies an error, it would be better if it were replaced with one that avoids the error", and that there is "something fishy" about defending a moral error theory while continuing to make moral judgements (1993, pp. 149, 152). For a different response to this objection, see Pigden 2007, pp. 446–50.

it, but because one does not *want* to believe it. By coming close to believing the error theory in the ways I have described, I think I am as far from being in bad faith as it is possible to be.

Wright and Blackburn both use the objection from bad faith as a starting point for further objections. Wright's further objection is what we can call

> *The objection from compliance with a different norm.* Even if the belief that murder is wrong and the belief that murder is right both ascribe a non-existent property to murder, the first belief is clearly more acceptable than the second. This shows that a normative judgement's acceptability does not depend on whether the object to which it ascribes a normative property really has this property. Instead, it depends on whether this judgement complies with a certain norm, such as a norm according to which a normative judgement is acceptable if and only if it promotes peaceful cooperation. We should therefore construe a normative judgement's truth in terms of its compliance with this norm. Since this means that some normative judgements are true, it means that the error theory is false.[21]

This objection may have some force against moral error theories, but it has no force against the error theory about all normative judgements that I defend. For the claim that a normative judgement is acceptable itself expresses a normative judgement: it does not mean that we *can* accept this judgement, but that it is *appropriate* to accept this judgement or that we *should* accept this judgement.[22] If the error theory I defend is true, claims about the acceptability of normative judgements are therefore just as false as the normative judgements these claims are about.[23] This means that the error theory I defend cannot be refuted by construing the truth of normative judgements in terms of their acceptability.

Blackburn's further objection is what we can call

---

[21] See Wright 1995, p. 185, and 1992, pp. 10, 86–7. For discussion, see Miller 2002. Wright actually proposes that the truth of a moral judgement is constituted by its *superassertibility*, where "a statement is superassertible if it is assertible in some state of information and then remains so no matter how that state of information is enlarged upon or improved" (1995, p. 193; see also 1992, p. 48).

[22] Since Wright's notion of superassertibility is construed from assertibility, and since the judgement that a normative judgement is assertible is likewise a normative judgement, the same goes for the judgement that a normative judgement is superassertible.

[23] A similar point is made by Miller 2002, p. 102.

The objection from revision. If we came to believe the error theory, we should change our use of normative vocabulary to make it free of error: we should stop using normative predicates to express beliefs that ascribe normative properties, and we should instead start to use these predicates to express non-cognitive attitudes. But this change would make no difference to our normative practice. This shows that our normative practice does not commit us to the truth of the error theory. And it should therefore make us doubt that the error theory was true in the first place.[24]

I think, however, that replacing our normative judgements with non-cognitive attitudes would make a difference to our normative practice. If we made this change, we would have to replace our belief that

(A)   When two people make conflicting normative judgements, at most one of these judgements is correct

with a non-cognitive attitude, such as:

(A*)   Disapproval of two people approving and disapproving of a single thing.

If the arguments I gave in §33 are sound, we would then no longer take conflicts between normative judgements to be fundamentally different from conflicts between likes or dislikes. Of course, Blackburn could deny this by making quasi-realist moves: he could say, for example, that the thought that

Conflicts between normative judgements are fundamentally different from conflicts between likes or dislikes

itself expresses a non-cognitive attitude. But I argued in §34 that if non-cognitivists keep making such moves, my arguments against realism also apply to non-cognitivism. I therefore think that our normative practice does commit us to the truth of the error theory.

Alternatively, Blackburn's objection can be interpreted as a defence of a revisionary version of non-cognitivism. In that case, it may have some force against moral error theories, but it has no force against the error theory about all normative judgements that I defend. For I will argue in

[24] See Blackburn 1993, pp. 149–52, and 1999, p. 214. See also Lenman 2013.

§74 that our inability to believe this error theory undermines revisionary alternatives to the theory, including this revisionary version of non-cognitivism.

73. Rejecting My Arguments

Another way in which our inability to believe the error theory makes this theory more likely to be true is by making it harder to reject my arguments. I said in §3 that we take the following claims to be true:

(S)   For all possible worlds W and W*, if the instantiation of descriptive properties in W and W* is exactly the same, then the instantiation of normative properties in W and W* is also exactly the same.

(G)   There are no descriptively specified conditions in which people's normative judgements are guaranteed to be correct.

(A)   When two people make conflicting normative judgements, at most one of these judgements is correct.

And I argued in §§6–8 that if properties are ways objects can be, the following criterion of property identity is correct:

(N)   Two predicates ascribe the same property if and only if they are necessarily coextensive.

These claims played an important role in the arguments I gave in chapters II to VII.[25] Now that you have seen where these arguments lead, you may therefore have started to doubt whether these claims are true.

Reductive realists will encourage you to doubt this. For example, David Lewis admits that his version of reductive realism does not "feel quite right".[26] But he thinks that if we amend his view, "requiring values to be all that we might wish them to be, we bring on the error theory".[27] And he concludes:

---

[25] Strictly speaking, my arguments need not appeal to (S): as we saw in §12, the second version of the reduction argument instead appeals to the claim that whether normative properties are identical to descriptive properties cannot depend on which first-order normative view is correct.

[26] Lewis 1989, p. 92.   [27] Lewis 1989, p. 90.

Strictly speaking, Mackie is right: genuine values would have to meet an impossible condition, so it is an error to think that there are any. Loosely speaking, the name may go to a claimant that deserves it imperfectly. Loosely speaking, common sense is right. There are values, and lots of them.[28]

Frank Jackson similarly suggests that defenders of reductive realism are allowed to make "a limited change of subject".[29] He writes:

There is nothing sacrosanct about folk theory. It has served us well but not so well that it would be irrational to make changes to it in the light of reflection on exactly what it involves, and in the light of one or another empirical discovery about us and the world.[30]

As I said in §3, however, I take (S), (G), and (A) to be central thoughts about normative judgements and properties: I take these claims to reflect the nature of these judgements and properties. And I take my arguments in §§6–8 to show that (N) is a central thought about properties in the sense of ways objects can be, since I take these arguments to show that those who reject (N) tacitly take properties to be shadows of concepts rather than ways objects can be.[31] I agree with Lewis and Jackson that if there is no defensible view that is compatible with (S), (G), (A), and (N), we should perhaps accept a revisionary view that is incompatible with one of these claims. But if my arguments are sound, there is a defensible view that is compatible with all of these claims: the error theory. Our inability to believe this theory may make it *seem* legitimate to reject (S), (G), (A), or (N), since this inability may make us think that there is no defensible view that is compatible with all of these claims. But it is not legitimate to reject one of our central thoughts about a topic merely because we cannot believe the only defensible view that is compatible with these thoughts.

Philosophers who defend one of the alternatives to the error theory could try to undermine my claim that (S), (G), and (A) are central thoughts about normative judgements and properties. They could say, for example,

---

[28] Lewis 1989, p. 93.   [29] Jackson 1998, p. 45.

[30] Jackson 1998, p. 44. Jackson also writes that the descriptive properties $x_1, x_2, x_3, \ldots$ only need to make the modified Ramsey sentence "near enough true", and adds that we "should not expect perfect solutions here any more than in physics where we found what the term 'atom' denoted by finding something that near enough satisfied atomic theory" (pp. 141–2).

[31] Of course, (N) is not a central thought, or even a true claim, about properties in the sense of shadows of concepts.

that before Einstein formulated his special theory of relativity, people's beliefs about motion presupposed that

(1)   Motion is absolute, in the sense that it is not relative to a spatio-temporal framework.

The special theory of relativity denies that motion is absolute. But as Gilbert Harman writes, "it would be mean-spirited to invoke an 'error theory' and conclude that these pre-Einsteinian judgements were all false".[32] Philosophers who reject the error theory could admit that our normative judgements presuppose that (S), (G), and (A) are true, but they could say that it would be similarly mean-spirited to conclude that these judgements are all false. And they could take this to show that (S), (G), and (A) are not central thoughts about normative judgements and properties.

As Paul Boghossian writes, however, "we can be perfectly nice to our ancestors even while we accuse them of systematic error in certain domains".[33] Moreover, before Einstein formulated his theory people probably did not have a determinate belief about whether (1) is true. They instead seem to have had what Boghossian describes as "a more general concept, MOTION, itself neither absolutist or relativist, such that both the absolutist and the relativistic notions [can] be seen to be sub-species of it".[34] By contrast, we *do* have determinate beliefs about whether (S), (G), and (A) are true. If we did not think that (S) is true, we would think that an action that is right could have failed to be right without any change in any object's descriptive properties. If we did not think that (G) is true, Jackson and Lewis would see no need to say that their versions of reductive realism do not "feel quite right" and make "a limited change of subject". And if we did not think that (A) is true, we would not take conflicts between normative judgements to be fundamentally different from conflicts between likes or dislikes.

Stephen Finlay also compares normative judgements to beliefs about motion. He writes that if

---

[32] Harman 1996, p. 4.   [33] Boghossian 2006, p. 17.

[34] Boghossian 2006, p. 32. Joyce similarly writes that "regarding motion the best thing to say is that we were uncommitted on the issue of relativism versus absolutism: in so far as we endorsed absolute motion, it was because we had never thought very closely about relative motion" (2001, p. 97; see also 2006, p. 201, and 2007, p. 65).

there is no genuine absolute motion, or genuine absolute moral properties, the absolutist's judgements could not be responsive to these fictional properties. Rather, his judgements about motion are responsive to his sensitivity to motion relative to particular frameworks, and his judgements about moral wrongness are responsive to his sensitivity to the relation of actions to certain moral standards or ends.[35]

But the fact that our normative judgements are sensitive to certain ends does not mean that these judgements ascribe the descriptive property of promoting these ends. For which properties our normative judgements ascribe also depends on our central thoughts about these judgements and properties: in other words, it also depends on (S), (G), and (A). Our inability to believe the error theory may make us doubt that (S), (G) and (A) are central thoughts about these judgements and properties. But I think we should resist this doubt.[36]

Philosophers who defend one of the alternatives to the error theory could also say that my arguments show that if we endorse (S), (G), and (A), we must choose between either rejecting the claim that

(N)   Two predicates ascribe the same property if and only if they are necessarily coextensive,

or rejecting the claim that

(C)   Some normative judgements are correct.

They could point out that whereas (N) is an abstract metaphysical claim, (C) is a common-sense claim that we all endorse. And they could say that if we have to choose between rejecting an abstract metaphysical claim and rejecting a common-sense claim, we should reject the abstract metaphysical claim: in other words, we should reject (N).

But I argued in §37 that if (A) is a central thought about normative judgements in the sense that (A) reflects the nature of these judgements, then the symmetry objection shows that these judgements represent the world. And I argued that if normative judgements represent the world, (C) is not a central thought about these judgements in this sense. Moreover, as I have said, I take the arguments I gave in §§6–8

---

[35] Finlay 2008, pp. 364–5.
[36] For further discussion of Finlay's claims, see Joyce 2011, pp. 530–3. For a response, see Finlay 2011.

to show that (N) is a central thought about properties in the sense of ways objects can be. I therefore do not think that it is legitimate to reject (N) in this way. Our inability to believe the error theory may make us inclined to reject (N) in this way. But as before, I think we should resist this inclination.

Finally, philosophers who defend one of the alternatives to the error theory could say that the error theory I defend is guaranteed to be false. For I have argued that the following claims are true:

(2)   If there are normative properties, these properties are identical to descriptive properties.

(3)   If there are normative properties, these properties are not identical to descriptive properties.

They could say that if (2) and (3) are both true, normative predicates express incoherent or empty concepts. But we do seem to know how to use these predicates. And if we know how to use a predicate, they could say, the concept it expresses cannot be incoherent or empty. Joshua Gert expresses the thought behind this objection when he writes:

> Philosophers often claim that there is one or another kind of incoherence in some concept, and they sometimes argue for this incoherence by claiming to expose contradictory claims to which it commits us. A paradigm example of a concept that receives this kind of treatment is the notion of moral responsibility... I do not think there is any real hope of showing that the concept is incoherent. The bare fact that children can be taught to use the notion of moral responsibility (whether or not they use the phrase 'moral responsibility' itself) in recognizable ways – that certain claims about such responsibility are clearly acceptable, and others clearly not – is enough to show that there is some flaw in any argument that purports to show that it is incoherent.[37]

Why does Gert think this? Because, he writes,

> Words are tools. Knowing their meanings, which is the same as knowing the concepts associated with them, is knowing how to use them. There is no prospect of arguing that a tool that we have been using, and finding indispensable, for centuries is useless.[38]

Gert is right, of course, that the fact that we have been using certain predicates for centuries suggests that these predicates are useful to us. Normative predicates may even be indispensable. But this does not show

---

[37] Gert 2012, p. 7.   [38] Gert 2012, p. 8.

that the properties they ascribe must exist. As non-cognitivists rightly insist, predicates can be useful to us even if they do not ascribe properties. In a similar way, predicates can also be useful to us even if they ascribe non-existent properties.

74. Revisionary Alternatives to the Error Theory

Non-cognitivists and reductive realists could also say that if the error theory is true, normative judgements are false beliefs that we should give up. And they could then defend their views as revisionary alternatives to the error theory: as views about what we should replace these false beliefs with. A final way in which our inability to believe the error theory makes this theory more likely to be true is by undermining these alternatives.

There are three revisionary alternatives to the error theory. The first is *revisionary non-cognitivism*, according to which we should replace our normative judgements with non-cognitive attitudes.[39] If the symmetry objection is sound, this means that we will have to give up our belief that

(A) When two people make conflicting normative judgements, at most one of these judgements is correct,

and perhaps replace it with a non-cognitive attitude, such as

(A*) Disapproval of two people approving and disapproving of a single thing.

The second is *revisionary reductive realism*, according to which we should replace our normative judgements with beliefs that ascribe normative properties that are identical to descriptive properties.[40] If the false guarantee objection is sound, this means that we will have to give up our belief that

---

[39] See Köhler and Ridge 2013.

[40] Loeb 2008 rightly notes that changing the subject "often *presupposes* irrealism with respect to the referents of the original terms" (p. 377; see also pp. 357, 365). Lewis and Jackson's versions of reductive realism may therefore really be revisionary alternatives to the error theory. Boghossian 2006, p. 19, argues that relativism should also be regarded as a revisionary view of this kind.

(G)   There are no descriptively specified conditions in which people's normative judgements are guaranteed to be correct.

The revisionary view about reasons for belief that I mentioned in §60 is, in part, a view of this kind.

The third alternative is *revisionary fictionalism*, which is defended by Richard Joyce. According to Joyce, if we came to believe his moral error theory, we could continue to make moral utterances while no longer regarding these utterances as assertions. He thinks that if a sufficiently large number of us did this together, our moral utterances would stop being assertions and would cease to express beliefs.[41] A kind of non-cognitivism would then become true instead. Revisionary fictionalists could make similar claims about the error theory I defend.

These revisionary alternatives to the error theory all rely on a version of the following argument:

> If the error theory is true, normative judgements are false beliefs. Since we should give up false beliefs, we should then give up all of our normative judgements. But normative judgements are too useful for us to simply give them all up. We should therefore replace these judgements with non-cognitive attitudes or with beliefs that ascribe normative properties that are identical to descriptive properties.

But if we cannot believe the error theory, this argument is problematic. For its first premise says that

(1)   If the error theory is true, normative judgements are false beliefs.

And if we cannot believe the error theory, we cannot believe the antecedent of (1). This argument therefore has no force for us: since we cannot believe the antecedent of (1), we cannot move through the argument's premises to reach its conclusion.

Defenders of these revisionary alternatives could reply that we can *partly* believe the antecedent of (1), by being only somewhat confident that the error theory is true. They could say that this partial belief will be enough to make us move through the argument's premises and reach a partial belief in its conclusion. And they could say that this partial belief in the argument's conclusion will be enough to make us replace our

---

[41]   Joyce 2001, pp. 199–204.

normative judgements with non-cognitive attitudes or with beliefs that ascribe normative properties that are identical to descriptive properties.

But as I explained in §63, we can form only a very weak partial belief in the error theory. If we reach a partial belief in the argument's conclusion in this way, this partial belief will therefore be too weak to make us replace our normative judgements with non-cognitive attitudes or with beliefs that ascribe normative properties that are identical to descriptive properties. Moreover, the argument's next premise says that

(2) Since we should give up false beliefs, we should give up all of our normative judgements.

And the antecedent of (2) is a normative claim that is false if the error theory is true. To the extent that we form a partial belief in the consequent of (1), we will therefore form a partial belief in the *negation* of the antecedent of (2). This means that even if a weak partial belief in the conclusion of the argument were enough to make us replace our normative judgements with non-cognitive attitudes or with beliefs that ascribe normative properties that are identical to descriptive properties, we *still* could not move through the argument's premises to reach its conclusion. Instead of getting stuck at (1), we would now get stuck at (2).

Defenders of these revisionary alternatives could reply that this does not matter. What matters, they could say, is whether the conclusion of the argument is supported by its premises, not whether we can move through the argument's premises to reach its conclusion. But as we have just seen, the antecedent of (2) is a normative claim that is false if the error theory is true. This means that the conclusion of the argument is in fact *not* supported by its premises. More generally, if the error theory is true, it cannot be true that

(3) We should replace our normative judgements with non-cognitive attitudes, or with beliefs that ascribe normative properties that are identical to descriptive properties.

For (3) is a normative claim that is false if the error theory is true.

Defenders of these revisionary alternatives could reply that *after* we have replaced our normative judgements with non-cognitive attitudes or with beliefs that ascribe normative properties that are identical to descriptive properties, it will be true that we *should have made* this change. For we will then have changed the nature of our normative judgements in such a way that non-cognitivism or reductive realism has become true. But for (3) to play the role it plays in this argument, (3) must say that it is *currently* true that we should replace our normative judgements with non-cognitive attitudes or with beliefs that ascribe normative properties that are identical to descriptive properties. Defenders of these revisionary alternatives could now say that the change they recommend cannot be rationally assessed: they could compare it to Kierkegaard's "qualitative transition of the leap from unbeliever to believer", disregarding "probabilities and guarantees".[42] But if a change cannot be rationally assessed, it also cannot be rationally defended. I therefore think that our inability to believe the error theory undermines these revisionary alternatives to the theory.

75. Conclusion

I conclude that our inability to believe the error theory makes this theory more likely to be true, by undermining objections to the theory, by making it harder to reject my arguments for the theory, and by undermining revisionary alternatives to the theory.

While reading this book, you may have felt that there must be something wrong with my arguments. I felt the same way while I was writing it. But I think we should resist this feeling. For there is a debunking explanation of why we have it: we have this feeling not because there is something wrong with my arguments, but because my arguments support a conclusion that we cannot believe.

---

[42] Kierkegaard 1846, p. 13.

XII

Effects, Parallels, Progress

I will now describe the effects that coming close to believing the error theory has had on me. I will end by explaining how my arguments can help us to make broader philosophical progress.

76. The Effects of Coming Close to Believing the Error Theory

I have come close to believing the error theory in three of the ways I described in §63: I have a weak partial belief in the error theory, I believe that there are sound arguments that together seem to show that the error theory is true, and I believe different parts of the error theory at different times, while implicitly changing some of my other beliefs.

How has this affected my confidence in my normative judgements? We can distinguish the *contrary* of a normative judgement from the *negation* of this judgement. Consider, for example, the judgement that euthanasia is permissible. The contrary of this judgement is the belief that

Euthanasia is impermissible.

Since this belief ascribes the property of being impermissible to euthanasia, it is itself a normative judgement. By contrast, the negation of the judgement that euthanasia is permissible is the belief that

Euthanasia is not permissible.

Since this belief merely says that euthanasia lacks the property of being permissible, it is not itself a normative judgement.

Coming close to believing the error theory has not affected my confidence in my normative judgements relative to their contraries. For since the contrary of a normative judgement is itself a normative judgement, any decrease in my confidence in my normative judgements as a result of coming close to believing the error theory has been matched by a similar decrease in my confidence in their contraries. But coming close to believing the error theory has affected my confidence in my normative judgements relative to their negations. For since the negation of a normative judgement is not itself a normative judgement, the decrease in my confidence in my normative judgements as a result of coming close to believing the error theory has not been matched by a decrease in my confidence in their negations. Fortunately, as I explained in §63, we can form only a very weak partial belief in the error theory. This weak partial belief has decreased my confidence in my normative judgements relative to their negations to some extent, but it has not made me give up any of my normative judgements. It also has not affected *which* normative judgements I make, since it has affected my confidence in all possible normative judgements in the same way.

Moreover, even a strong partial belief in the error theory should not affect how we act. Suppose I had a 0.99 degree of belief in the error theory and a 0.01 degree of belief in the following claim:

(1)   There is more reason to do A than to do B.

As Jacob Ross argues, this 0.01 degree of belief in (1) would then make it to some extent rational to do A. Doing A could only fail to be the most rational option if my 0.99 degree of belief in the error theory made it at least equally rational to do B. But since the error theory entails that there are no reasons, it entails that doing B is *not* more rational than doing A. My degrees of belief would therefore make doing A the most rational option, despite my 0.99 degree of belief in the error theory.[1]

Ross thinks that this argument "does not address a more radical form of nihilism that rejects the very idea of subjective practical rationality".[2] But suppose I had a 0.99 degree of belief in this more radical error theory, and suppose that, on the basis of Ross's argument, I had a 0.01 degree of belief in the following claim:

(2)   If I have a 0.99 degree of belief in this radical error theory and a 0.01 degree of belief in (1), it is rational for me to do A.

---

[1] See Ross 2006.   [2] Ross 2006, p. 749 n. 3.

My 0.01 degree of belief in (2) would then make it to some extent subjectively rational to do A. Doing A could only fail to be the most subjectively rational option if my 0.99 degree of belief in this radical error theory made it at least equally rational to do B. But since this radical error theory entails that nothing is subjectively rational, it entails that doing B is *not* more subjectively rational than doing A. As before, my degrees of belief would therefore make doing A the most subjectively rational option, despite my 0.99 degree of belief in this radical error theory. And we can in fact have only a very weak partial belief in this error theory.

Coming close to believing the error theory has also had another effect on me: it has made me realize that the gap between philosophy and rhetoric is even larger than philosophers since Plato have taken it to be. As I said in the preface, whereas philosophy is the art of giving sound arguments for true conclusions, rhetoric is the art of convincing others with arguments, irrespective of whether these arguments are sound and of whether their conclusions are true. Philosophers rightly care most about whether an argument is sound, not about whether it convinces others. But they do tend to assume that a sound argument *can* convince others, at least if these others are sufficiently rational. Coming close to believing the error theory has made me give up this assumption. I now think that there may be sound arguments that cannot convince anyone. To enable us to come as close as possible to the truth, philosophers should give such arguments even if this leads to disbelief and ridicule. I think Plato would have agreed.

These are the effects that coming close to believing the error theory has had on me. I hope and expect that the effects on you will be similar.

77. Parallels in Other Areas of Philosophy

This book has been about normative judgements and properties. But certain other philosophical views can perhaps also be defended by arguing that we cannot believe them.

Consider first moral responsibility. Galen Strawson has given the following argument to show that we are not morally responsible for what we do:

(1) We do what we do partly because of the way we are, at least in certain crucial mental respects.

(2)   To be morally responsible for what we do, we must be morally responsible for the way we are, at least in these crucial mental respects.[3]

(3)   To be morally responsible for the way we are, we must have done something in the past, for which we were also morally responsible, to make ourselves at least partly the way we are.

(4)   If we were morally responsible for doing something in the past to make ourselves at least partly the way we are now, we must have been morally responsible for the way we were then.

(5)   To have been morally responsible for the way we were then, we must have done something even earlier, for which we were also morally responsible, to make ourselves at least partly the way we were then ... and so on to infinity.

(6)   We cannot perform such an infinite series of self-forming actions.

(7)   Therefore, we are not morally responsible for what we do.[4]

Most philosophers suspect that there is something wrong with this argument. But it has been hard to make this suspicion stick.[5] And Strawson can perhaps defend the argument against this suspicion by

---

[3] In the rest of the argument, I will leave out 'in these crucial mental respects'.

[4] See Strawson 1994 and 2002.

[5] For example, according to Clarke 1997 and 2005, the argument mistakenly assumes that we are nothing but collections of mental states, whereas we are in fact 'agent-causes': enduring substances that agent-cause their mental states in a way that cannot be reduced to event-causation. But suppose that we are agent-causes. Do we then agent-cause our mental states because of the way we are? If so, the argument applies to agent-causes as well. If not, the claim that we agent-cause our mental states is hard to distinguish from the claim that our mental states just pop into existence without any cause at all, in which case it is hard to see how we could be responsible for them. And according to Fischer 2006, the argument mistakenly assumes that to be morally responsible for what we do, we must be responsible for *all* causes and enabling conditions of what we do. But the argument does not assume this. It only assumes that to be morally responsible for what we do, we must be responsible for the way we are *in certain crucial mental respects*. And if we are not responsible for *any* of the *mental* causes and enabling conditions of what we do, it does seem to follow that we are not morally responsible for what we do. That is why we think, for example, that young children and people with compulsive behaviour are not morally responsible for what they do. For further objections to the argument, see, among others, Mele 1995, pp. 221–30, and Hurley 2000. For replies to these and other objections, see Istvan 2011.

arguing that we cannot believe one of its crucial steps.[6] As premise (2) makes clear, the argument aims to show that we are not morally responsible for what we do by showing that we are not what we can call *mentally responsible*: responsible for our mental states. And Strawson could try to argue that

(RM)   There can be a reason for a person to have a certain mental state only if this person is mentally responsible.[7]

If (RM) is true and if we are not mentally responsible, there are no reasons for us to have beliefs. If we realize this, and if it is true that

(B4)   A person believes that *p* only if this person does not believe that there is no reason to believe that *p*,

it follows that we cannot believe that we are not mentally responsible. This could explain why most philosophers suspect that there is something wrong with Strawson's argument, in a way that is compatible with its actually being sound.

Consider next propositional attitudes. Some philosophers think that we ascribe these attitudes to each other on the basis of an implicit folk theory, which consists of theoretical posits, such as beliefs and desires, and generalizations about these posits, such as the claim that

If someone desires that *p* and believes that doing A is the most efficient way to make it the case that *p*, this person will tend to do A.[8]

According to eliminativists about propositional attitudes, such as Paul and Patricia Churchland, this folk theory is false. The Churchlands think that this theory will in the future be replaced by a very different

---

[6] Strawson himself suggests that we cannot believe the conclusion of the argument: he writes that "human beings cannot help believing they are free agents, in the ordinary, strong, true-responsibility-entailing sense of the word" (2010, p. 64).

[7] Smith 2007, p. 10, suggests that "those normative claims that entail the possibility of holding some agent responsible are deontic, whereas normative claims that do not entail such a possibility are evaluative". If claims about reasons for a person to have a certain mental state are deontic, as they seem to be, this means that they entail that this person is responsible for having or not having this mental state. See also Tappolet 2013.

[8] Paul Churchland 1981, p. 71, lists some of these generalisations.

scientific theory that does not posit beliefs, desires, and other propositional attitudes. They therefore think that these attitudes do not exist.[9]

Most philosophers suspect that eliminativism is incoherent. But as before, it has been hard to make this suspicion stick. Since eliminativism says that there are no beliefs, it is clearly true that

(8)   If eliminativism is true, no one can believe that it is true.

And since we can sincerely assert something only if we believe it, (8) implies that

(9)   If eliminativism is true, no one can sincerely assert that it is true.

More strongly, perhaps there can be assertions only if there are beliefs.[10] If so, (8) also implies that

(10)   If eliminativism is true, no one can assert that it is true.

Even more strongly, perhaps sentences can have meaning only if there are propositional attitudes.[11] If so, it follows that

(11)   If eliminativism is true, the sentence 'Eliminativism is true' is meaningless.

But none of this shows that eliminativism is incoherent, at least not in the sense that it contradicts itself. And eliminativists can perhaps defend their view against the suspicion that it is incoherent by arguing that we cannot believe it. They could say that anyone who understands eliminativism well enough to believe it knows that this view entails that there are no beliefs. Given that

(B3)   A person believes that p only if this person believes what he or she believes to be entailed by p,

---

[9] See Paul Churchland 1981 and 1988, pp. 43–9, and Patricia Churchland 1986, pp. 395–9. A similar view is defended by Stich 1983, though Stich 1996 abandons this view. Dennett 1978, p. 63, suggests that the "validity of our conceptual scheme of moral agents having dignity, freedom and responsibility stands or falls on the question: can men ever be *truly* said to have beliefs, desires, intentions?" Baker 1987, p. 131, agrees. If so, eliminativism entails that we are not morally responsible for what we do.

[10] See Baker 1987, pp. 138–42.

[11] See Baker 1987, pp. 139–40, and Boghossian 1990, pp. 170–3. Churchland 1981, pp. 89–90, tries to pre-empt such objections. For discussion, see Lockie 2003.

they could say that anyone who believes eliminativism believes that he or she does not believe it. And they could try to argue that if we use the term 'belief' to mean full, explicit, and occurrent belief,

(B5)   A person believes that p only if this person does not believe that he or she does not believe that p.

If so, it follows that we cannot believe eliminativism. This could explain why most philosophers suspect that this view is incoherent, in a way that is compatible with its actually being coherent.

Finally, consider truth. In an influential early essay, Nietzsche wrote:

What then is truth? A movable host of metaphors, metonymies, and anthropomorphisms: in short, a sum of human relations which have been poetically and rhetorically intensified, transferred, and embellished, and which, after long usage, seem to a people to be fixed, canonical, and obligatory. Truths are illusions we have forgotten are illusions.[12]

Since illusions are not true, truths cannot literally be illusions. But Nietzsche is here using the term 'truth' in scare quotes: he is saying that what we call 'truths' are in fact illusions. In other words, he is saying that

(12)   There are no truths.

Most people, including me, take (12) to be an outrageous falsehood. And Nietzsche clearly cannot defensibly have thought that (12) is true. But he may have thought that (12) is neither true nor false. And he could have tried to defend (12) against the charge that it is false by arguing that if we use the term 'belief' to mean full, explicit, and occurrent belief,

(B6)   A person believes that p only if this person does not believe that it is not true that p.

If so, we cannot believe (12). This could explain why we take (12) to be false, in a way that is compatible with its actually being neither true nor false.[13]

---

[12] Nietzsche 1873, p. 117. This view was enthusiastically embraced by Derrida and other deconstructivists. For discussion of Nietzsche's early view on truth and deconstructivist interpretations of this view, see Clark 1990, pp. 63–93.

[13] According to Baker, eliminativism also implies (12). For eliminativism says that there are no beliefs, and Baker thinks that there can be truths only if there are true beliefs

Dialetheists about truth can perhaps also make use of (B6). Consider the sentence

(13)   This sentence is not true.

Is (13) true or not? If it is true, it is not true. And if it is not true, it is true. Dialetheists take this to show that (13) is *both* true *and* not true.[14] As before, many philosophers suspect that this view is incoherent. But dialetheists can perhaps defend their view against this suspicion by arguing that if we use the term 'belief' to mean full, explicit, and occurrent belief,

(B7)   A person believes that *p* is true only if this person believes that *p*.

If it is also true that

(B6)   A person believes that *p* only if this person does not believe that it is not true that *p*,

it would follow that we cannot believe that (13) is both true and not true. This could explain why many philosophers suspect that dialetheism is incoherent, in a way that is compatible with its actually being coherent.

I do not mean to endorse these views. I am inclined to think that Strawson's argument against moral responsibility is sound, but I am not convinced by the arguments for eliminativism, and there clearly cannot be sound arguments for Nietzsche's view about truth. I do think, however, that noticing that certain other philosophical views can perhaps also be defended by arguing that we cannot believe them can help us to make broader philosophical progress.

78. Reflective Equilibrium

If there can be true philosophical theories that we cannot believe, I think we should modify the method we normally use in philosophy. This method

---

(1987, pp. 143–7). Eliminativists can perhaps answer this objection in a similar way. As Paul Churchland 1981, p. 87, writes, the states posited by the scientific theory that will replace folk psychology can perhaps be expressed with 'Übersatzen', which "are not evaluated as true or false".

[14]   For a defence of this view, see Priest 1998, 2006a, and 2006b.

is a form of coherentism, or defeasible foundationalism, that John Rawls calls 'reflective equilibrium'.[15] We start with our beliefs about a certain topic. We then try to construct a philosophical theory about this topic that coheres as well as possible with these beliefs. While constructing this theory, we go back and forth between our beliefs and the theory we are constructing, and we keep modifying both the theory and our beliefs until they match. At that point we have reached what Rawls calls 'narrow reflective equilibrium'. If we have considered all theories that bear on this topic while constructing our theory, we have reached what he calls 'wide reflective equilibrium'.[16]

Philosophers disagree about which beliefs should be this method's starting points. Gilbert Harman, who calls this method 'general foundationalism', thinks that we should start with all of our beliefs.[17] Rawls himself thinks that we should start with what he calls our 'considered judgements': the beliefs that we are confident about and that we formed when we had "the ability, the opportunity, and the desire to reach a correct decision".[18] Thomas Kelly and Sarah McGrath suggest that we should start with the beliefs that we are "justified in holding".[19] And Timothy Williamson, who claims to reject the reflective equilibrium method, thinks that we should start with our knowledge. He writes:

A popular remark is that we have no choice but to start from where we are, with our current beliefs. But where we are is not only having various beliefs about the world; it is also having significant knowledge of the world.... To characterize our method as one of achieving reflective equilibrium is to fail to engage with epistemologically crucial features of our situation.[20]

---

[15] Rawls 1971, pp. 19–21, 46–51, and 1974, pp. 7–10. As Rawls 1971, p. 20, notes, a similar method is proposed by Goodman 1954, pp. 65–8. See also Daniels 1996. Reflective equilibrium is usually taken to be a coherentist method, but Ebertz 1993 and McMahan 2000, pp. 102–6, outline a defeasibly foundationalist version.

[16] Rawls 1971, pp. 49–50, and 1974, p. 8. Daniels 1979, p. 258, calls the other theories that bear on this topic 'background theories', and says that in Rawls's defence of his principles of justice, these are "a theory of the person, a theory of procedural justice, general social theory, and a theory of the role of morality in society". But Rawls himself seems to take these other theories to be competing conceptions of justice (see Rawls 2001, p. 31).

[17] Harman 2003, p. 416.

[18] Rawls 1971, pp. 47–8. Rawls is here talking about moral judgements, but adds that these criteria are "similar to those that single out considered judgments of any kind" (p. 48). See also Scanlon 2002, p. 143.

[19] Kelly and McGrath 2010, p. 348.   [20] Williamson 2007, p. 5; see also pp. 244–6.

What Williamson rejects here, however, is only Harman's and Rawls's views about the starting points of the method. That does not amount to rejecting the reflective equilibrium method itself. To the extent that we do not construct philosophical theories on the basis of empirical research, there are few other methods we can use.[21]

Suppose, however, that there are true philosophical theories that we cannot believe. In that case, we are likely to have many beliefs that are incompatible with these theories. Some of these beliefs may be considered judgements in Rawls's sense, may seem to us to be justified, and may seem to us to be knowledge. No matter which view we accept about the starting points of the reflective equilibrium method, some of these beliefs may therefore be among our starting points when we are constructing philosophical theories. If so, this method may lead us away from the truth rather than towards it.

I therefore think we should modify the reflective equilibrium method as follows. Suppose that sound arguments seem to show, in the sense I explained in §63, that the true theory about a topic is unbelievable. We should then bracket all beliefs that are false if this theory is true, except for those beliefs that are central thoughts about this topic. For example, in the case of the error theory, we should bracket all normative judgements, in the case of scepticism about moral responsibility, we should bracket all beliefs that ascribe moral responsibility to people, and so on. And we should then construct a philosophical theory by appealing only to the beliefs that we have not bracketed. When we have done this, we may find that the most defensible arguments support a theory that we cannot believe. If so, we cannot reach reflective equilibrium about this topic. But we can then nevertheless try to approach such equilibrium by rejecting the alternatives to this theory and by trying to come as close as possible to believing the theory. That is what I have tried to do in this book.[22]

---

[21] The only alternative seems to be a form of indefeasible foundationalism, according to which philosophical theories should be based on self-evident or indubitable beliefs.

[22] You may think that this is not really a modification of the reflective equilibrium method, since when trying to reach reflective equilibrium we already have to take into account potential debunking explanations of our beliefs. But I am here considering cases in which we cannot believe what these debunking explanations seem to show. In such cases, I think using the unmodified method will lead us away from the truth.

Unless there are sound arguments that seem to show that the correct theory in normative ethics or in political philosophy is unbelievable, this will not make any difference to the way we construct theories in normative ethics or in political philosophy. This fits with Rawls's purpose in formulating the reflective equilibrium method: he formulated this method to enable him to defend his principles of justice without having to worry about the nature of normative judgements and properties. If we modify the method in the way I propose, I think moral and political philosophers can continue to defend their views in this way.

79. Progress

Philosophers sometimes reject a theory by claiming that it is 'hard to believe'. Strictly speaking, this is not a reason to reject a theory, since it is not a reason to think that the theory is false. But that is not what these philosophers mean. As Peter Hacker writes, this claim

does not mean that it is hard to get oneself into a certain state of mind – as it is hard to be cheerful in the face of adversity. It means that it is hard to explain away all the evidence that speaks against [this theory].[23]

Hacker is clearly right that this is the usual speaker meaning of the claim that a theory is hard to believe. But we should take care not to conflate this claim's usual speaker meaning with its literal meaning. To make progress in philosophy, we should sharply distinguish the truth of a theory from our ability to believe it.

---

[23] Hacker 2004, p. 201.

Conclusion

I have argued that there are sound arguments that together seem to show that the error theory is true. I have argued that we cannot believe the error theory and that there is therefore no reason for us to believe this theory. And I have argued that this makes the error theory more likely to be true.

Am I certain that I am right? I am not. But that is exactly what my arguments predict. Since I cannot believe the error theory, I cannot be convinced by all of my arguments at the same time. Neither can you. But that does not show that these arguments are unsound or that the error theory is false.

Am I certain that the central thoughts about normative judgements and properties that play a role in my arguments are true? I am not. When I started to see that the error theory is the only defensible theory that is compatible with these thoughts, I became inclined to reject one of them. But I have resisted this inclination. For I think I have this inclination not because (S), (G), (A), and (N) are false, but merely because I cannot believe the error theory. I therefore think that you should resist this inclination too.

Leszek Kołakowski famously wrote that a modern philosopher "who has never once suspected himself of being a charlatan must be such a shallow mind that his work is probably not worth reading".[1] I comfortably meet this requirement: since I defend a view that I do not believe, I suspect myself of being a charlatan whenever I consider my defence of this view. But my arguments explain why this happens. And if they are sound, the suspicion that I am a charlatan is unfounded.

---

[1] Kołakowski 2001, p. 1.

Bibliography

Antony, Louise. 2003. 'Who's Afraid of Disjunctive Properties?' *Philosophical Perspectives* 13: 1–21.

Armstrong, D. M. 1980. 'Against "Ostrich" Nominalism: A Reply to Michael Devitt'. Reprinted in D. H. Mellor and Alex Oliver, eds., *Properties*. Oxford: Oxford University Press, 1997, pp. 101–11.

Armstrong, D. M. 1997. *A World of States of Affairs*. Cambridge: Cambridge University Press.

Aune, Bruce. 2002. 'Universals and Predication'. In Richard Gale, ed., *The Blackwell Guide to Metaphysics*. Oxford: Blackwell, pp. 131–50.

Ayer, A. J. 1946. *Language, Truth and Logic* (second edition). London: Gollancz.

Bagnoli, Carla, ed. 2013. *Constructivism in Ethics*. Cambridge: Cambridge University Press.

Baker, Lynne Rudder. 1987. *Saving Belief*. Princeton, NJ: Princeton University Press.

Bedke, Matthew. 2010. 'Might All Normativity Be Queer?' *Australasian Journal of Philosophy* 88: 41–58.

Bennett, Karen and Brian McLaughlin. 2011. 'Supervenience'. *Stanford Encyclopedia of Philosophy*, Winter 2011 edition, http://plato.stanford.edu/archives/win2011/entries/supervenience/.

Bergamaschi Ganapini, Marianna. 2016. 'Why We Can Still Believe the Error Theory'. *International Journal of Philosophical Studies* 24: 523–36.

Björnsson, Gunnar. 2015. 'Disagreement, Correctness, and the Evidence for Metaethical Absolutism'. In Russ Shafer-Landau, ed., *Oxford Studies in Metaethics, Volume 10*. Oxford: Oxford University Press, pp. 160–87.

Björnsson, Gunnar and Caj Strandberg, Ragnar Francén Olinder, John Eriksson, and Fredrik Björklund, eds. 2015. *Motivational Internalism*. Oxford: Oxford University Press.

Blackburn, Simon. 1984. *Spreading the Word*. Oxford: Oxford University Press.

Blackburn, Simon. 1993. *Essays in Quasi-Realism*. Oxford: Oxford University Press.

Blackburn, Simon. 1996. 'Securing the Nots'. In Walter Sinnott-Armstrong and Mark Timmons, eds., *Moral Knowledge?* Oxford: Oxford University Press, pp. 82–100.

Blackburn, Simon. 1998. *Ruling Passions*. Oxford: Oxford University Press.

Blackburn, Simon. 1999. 'Is Objective Moral Justification Possible on a Quasi-Realist Foundation?' *Inquiry* 42: 213–28.

Blackburn, Simon. 2013. 'Pragmatism: All or Some?' In Price 2013, pp. 67–84.

Boghossian, Paul. 1990. 'The Status of Content'. *Philosophical Review* 99: 157–84.

Boghossian, Paul. 2006. 'What is Relativism?' In Patrick Greenough and Michael Lynch, eds., *Truth and Relativism*. Oxford: Oxford University Press, pp. 13–37.

Boisvert, Daniel. 2008. 'Expressive-Assertivism'. *Pacific Philosophical Quarterly* 89: 169–203.

Bortolotti, Lisa. 2010. *Delusions and Other Irrational Beliefs*. Oxford: Oxford University Press.

Boyd, Richard. 1988. 'How to Be a Moral Realist'. In Geoffrey Sayre-McCord, ed., *Essays on Moral Realism*. Ithaca, NY: Cornell University Press, pp. 181–228.

Boyd, Richard. 2003. 'Finite Beings, Finite Goods: The Semantics, Metaphysics and Ethics of Naturalist Consequentialism, Part I'. *Philosophy and Phenomenological Research* 66: 505–53.

Brink, David. 1984. 'Moral Realism and the Sceptical Arguments from Disagreement and Queerness'. *Australasian Journal of Philosophy* 62: 111–25.

Brink, David. 1989. *Moral Realism and the Foundations of Ethics*. Cambridge: Cambridge University Press.

Brink, David. 2001. 'Realism, Naturalism, and Moral Semantics'. *Social Philosophy and Policy* 18: 154–76.

Broome, John. 1999. 'Normative Requirements'. *Ratio* 12: 398–419.

Brown, Campbell. 2011. 'A New and Improved Supervenience Argument for Ethical Descriptivism'. In Russ Shafer-Landau, ed., *Oxford Studies in Metaethics, Volume 6*. Oxford: Oxford University Press, pp. 205–18.

Brown, Campbell. 2014. 'Minding the Is-Ought Gap'. *Journal of Philosophical Logic* 43: 53–69.

Brown, Campbell. 2015. 'Two Versions of Hume's Law'. *Journal of Ethics and Social Philosophy*, discussion note, May, http://www.jesp.org.

Burgess, John. 2007. 'Against Ethics'. *Ethical Theory and Moral Practice* 10: 427–39.

Campbell, Keith. 1990. *Abstract Particulars*. Oxford: Blackwell.

Chisholm, Roderick. 1989. *Theory of Knowledge* (third edition). Englewood Cliffs, NJ: Prentice Hall.

Christensen, David. 1994. 'Conservatism in Epistemology'. *Noûs* 28: 69–89.

Churchland, Patricia. 1986. *Neurophilosophy*. Cambridge, MA: MIT Press.

Churchland, Paul. 1981. 'Eliminative Materialism and the Propositional Attitudes'. *Journal of Philosophy* 78: 67–90.

Churchland, Paul. 1988. *Matter and Consciousness* (revised edition). Cambridge, MA: MIT Press.

Clark, Maudemarie. 1990. *Nietzsche on Truth and Philosophy*. Cambridge: Cambridge University Press.

Clarke, Randolph. 1997. 'On the Possibility of Rational Free Action'. *Philosophical Studies* 88: 37–57.

Clarke, Randolph. 2005. 'On an Argument for the Impossibility of Moral Responsibility'. *Midwest Studies in Philosophy* 29: 13–24.

Cohen, G. A. 2008. *Rescuing Justice and Equality*. Cambridge, MA: Harvard University Press.

Copp, David. 1995. *Morality, Normativity, and Society*. Oxford: Oxford University Press.

Copp, David. 1997. 'Defending the Principle of Alternate Possibilities: Blameworthiness and Moral Responsibility'. *Noûs* 31: 441–56.

Copp, David. 2001. 'Realist-Expressivism: A Neglected Option for Moral Realism'. *Social Philosophy and Policy* 18: 1–43.

Cowie, Christopher. 2014. 'Why Companions in Guilt Arguments Won't Work'. *Philosophical Quarterly* 64: 407–22.

Crisp, Roger. 2006. *Reasons and the Good*. Oxford: Oxford University Press.

Cuneo, Terence. 2006. 'Saying What We Mean: An Argument Against Expressivism'. In Russ Shafer-Landau, ed., *Oxford Studies in Metaethics, Volume 1*. Oxford: Oxford University Press, pp. 35–71.

Cuneo, Terence. 2007. *The Normative Web*. Oxford: Oxford University Press.

Cuneo, Terence and Russ Shafer-Landau. 2014. 'The Moral Fixed Points: New Directions for Moral Nonnaturalism'. *Philosophical Studies* 171: 399–443.

Daly, Chris and David Liggins. 2010. 'In Defence of Error Theory'. *Philosophical Studies* 149: 209–30.

Dancy, Jonathan. 1993. *Moral Reasons*. Oxford: Blackwell.

Dancy, Jonathan. 2004a. 'On the Importance of Making Things Right'. *Ratio* 17: 229–37.

Dancy, Jonathan. 2004b. *Ethics Without Principles*. Oxford: Oxford University Press.

Dancy, Jonathan. 2005. 'Nonnaturalism'. In David Copp, ed., *The Oxford Handbook of Ethical Theory*. Oxford: Oxford University Press, pp. 122–45.

Daniels, Norman. 1979. 'Wide Reflective Equilibrium and Theory Acceptance in Ethics'. *Journal of Philosophy* 76: 256–82.

Daniels, Norman. 1996. *Justice and Justification*. Cambridge: Cambridge University Press.

Davidson, Donald. 1980. *Essays on Actions and Events*. Oxford: Oxford University Press, republished in 2001.

Davidson, Donald. 1984. *Inquiries into Truth and Interpretation*. Oxford: Oxford University Press, republished in 2001.

Dennett, Daniel. 1978. *Brainstorms*. Cambridge, MA: MIT Press.

Dennett, Daniel. 1987. *The Intentional Stance*. Cambridge, MA: MIT Press.

Devitt, Michael. 1980. '"Ostrich Nominalism" or "Mirage Realism"?' Reprinted in D. H. Mellor and Alex Oliver, eds., *Properties*. Oxford: Oxford University Press, 1997, pp. 93–100.

Divers, John and Alexander Miller. 1994. 'Why Expressivists About Value Should Not Love Minimalism About Truth'. *Analysis* 54: 12–19.

Divers, John and Alexander Miller. 1995. 'Platitudes and Attitudes: A Minimalist Conception of Belief'. *Analysis* 55: 37–44.

Dowell, Janice. 2016. 'The Metaethical Insignificance of Moral Twin Earth'. In Russ Shafer-Landau, ed., *Oxford Studies in Metaethics, Volume 11*. Oxford: Oxford University Press, pp. 1–27.

Dreier, James. 1990. 'Internalism and Speaker Relativism'. *Ethics* 101: 6–26.

Dreier, James. 1996. 'Expressivist Embeddings and Minimalist Truth'. *Philosophical Studies* 83: 29–51.

Dreier, James. 2004. 'Meta-Ethics and the Problem of Creeping Minimalism'. *Philosophical Perspectives* 18: 23–44.

Dreier, James. Unpublished. 'Is There a Supervenience Problem for Robust Moral Realism?'

Dretske, Fred. 1988. *Explaining Behavior*. Cambridge, MA: MIT Press.

Dunaway, Billy. 2015. 'Supervenience Arguments and Normative Non-Naturalism'. *Philosophy and Phenomenological Research* 91: 627–55.

Dworkin, Ronald. 1996. 'Objectivity and Truth: You'd Better Believe It'. *Philosophy and Public Affairs* 25: 87–139.

Dworkin, Ronald. 2011. *Justice for Hedgehogs*. Cambridge, MA: Harvard University Press.

Ebertz, Roger. 1993. 'Is Reflective Equilibrium a Coherentist Model?' *Canadian Journal of Philosophy* 23: 193–214.

Eklund, Matti. 2009. 'The Frege-Geach Problem and Kalderon's Moral Fictionalism'. *Philosophical Quarterly* 59: 705–12.

Eklund, Matti. 2015. 'Fictionalism'. *Stanford Encyclopedia of Philosophy*, Winter 2015 edition, http://plato.stanford.edu/archives/win2015/entries/fictionalism/.

Enoch, David. 2006. 'Agency, Shmagency: Why Normativity Won't Come from What Is Constitutive of Action'. *Philosophical Review* 115: 169–98.

Enoch, David. 2009. 'Can There Be a Global, Interesting, Coherent Constructivism About Practical Reason?' *Philosophical Explorations* 12: 319–39.

Enoch, David. 2011a. *Taking Morality Seriously*. Oxford: Oxford University Press.

Enoch, David. 2011b. 'Shmagency Revisited'. In Michael Brady, ed., *New Waves in Metaethics*. Basingstoke: Palgrave MacMillan, pp. 208–33.

Evans, Matthew and Nishi Shah. 2012. 'Mental Agency and Metaethics'. In Russ Shafer-Landau, ed., *Oxford Studies in Metaethics, Volume 7*. Oxford: Oxford University Press, pp. 80–109.

Evers, Daan and Bart Streumer. 2016. 'Are the Moral Fixed Points Conceptual Truths?' *Journal of Ethics and Social Philosophy*, discussion note, March, http://www.jesp.org.

Finlay, Stephen. 2006. 'The Reasons that Matter'. *Australasian Journal of Philosophy* 84: 1–20.

Finlay, Stephen. 2008. 'The Error in the Error Theory'. *Australasian Journal of Philosophy* 86: 347–69.

Finlay, Stephen. 2009. 'Oughts and Ends'. *Philosophical Studies* 143: 315–40.

Finlay, Stephen. 2011. 'Errors upon Errors: A Reply to Joyce'. *Australasian Journal of Philosophy* 89: 535–47.

Finlay, Stephen. 2014. *Confusion of Tongues*. Oxford: Oxford University Press.

Fischer, John Martin. 2006. 'The Cards That Are Dealt You'. *Journal of Ethics* 10: 107–29.

Fischer, John Martin. 2011. 'Frankfurt-Type Examples and Semicompatibilism: New Work'. In Robert Kane, ed., *The Oxford Handbook of Free Will* (second edition). Oxford: Oxford University Press, pp. 243–65.

FitzPatrick, William. 2008. 'Robust Ethical Realism, Non-Naturalism, and Normativity'. In Russ Shafer-Landau, ed., *Oxford Studies in Metaethics, Volume 3*. Oxford: Oxford University Press, pp. 159–205.

Fletcher, Guy and Michael Ridge, eds. 2015. *Having It Both Ways*. Oxford: Oxford University Press.

Foley, Richard. 1987. *The Theory of Epistemic Rationality*. Cambridge, MA: Harvard University Press.

Forcehimes, Andrew and Robert Talisse. 2016. 'Belief and the Error Theory'. *Ethical Theory and Moral Practice* 19: 849–56.

Frankfurt, Harry. 1969. 'Alternate Possibilities and Moral Responsibility'. *Journal of Philosophy* 66: 829–39.

Gärdenfors, Peter. 2000. *Conceptual Spaces*. Cambridge, MA: MIT Press.

Gärdenfors, Peter. 2014. *The Geometry of Meaning*. Cambridge, MA: MIT Press.

Garner, Richard. 1990. 'On the Genuine Queerness of Moral Properties and Facts'. *Australasian Journal of Philosophy* 68: 137–46.

Garner, Richard. 1994. *Beyond Morality*. Philadelphia, PA: Temple University Press.

Garner, Richard. 2007. 'Abolishing Morality'. *Ethical Theory and Moral Practice* 10: 499–513.

Gert, Joshua. 2012. *Normative Bedrock*. Oxford: Oxford University Press.

Gibbard, Allan. 1990. *Wise Choices, Apt Feelings*. Oxford: Oxford University Press.

Gibbard, Allan. 1999. 'Morality as Consistency in Living: Korsgaard's Kantian Lectures'. *Ethics* 110: 140–64.

Gibbard, Allan. 2002a. 'Normative and Recognitional Concepts'. *Philosophy and Phenomenological Research* 64: 151–67.

Gibbard, Allan. 2002b. 'Reply to Hawthorne'. *Philosophy and Phenomenological Research* 64: 179–83.

Gibbard, Allan. 2003. *Thinking How to Live*. Cambridge, MA: Harvard University Press.

Gibbard, Allan. 2006. 'Normative Properties'. In Terry Horgan and Mark Timmons, eds., *Metaethics After Moore*. Oxford: Oxford University Press, pp. 319–37.

Goodman, Nelson. 1954. *Fact, Fiction, and Forecast*. London: Athlone Press.

Hacker, P. M. S. 2004. 'Of the Ontology of Belief'. In Mark Siebel and Mark Textor, eds., *Semantik und Ontologie*. Frankfurt: Ontos Verlag, pp. 185–222.

Hájek, Alan. 2007. 'My Philosophical Position Says $\ulcorner p \urcorner$ and I Don't Believe $\ulcorner p \urcorner$'. In Mitchell Green and John Williams, eds., *Moore's Paradox*. Oxford: Oxford University Press, pp. 217–31.

Haji, Ishtiyaque. 2002. *Deontic Morality and Control*. Cambridge: Cambridge University Press.

Hare, R. M. 1952. *The Language of Morals*. Oxford: Oxford University Press.

Harman, Gilbert. 1986. *Change in View*. Cambridge, MA: MIT Press.

Harman, Gilbert. 1996. 'Moral Relativism'. In Gilbert Harman and Judith Jarvis Thomson, *Moral Relativism and Moral Objectivity*. Oxford: Blackwell, pp. 1–64.

Harman, Gilbert. 2003. 'Three Trends in Moral and Political Philosophy'. *Journal of Value Inquiry* 37: 415–25.

Hawthorne, John. 2002. 'Practical Realism?' *Philosophy and Phenomenological Research* 64: 169–78.

Heathwood, Chris. 2009. 'Moral and Epistemic Open Question Arguments'. *Philosophical Books* 50: 83–98.

Heuer, Ulrike. 2010. 'Reasons and Impossibility'. *Philosophical Studies* 147: 235–46.

Hinckfuss, Ian. 1987. *The Moral Society*. Department of Philosophy, Australian National University.

Horgan, Terry and Mark Timmons. 1991. 'New Wave Moral Realism Meets Moral Twin Earth'. *Journal of Philosophical Research* 16: 447–65.

Horgan, Terry and Mark Timmons. 1992a. 'Troubles for New Wave Moral Semantics: The Open Question Argument Revived'. *Philosophical Papers* 21: 153–75.

Horgan, Terry and Mark Timmons. 1992b. 'Troubles on Moral Twin Earth: Moral Queerness Revived'. *Synthese* 92: 221–60.

Horgan, Terry and Mark Timmons. 2000. 'Nondescriptivist Cognitivism: Framework for a New Metaethic'. *Philosophical Papers* 29: 121–53.

Horgan, Terry and Mark Timmons. 2006a. 'Cognitivist Expressivism'. In Terry Horgan and Mark Timmons, eds., *Metaethics After Moore*. Oxford: Oxford University Press, pp. 255–98.

Horgan, Terry and Mark Timmons. 2006b. 'Expressivism, Yes! Relativism, No!' In Russ Shafer-Landau, ed., *Oxford Studies in Metaethics, Volume 1*. Oxford: Oxford University Press, pp. 73–98.

Horgan, Terry and Mark Timmons. 2009. 'Analytical Moral Functionalism Meets Moral Twin Earth'. In Ian Ravenscroft, ed., *Minds, Ethics, and Conditionals*. Oxford: Oxford University Press, pp. 221–36.

Horwich, Paul. 1993. 'Gibbard's Theory of Norms'. *Philosophy and Public Affairs* 22: 67–78.

Howard-Snyder, Frances. 2006. '"Cannot" Implies "Not Ought"'. *Philosophical Studies* 130: 233–46.

Huemer, Michael. 2005. *Ethical Intuitionism*. Basingstoke: Palgrave Macmillan.

Hurley, S. L. 2000. 'Is Responsibility Essentially Impossible?' *Philosophical Studies* 99: 229–68.

Husi, Stan. 2011. 'Why Reasons Skepticism is Not Self-Defeating'. *European Journal of Philosophy* 21: 424–49.

Hussain, Nadeem. 2012. 'A Problem for Metanormative Constructivism'. In Lenman and Shemmer 2012, pp. 180–94.

Hussain, Nadeem and Nishi Shah. 2006. 'Misunderstanding Metaethics: Korsgaard's Rejection of Realism'. In Russ Shafer-Landau, ed., *Oxford Studies in Metaethics, Volume 1*. Oxford: Oxford University Press, pp. 265–94.

Hussain, Nadeem and Nishi Shah. 2013. 'Meta-Ethics and its Discontents: A Case Study of Korsgaard'. In Bagnoli 2013, pp. 82–107.

Hyun, Alexander and Eric Sampson. 2014. 'On Believing the Error Theory'. *Journal of Philosophy* 111: 631–40.

Istvan, Michael Anthony. 2011. 'Concerning the Resilience of Galen Strawson's Basic Argument'. *Philosophical Studies* 155: 399–420.

Jackson, Frank. 1992. 'Critical Notice of Susan Hurley, *Natural Reasons*'. *Australasian Journal of Philosophy* 70: 475–88.

Jackson, Frank. 1998. *From Metaphysics to Ethics*. Oxford: Oxford University Press.

Jackson, Frank. 2000. 'Reply to Yablo: What Do We Communicate When We Use Ethical Terms?' *Philosophical Books* 41: 24–9.

Jackson, Frank. 2001. 'Responses'. *Philosophy and Phenomenological Research* 62: 653–64.

Jackson, Frank. 2003. 'Cognitivism, A Priori Deduction, and Moore'. *Ethics* 113: 557–75.

Jackson, Frank. 2005. 'What Are Cognitivists Doing When They Do Normative Ethics?' *Philosophical Perspectives* 15: 94–106.

Jackson, Frank. 2009. 'Replies to My Critics'. In Ian Ravenscroft, ed., *Minds, Ethics, and Conditionals*. Oxford: Oxford University Press, pp. 387–474.

Jackson, Frank, Graham Oppy, and Michael Smith. 1994. 'Minimalism and Truth Aptness'. *Mind* 103: 287–302.

Jackson, Frank and Philip Pettit. 1995. 'Moral Functionalism and Moral Motivation'. *Philosophical Quarterly* 45: 20–40.

Jackson, Frank and Philip Pettit. 1996. 'Moral Functionalism, Supervenience and Reductionism'. *Philosophical Quarterly* 46: 82–6.

Joyce, Richard. 2001. *The Myth of Morality*. Cambridge: Cambridge University Press.

Joyce, Richard. 2006. *The Evolution of Morality*. Cambridge, MA: MIT Press.

Joyce, Richard. 2007. 'Morality, Schmorality.' In Paul Bloomfield, ed., *Morality and Self-Interest*. Oxford: Oxford University Press, pp. 51–75.

Joyce, Richard. 2011. 'The Error in "The Error in the Error Theory"'. *Australasian Journal of Philosophy* 89: 519–34.

Joyce, Richard. 2015. 'Moral Anti-Realism'. *Stanford Encyclopedia of Philosophy*, Fall 2015 edition, http://plato.stanford.edu/archives/fall2015/entries/moral-anti-realism/.

Kalderon, Mark. 2005. *Moral Fictionalism*. Oxford: Oxford University Press.

Kane, Robert. 1998. *The Significance of Free Will*. Oxford: Oxford University Press.

Kane, Robert. 2005. *A Contemporary Introduction to Free Will*. Oxford: Oxford University Press.

Karmo, Toomas. 1988. 'Some Valid (but No Sound) Arguments Trivially Span the "Is"-"Ought" Gap'. *Mind* 97: 252–7.

Kearns, Stephen and Daniel Star. 2009. 'Reasons as Evidence'. In Russ Shafer-Landau, ed., *Oxford Studies in Metaethics, Volume 4*. Oxford: Oxford University Press, pp. 215–42.

Kelly, Thomas. 2003. 'Epistemic Rationality as Instrumental Rationality: A Critique'. *Philosophy and Phenomenological Research* 66: 612–40.

Kelly, Thomas. 2005. 'Moorean Facts and Belief Revision, or Can the Skeptic Win?' *Philosophical Perspectives* 19: 179–209.

Kelly, Thomas. 2007. 'Evidence and Normativity: Reply to Leite'. *Philosophy and Phenomenological Research* 75: 465–74.

Kelly, Thomas. 2008. 'Evidence'. *Stanford Encyclopedia of Philosophy*, Fall 2008 edition, http://plato.stanford.edu/archives/fall2008/entries/evidence/.

Kelly, Thomas and Sarah McGrath. 2010. 'Is Reflective Equilibrium Enough?' *Philosophical Perspectives* 24: 325–59.

Kierkegaard, Søren. 1846. *Concluding Unscientific Postscript*. Edited by Alastair Hannay. Cambridge: Cambridge University Press, 2009.

Kim, Jaegwon. 1993. *Supervenience and Mind*. Cambridge: Cambridge University Press.

Köhler, Sebastian and Michael Ridge. 2013. 'Revolutionary Expressivism'. *Ratio* 26: 428–49.

Kołakowski, Leszek. 2001. *Metaphysical Horror*. London: Penguin.

Korsgaard, Christine. 1996. *The Sources of Normativity*. Cambridge: Cambridge University Press.

Korsgaard, Christine. 2008. *The Constitution of Agency*. Oxford: Oxford University Press.

Korsgaard, Christine. 2009. *Self-Constitution*. Oxford: Oxford University Press.

Kramer, Matthew. 2009. *Moral Realism as a Moral Doctrine*. Oxford: Wiley-Blackwell.

Lehrer, Keith. 1990. *Metamind*. Oxford: Oxford University Press.

Lenman, James. 2013. 'Ethics Without Errors'. *Ratio* 26: 391–409.

Lenman, James. 2014. 'Deliberation, Schmeliberation: Enoch's Indispensability Argument'. *Philosophical Studies* 168: 835–42.

Lenman, James and Yonatan Shemmer, eds. 2012. *Constructivism in Practical Philosophy*. Oxford: Oxford University Press.

Lewis, David. 1970. 'How to Define Theoretical Terms'. Reprinted in Lewis 1983, pp. 78–95.

Lewis, David. 1980. 'Mad Pain and Martian Pain'. Reprinted in Lewis 1983, pp. 122–32.

Lewis, David. 1983. *Philosophical Papers, Volume I*. Oxford: Oxford University Press.

Lewis, David. 1986. *On the Plurality of Worlds*. Oxford: Blackwell.

Lewis, David. 1989. 'Dispositional Theories of Value'. Reprinted in David Lewis, *Papers in Ethics and Social Philosophy*. Cambridge: Cambridge University Press, 2000, pp. 68–94.

Lewis, David. 1994. 'Reduction of Mind'. Reprinted in David Lewis, *Papers in Metaphysics and Epistemology*. Cambridge: Cambridge University Press, 1999, pp. 291–324.

Lillehammer, Hallvard and Niklas Möller. 2015. 'We Can Believe the Error Theory'. *Ethical Theory and Moral Practice* 18: 453–9.

Lockie, Robert. 2003. 'Transcendental Arguments Against Eliminativism'. *British Journal for the Philosophy of Science* 54: 569–89.

Loeb, Don. 2008. 'Moral Incoherentism: How to Pull a Metaphysical Rabbit out of a Semantic Hat'. In Walter Sinnott-Armstrong, ed., *Moral Psychology, Volume 2*. Cambridge, MA: MIT Press, pp. 355–86.

Lowe, E. J. 2006. *The Four-Category Ontology*. Oxford: Oxford University Press.

MacBride, Fraser. 2005. 'The Particular-Universal Distinction: A Dogma of Metaphysics?' *Mind* 114: 565–614.

Mackie, J. L. 1977. *Ethics*. Harmondsworth: Penguin.

Maitzen, Stephen. 1998. 'Closing the 'Is'-'Ought' Gap'. *Canadian Journal of Philosophy* 28: 349–65.

Maitzen, Stephen. 2010. 'Moral Conclusions from Non-Moral Premises'. In Pigden 2010, pp. 290–309.

Majors, Brad. 2005. 'Moral Discourse and Descriptive Properties'. *Philosophical Quarterly* 55: 475–94.

McMahan, Jeff. 2000. 'Moral Intuition'. In Hugh LaFollette, ed., *The Blackwell Guide to Ethical Theory*. Oxford: Blackwell, pp. 92–110.

McNaughton, David and Piers Rawling. 2003. 'Naturalism and Normativity'. *Proceedings of the Aristotelian Society, Supplementary Volume* 77: 23–45.

McPherson, Tristram. 2009. 'Moorean Arguments and Moral Revisionism'. *Journal of Ethics and Social Philosophy*, vol. 3 no. 2, http://www.jesp.org.

McPherson, Tristram. 2011. 'Against Quietist Normative Realism'. *Philosophical Studies* 154: 223–40.

McPherson, Tristram and David Plunkett. 2015. 'Deliberative Indispensability and Epistemic Justification'. In Russ Shafer-Landau, ed., *Oxford Studies in Metaethics, Volume 10*. Oxford: Oxford University Press, pp. 104–33.

Mele, Alfred. 1995. *Autonomous Agents*. Oxford: Oxford University Press.

Merli, David. 2002. 'Return to Moral Twin Earth'. *Canadian Journal of Philosophy* 32: 207–40.

Miller, Alexander. 2002. 'Wright's Argument Against Error-Theories'. *Analysis* 62: 98–103.

Moore, G. E. 1925. 'A Defence of Common Sense'. Reprinted in G. E. Moore, *Philosophical Papers*. London: George Allen and Unwin, 1959, pp. 32–59.

Moore, G. E. 1939. 'Proof of an External World'. Reprinted in G. E. Moore, *Philosophical Papers*. London: George Allen and Unwin, 1959, pp. 127–50.

Nagel, Thomas. 1986. *The View From Nowhere*. Oxford: Oxford University Press.

Nagel, Thomas. 1997. *The Last Word*. Oxford: Oxford University Press.

Naylor, Margery Bedford. 1984. 'Frankfurt on the Principle of Alternate Possibilities'. *Philosophical Studies* 46: 249–58.

Nietzsche, Friedrich. 1873. 'On Truth and Lies in a Nonmoral Sense'. In Keith Ansell Pearson and Duncan Large, eds., *The Nietzsche Reader*. Oxford: Blackwell, 2006, pp. 114–23.

Oddie, Graham. 2005. *Value, Reality, and Desire*. Oxford: Oxford University Press.

Olson, Jonas. 2012. 'Skorupski's Middle Way in Metaethics'. *Philosophy and Phenomenological Research* 85: 192–200.

Olson, Jonas. 2014. *Moral Error Theory*. Oxford: Oxford University Press.

Owens, David. 2000. *Reason Without Freedom*. London: Routledge.

Owens, David. 2002. 'Epistemic Akrasia'. *The Monist* 85: 381–97.

Parfit, Derek. 2006. 'Normativity'. In Russ Shafer-Landau, ed., *Oxford Studies in Metaethics, Volume 1*. Oxford: Oxford University Press, pp. 325–80.

Parfit, Derek. 2011a. *On What Matters, Volume One*. Oxford: Oxford University Press.

Parfit, Derek. 2011b. *On What Matters, Volume Two*. Oxford: Oxford University Press.

Pigden, Charles. 2007. 'Nihilism, Nietzsche and the Doppelganger Problem'. *Ethical Theory and Moral Practice* 10: 441–56.

Pigden, Charles, ed. 2010. *Hume on Is and Ought*. Basingstoke: Palgrave MacMillan.

Plantinga, Alvin. 2010. 'Naturalism, Theism, Obligation and Supervenience'. *Faith and Philosophy* 27: 247–72.

Plato. *Complete Works*. Edited by John Cooper and D. S. Hutchinson. Indianapolis: Hackett, 1997.

Plunkett, David and Tim Sundell. 2013. 'Disagreement and the Semantics of Normative and Evaluative Terms'. *Philosophers' Imprint*, vol. 13 no. 23, http://www.philosophersimprint.org.

Price, Huw. 2011. *Naturalism Without Mirrors*. Oxford: Oxford University Press.

Price, Huw. 2013. *Expressivism, Pragmatism and Representationalism*. Cambridge: Cambridge University Press.

Priest, Graham. 1998. 'What's So Bad About Contradictions?' *Journal of Philosophy* 95: 410–26.

Priest, Graham. 2006a. *In Contradiction* (second edition). Oxford: Oxford University Press.

Priest, Graham. 2006b. *Doubt Truth to Be a Liar*. Oxford: Oxford University Press.

Prinz, Jesse. 2007. *The Emotional Construction of Morals*. Oxford: Oxford University Press.

Prior, Arthur. 1960. 'The Autonomy of Ethics'. *Australasian Journal of Philosophy* 38: 199–206.

Quine, Willard Van Orman. 1953. 'On What There Is'. In Willard Van Orman Quine, *From a Logical Point of View*. Cambridge, MA: Harvard University Press, pp. 1–19.

Railton, Peter. 1986. 'Moral Realism'. Reprinted in Peter Railton, *Facts, Values and Norms*. Cambridge: Cambridge University Press, 2003, pp. 3–42.

Railton, Peter. 1989. 'Naturalism and Prescriptivity'. *Social Philosophy and Policy* 7: 151–74.

Ramsey, Frank. 1925. 'Universals'. *Mind* 34: 401–17.

Rawls, John. 1971. *A Theory of Justice*. Cambridge, MA: Harvard University Press.

Rawls, John. 1974. 'The Independence of Moral Theory'. *Proceedings and Addresses of the American Philosophical Association* 48: 5–22.

Rawls, John. 1993. *Political Liberalism*. New York, NY: Columbia University Press.

Rawls, John. 2001. *Justice as Fairness*. Cambridge, MA: Harvard University Press.

Ridge, Michael. 2006. 'Ecumenical Expressivism: Finessing Frege'. *Ethics* 116: 302–36.

Ridge, Michael. 2007. 'Ecumenical Expressivism: The Best of Both Worlds?' In Russ Shafer-Landau, ed., *Oxford Studies in Metaethics, Volume 2*. Oxford: Oxford University Press, pp. 51–76.

Ridge, Michael. 2009. 'The Truth in Ecumenical Expressivism'. In David Sobel and Steven Wall, eds., *Reasons for Action*. Cambridge: Cambridge University Press, pp. 219–42.

Ridge, Michael. 2014. *Impassioned Belief*. Oxford: Oxford University Press.

Rosen, Gideon. 1998. 'Blackburn's *Essays in Quasi-Realism*'. *Noûs* 32: 386–405.

Rosen, Gideon. Unpublished. 'What is Normative Necessity?'

Ross, Jacob. 2006. 'Rejecting Ethical Deflationism'. *Ethics* 116: 742–68.

Rowland, Richard. 2013. 'Moral Error Theory and the Argument from Epistemic Reasons'. *Journal of Ethics and Social Philosophy*, vol. 7 no. 1, http://www.jesp.org.

Sayre-McCord, Geoffrey. 1997. ' "Good" on Twin Earth'. *Philosophical Issues* 8: 267–92.

Scanlon, T. M. 1998. *What We Owe to Each Other*. Cambridge, MA: Harvard University Press.

Scanlon, T. M. 2002. 'Rawls on Justification'. In Samuel Freeman, ed., *The Cambridge Companion to Rawls*. Cambridge: Cambridge University Press, pp. 139–67.

Scanlon, T. M. 2003. 'Metaphysics and Morals'. *Proceedings and Addresses of the American Philosophical Association* 77: 7–22.

Scanlon, T. M. 2014. *Being Realistic About Reasons*. Oxford: Oxford University Press.

Schiffer, Stephen. 2003. *The Things We Mean*. Oxford: Oxford University Press.

Schmitt, Johannes and Mark Schroeder. 2011. 'Supervenience Arguments Under Relaxed Assumptions'. *Philosophical Studies* 155: 133–60.

Schroeder, Mark. 2004. 'The Scope of Instrumental Reason'. *Philosophical Perspectives* 18: 337–64.

Schroeder, Mark. 2007. *Slaves of the Passions*. Oxford: Oxford University Press.

Schroeder, Mark. 2009. 'Hybrid Expressivism: Virtues and Vices'. *Ethics* 119: 257–309.

Schroeter, Laura and François Schroeter. 2005. 'Is Gibbard a Realist?' *Journal of Ethics and Social Philosophy*, vol. 1 no. 2, http://www.jesp.org.

Schroeter, Laura and François Schroeter. 2009. 'A Third Way in Metaethics'. *Noûs* 43: 1–30.

Schroeter, Laura and François Schroeter. 2013. 'Normative Realism: Co-Reference Without Convergence?' *Philosophers' Imprint*, vol. 13 no. 13, http://www.philosophersimprint.org.

Schwitzgebel, Eric. 2002. 'A Phenomenal, Dispositional Account of Belief'. *Noûs* 36: 249–75.

Shah, Nishi. 2010. 'The Limits of Normative Detachment.' *Proceedings of the Aristotelian Society* 110: 347–71.

Shah, Nishi. 2011. 'Can Reasons for Belief Be Debunked?' In Andrew Reisner and Asbjørn Steglich-Petersen, eds., *Reasons for Belief*. Cambridge: Cambridge University Press, pp. 94–107.

Shafer-Landau, Russ. 2003. *Moral Realism*. Oxford: Oxford University Press.

Shepski, Lee. 2008. 'The Vanishing Argument from Queerness'. *Australasian Journal of Philosophy* 86: 371–87.

Sinnott-Armstrong, Walter. 1984. '"Ought" Conversationally Implies "Can"'. *Philosophical Review* 93: 249–61.

Sinnott-Armstrong, Walter. 2006. *Moral Skepticisms*. Oxford: Oxford University Press.

Skorupski, John. 2010. *The Domain of Reasons*. Oxford: Oxford University Press.

Smith, Michael. 1994a. *The Moral Problem*. Oxford: Blackwell.

Smith, Michael. 1994b. 'Why Expressivists About Value Should Love Minimalism About Truth'. *Analysis* 54: 1–11.

Smith, Michael. 1994c. 'Minimalism, Truth-Aptitude and Belief'. *Analysis* 54: 21–6.

Smith, Michael. 2007. 'Meta-Ethics'. In Frank Jackson and Michael Smith, eds., *The Oxford Handbook of Contemporary Philosophy*. Oxford: Oxford University Press, pp. 3–30.

Sober, Elliott. 1982. 'Why Logically Equivalent Predicates May Pick Out Different Properties'. *American Philosophical Quarterly* 19: 183–9.

Sorensen, Roy. 1988. *Blindspots*. Oxford: Oxford University Press.

Stevenson, Charles. 1963. *Facts and Values*. New Haven, CT: Yale University Press.

Stevenson, Leslie. 2002. 'Six Levels of Mentality'. *Philosophical Explorations* 5: 105–24.

Stich, Stephen. 1983. *From Folk Psychology to Cognitive Science*. Cambridge, MA: MIT Press.

Stich, Stephen. 1996. *Deconstructing the Mind*. Oxford: Oxford University Press.

Stocker, Michael. 1979. 'Desiring the Bad: An Essay in Moral Psychology'. *Journal of Philosophy* 76: 738–53.

Stratton-Lake, Philip. 2002. 'Introduction'. In W. D. Ross, *The Right and the Good*. Oxford: Oxford University Press, pp. ix–l.

Strawson, Galen. 1994. 'The Impossibility of Moral Responsibility'. *Philosophical Studies* 75: 5–24.

Strawson, Galen. 2002. 'The Bounds of Freedom'. In Robert Kane, ed., *The Oxford Handbook of Free Will*. Oxford: Oxford University Press, pp. 441–6.

Strawson, Galen. 2010. *Freedom and Belief* (revised edition). Oxford: Oxford University Press.

Strawson, P. F. 1950. 'On Referring'. *Mind* 59: 320–44.

Strawson, P. F. 1952. *Introduction to Logical Theory*. London: Methuen.

Street, Sharon. 2008. 'Constructivism About Reasons'. In Russ Shafer-Landau, ed., *Oxford Studies in Metaethics, Volume 3*. Oxford: Oxford University Press, pp. 207–45.

Street, Sharon. 2009. 'In Defence of Future Tuesday Indifference: Ideally Coherent Eccentrics and the Contingency of What Matters'. *Philosophical Issues* 19: 273–98.

Street, Sharon. 2010. 'What is Constructivism in Ethics and Metaethics?' *Philosophy Compass* 5: 363–84.

Street, Sharon. 2012. 'Coming to Terms with Contingency: Humean Constructivism About Practical Reason'. In Lenman and Shemmer 2012, pp. 40–59.

Streumer, Bart. 2003. 'Does "Ought" Conversationally Implicate "Can"?' *European Journal of Philosophy* 11: 219–28.

Streumer, Bart. 2007. 'Reasons and Impossibility'. *Philosophical Studies* 136: 351–84.

Streumer, Bart. 2008. 'Are There Irreducibly Normative Properties?' *Australasian Journal of Philosophy* 86: 537–61.

Streumer, Bart. 2010. 'Reasons, Impossibility and Efficient Steps: Reply to Heuer'. *Philosophical Studies* 151: 79–86.

Streumer, Bart. 2011. 'Are Normative Properties Descriptive Properties?' *Philosophical Studies* 154: 325–48.

Streumer, Bart. 2013a. 'Can We Believe the Error Theory?' *Journal of Philosophy* 110: 194–212.

Streumer, Bart. 2013b. 'Why There Really Are No Irreducibly Normative Properties'. In David Bakhurst, Brad Hooker, and Margaret Little, eds., *Thinking About Reasons: Essays in Honour of Jonathan Dancy*. Oxford: Oxford University Press, pp. 310–36.

Streumer, Bart. 2013c. 'Do Normative Judgements Aim to Represent the World?' *Ratio* 26: 450–70.

Streumer, Bart. 2016a. 'Why Jonas Olson Cannot Believe the Error Theory Either'. *Journal of Moral Philosophy* 13: 419–36.

Streumer, Bart. 2016b. 'No, We Cannot'. *International Journal of Philosophical Studies* 24: 537–46.

Streumer, Bart. Forthcoming. 'Reasons and Ability'. In Daniel Star, ed., *The Oxford Handbook of Reasons and Normativity*. Oxford: Oxford University Press.

Sturgeon, Nicholas. 1985. 'Moral Explanations'. In David Copp and David Zimmerman, eds., *Morality, Reason, and Truth*. Totowa, NJ: Rowman and Allanheld, pp. 49–78.

Sturgeon, Nicholas. 2005. 'Ethical Naturalism'. In David Copp, ed., *The Oxford Handbook of Ethical Theory*. Oxford: Oxford University Press, pp. 91–121.

Sturgeon, Nicholas. 2009. 'Doubts About the Supervenience of the Evaluative'. In Russ Shafer-Landau, ed., *Oxford Studies in Metaethics, Volume 4*. Oxford: Oxford University Press, pp. 53–90.

Suikkanen, Jussi. 2010. 'Non-Naturalism: The Jackson Challenge'. In Russ Shafer-Landau, ed., *Oxford Studies in Metaethics, Volume 5*. Oxford: Oxford University Press, pp. 87–110.

Tappolet, Christine. 2013. 'Evaluative vs. Deontic Concepts'. In Hugh LaFollette, ed., *The International Encyclopedia of Ethics*. Oxford: Wiley-Blackwell, pp. 1791–9.

Timmons, Mark. 1999. *Morality Without Foundations*. Oxford: Oxford University Press.

Vahid, Hamid. 2004. 'Varieties of Epistemic Conservatism'. *Synthese* 141: 97–122.

van Roojen, Mark. 1996. 'Moral Functionalism and Moral Reductionism'. *Philosophical Quarterly* 46: 77–81.

van Roojen, Mark. 2006. 'Knowing Enough to Disagree: A New Response to the Moral Twin Earth Argument'. In Russ Shafer-Landau, ed., *Oxford Studies in Metaethics, Volume 1*. Oxford: Oxford University Press, pp. 161–93.

Väyrynen, Pekka. 2017. 'The Supervenience Challenge to Non-Naturalism'. In Tristram McPherson and David Plunkett, eds., *The Routledge Handbook of Metaethics*. London: Routledge.

Vranas, Peter. 2007. 'I Ought, Therefore I Can'. *Philosophical Studies* 136: 167–216.

Way, Jonathan. 2010. 'Defending the Wide-Scope Approach to Instrumental Reason'. *Philosophical Studies* 147: 213–33.

Wedgwood, Ralph. 2002. 'The Aim of Belief'. *Philosophical Perspectives* 16: 267–97.

Wedgwood, Ralph. 2007. *The Nature of Normativity*. Oxford: Oxford University Press.

White, Alan. 1975. *Modal Thinking*. Oxford: Blackwell.

Widerker, David. 1991. 'Frankfurt on "Ought Implies Can" and Alternative Possibilities'. *Analysis* 51: 222–4.

Williams, Bernard. 1985a. *Ethics and the Limits of Philosophy*. London: Fontana Press, republished in 1993.

Williams, Bernard. 1985b. 'Ethics and the Fabric of the World'. Reprinted in Bernard Williams, *Making Sense of Humanity*. Cambridge: Cambridge University Press, 1995, pp. 172–81.

Williamson, Timothy. 2001. 'Ethics, Supervenience and Ramsey Sentences'. *Philosophy and Phenomenological Research* 62: 625–30.

Williamson, Timothy. 2007. *The Philosophy of Philosophy*. Oxford: Blackwell.

Wright, Crispin. 1985. 'Review of Simon Blackburn's *Spreading the Word*'. *Mind* 94: 310–19.

Wright, Crispin. 1992. *Truth and Objectivity*. Cambridge, MA: Harvard University Press.

Wright, Crispin. 1995. 'Truth in Ethics'. Reprinted in Crispin Wright, *Saving the Differences*. Cambridge, MA: Harvard University Press, 2003, pp. 183–203.

Yablo, Stephen. 2000. 'Red, Bitter, Best'. *Philosophical Books* 41: 13–23.

Zangwill, Nick. 2000. 'Against Analytic Moral Functionalism'. *Ratio* 13: 275–86.

Zimmerman, Michael. 1996. *The Concept of Moral Obligation*. Cambridge: Cambridge University Press.

Index

Printed and bound by CPI Group (UK) Ltd, Croydon, CR0 4YY